Freedom, Democracy and Revolution
Explorations in JP's Thought

Freedom, Democracy and Revolution Explorations in JP's Thought

Edited by

Prof. Sachchidananda
Chairman, A.N. Sinha Institute of Social Studies, Patna

Dr. Nil Ratan
Reader in Political Science A.N. Sinha Institute of Social Studies, Patna

SERIALS PUBLICATIONS
New Delhi

First Published - 2005

ISBN : 81-86771-82-4

Published by

Head Office	:	**SERIALS PUBLICATIONS** 4, B.S.S. Hall, Khyber Pass Market Civil Lines, Delhi-110054 (India) Phone : 23245225 Fax : 91-11-23272135 E-mail: serials@satyam.net.in
Branch Office	:	4830/24, Prahlad Street, Ansari Road Darya Ganj, New Delhi-110002 (India)

Preface

In the JP Centenary year, the Board of Control of the A.N. Sinha Institute of Social Studies, Patna, took a decision to hold a seminar to discuss his seminal ideas on some of the burning social issues facing the country as well as his attempts to provide possible solutions. JP's entire life was a quest of a revolutionary for the creation of a social order based upon freedom, equity and parti-cipative democracy, JP's ideas were not only relevant in his time. They are more relevant today with the fast erosion of social values, acceleration of violence and fast decline of respect for human rights and democratic norms.

The present volume is a humble tribute to the memory of JP, who was the founder chairman of our institute for the first ten years.

We are deeply obliged to the academics and activists who responded to our invitation and participated in the seminar held at the A.N. Sinha Institute of Social Studies on Feb. 6-7, 2004. We are also grateful to some scholars who could not attend the seminar but sent their papers for inclusion in the present volume. We are indebted to the Indian Council of Social Science Research, New Delhi for providing subsidy for the publication of this book. Thanks are also due to Sri S.K. Jha, Director, Serials Publications, New Delhi for seeing the book through the press in a short time.

Sachchidananda
Nil Ratan

List of Contributors

Prof. L.N. Sharma, Univ. Prof. & HOD, P.U. (Retd.)

Dr. Jitendra Narayan, Reader, University Dept. of Pol. Science, L.N. Mithila University Darbhanga

Dr. D.M. Diwakar, Professor of Economic, Giri Institute of Development Studies, Lucknow, Uttar Pradesh.

Dr. Vijay Kumar, Professor, Department of Political Science, T.M. Bhagalpur University, Bhagalpur.

Dr. Ravindra Kumar Verma, P.G. Deptt. of Political Science, R.N. College, Hajipur (Vaishali)

Prof. Sachchidananda, A.N.S. Institute of Social Studies, Patna.

Dr. Manohar Lal, Reader, A.N. Sinha Institute of Social Studies, Patna.

Prof. B.B. Mandal, A.N. Sinha Institute of Social Studies, Patna.

Dr. Jagdish Prasad, A.N. Sinha Institute of Social Studies, Patna.

Sudhanshu Ranjan, Doordarshan, Patna.

Dr. K.K. Sinha, Former Professor of Economics, Magadh University.

Dr. Vijay Ranjan Dutta, Former Reader in Political Science, Gandhian Institute of Studies, Varanasi, Former Senior Research Fellow, Indian Council of Social Science Research.

Dr. Bimal Prasad, Former, Chairman, SIS, Jawahar Lal Nehru University.

Prof. Ramjee Singh, Founder, Gandhian Studies Department, Bhagalpur University, Bhagalpur.

Dr. Nil Ratan, Reader in Political Science, A.N. Sinha Institute of Social Studies, Patna.

Introduction

The Centenary volume reflects the leading areas where JP significantly contributed as thinker, innovator and activist. It focuses on JP's thought and action under five themes such as JP's concern for democracy and freedom; rural development; land reform; Panchayati Raj and JP as a Hero of the Past and Hope for the Future.

L.N. Sharma has analysed JP's concept of freedom and its significance at the individual as well as at societal level. He stresses that JP was a champion of liberty, equality, decentralization and autonomous values which he wanted to percolate in the entire society as an organic process of growth. JP stood, according to him, for the concept of a moral man.

Jitendra Narayan focuses on JP's concern for consistency with equality, freedom and peace as ideals which can only be achieved in a democracy, based on the people's faith and their capacity to manage their affairs themselves. JP, according to Narayan, placed great premium on the individual and the supremacy of the human spirit. He has critically analysed JP's view on political parties, western democracies, corruption and decline of institutions. He has brought out JP's concern to preserve morality and strengthen man's freedom to his satisfaction.

D.M. Diwakar has covered the economic, cultural and social aspects of life at the global level and trend to relate it to JP's seminal contributions on economic democracy vis-à-vis political democracy. He highlights the philosophical trends which converge with JP's thought on economic decentralization and peoples' mobilization to strengthen their will and democratic values.

Vijay Kumar examines the concept of Total Revolution in the era of globalization. He has attempted to delineate the concept of total revolution and its relevance in Indian society in particular, and developing world in general. JP conceived of a society free from corruption, and based on justice, equality, dignity of the human being and people's participation. He discusses JP's great faith on people's power, mobilization, mass involvement and the people's capacity to shape their own models of socio-economic polity for achieving larger good.

Ravindra Kumar Verma in his lucid presentation on "People's power in JP's thought' has analytically diagnosed JP's view on the concept of Marxism, socialism, democracy, people's participation etc. He discusses, JP's major contribution of People's power through Sarvodaya, Lokniti and Total Revolution.

Sachchidananda highlights prominently the valuable contribution of JP in the realm of rural development. He has underlined in some detail the vision of a village, which JP regarded as a natural and sensible formation at the primary unit of social organization. He stresses the consistency in JP's thought and action on this issue which revolved around reduction of land holdings, vigorous land reforms, and creation of watchdog village committees to safeguard and implement land laws. He brings out how JP practised what he preached, in the project of rural reconstruction in Sokhodeora. He also discusses how peace was established in Musahari area through Sarvodaya. Despite JP's sustained campaign it failed to achieve its goals and values in totality. The paper also details JP's efforts for rural industrialization. The setting up of the Association of Voluntary Agencies for Rural Development by JP at the national level reflected his great hopes about the potentialities of voluntary action in this field.

Manohar Lal's paper is a case study of Gram Nirman Mandal, a voluntary organization founded by JP in the Nawada district in Bihar. JP devoted all his time to nourish the Mandal and its diverse activities for several years. Lal has taken pains to critically analyse the growth of this organization and its contribution to rural reconstruction in the area.

B.B. Mandal has systematically explained JP's view on the ills of feudal socio-economic structure and the importance of setting up a new social order based on freedom and equity. He analyses JP's ideas about the implementation of land reform laws, specially relating to homestead, ceiling, share cropping, both in respect of title to land and share of produce, money lending and agricultural wages. He has discussed Gramdan in Musahari. Mandal has observed that JP was a firm believer of community approach, because of his conviction that unless village communities are built as self-governing, mutually cooperative and self-reliant bodies, the imbalance of power in the community would never be corrected and the land reforms would never bear fruit.

Jagdish Prasad brings out JP's concern for agrarian problems in contemporary Bihar. JP held that the development of the villages was constrained because of the lack of agrarian reform.

Sudhanshu Ranjan dwells on the deep involvement of JP from his early life on the problems of land reform and how Bhoodan movement of Vinoba could help in this process. He has highlighted JP's involvement in Bhoodan movement and how he perceived Bhoodan in socialistic perspective for creating an atmosphere for the redistribution of land. He lauds JP's supreme sacrifice and commitment to the cause by announcing the dedication of his life and how he synergiesed his life and thought process to achieve this goal.

Sachchidananda deals with JP's vision of Panchayati Raj and the contemporary scenario in Bihar. He has brought out the finer points of JP's views on decentralized autonomous communitarian society and how it should work for the general good of all without getting sucked into petty politicking and disruptive issues. He laments that JP's vision of Pachayati Raj remains a dream in Bihar as the attitude of political leadership in Bihar does not reflect JP's paradigm of decentralization and development, but hopes for a better future.

K.K. Sinha analyses the Gramdan Panchayats and Musahari experiment to stress the merits of decentralized governance at the grassroot for rural reconstruction. He suggests that to give a new life to the Gramdan Act, it should be incorporated in the Panchayat Act of 1993.

Vijay Rajan Dutt in his paper elaborates approach to Panchayati Raj and participatory democracy. He traces changes in JP's understanding of social, political and economic processes in decentralized participatory development in different phases of his life. He holds that JP understood the core of grassroot development with a larger role of Panchayat bodies as units of self government, participatory democracy and social engineering. He has made the plea for a social movement to move faster for a resurgence in contemporary Bihar.

Bimal Prasad in his paper on the ideological legacy of JP and the future of democracy in India has discussed the relevance of JP's contribution in the contemporary Indian situation. He stresses that the foundation of democracy will become much stronger than at present if political and economic decentralization are adopted on the lines suggested by JP. JP wanted the masses be given the opportunity to mange their affairs themselves through the Panchayati Raj institutions and thus help transform the present representative democracy into a participatory one. He is of the opinion that by emulating JP's path a new social order based on freedom, equality and human fellowship could be founded.

Ramjee Singh hails JP as a practical idealist. He expresses his concern for Green horns who fail to comprehend JP's seminal contribution through out his life. He has analysed JP's immense faith in the great potential and capacity of youth power to act as vanguard of society and democratic system. JP correctly chose the power of youth as an appropriate instrument of change.

K.K. Sinha has tried to analyse the views of Marx, Gandhi and JP, based on the common theme that the state power should give way to peoples' power, the state should wither away and the social changes take a quantum leap. He holds that JP talks of reconstruction of villages based on self-governance and communitarian ownership akin to Gandhi's Trusteeship, where the property owners treated themselves not as owners of the surplus but as just as its trustees. He feels that it is necessary to understand this commonality among them, to grasp the crux of poverty, decentralization, peoples' power and development.

Nil Ratan tries to focus on the larger role played by JP throughout his life. He has recounted JP's legacy and how relevant he is still today.

Contents

SECTION - III
JP and Land Reform

SECTION - IV
JP and Panchayati Raj

SECTION - V
JP as a Hero of Past and Hope for Future

SECTION - I

JP's Concerns for Democracy and Freedom

1
JP's Concepts of Freedom and Democracy

Prof. L. N. Sharma

JP has been a Communist, a socialist and a romantic anarchist. Above all, he has been a humanist and a communitarian. However, in this paper, we shall limit our discussion to an elucidation of his concepts of freedom and democracy which stand turned in his political treatises, speeches and activities.

JP's concept of freedom transcends liberation from foreign rule. A self-government of past-colonial parliamentary democratic government can amount to 'action' rule and an imposed or super-imposed governance in which people's wills may not be reflected. Hence, people are free to rise against misrule; even state's apparatuses like army, police and the bureaucracy should act according to "conscience" and law. The fact that some of JP's disciples now talk of colonial "cods of conduct" for the Police and try to curb freedom of speech does not undermine what JP stood and fought for.

JP's concept of freedom is very comprehensive. It embraces the "freedom of man everywhere and from every sort of trammel, above all, it meant freedom of the human personality, freedom of the mind, freedom of the spirit"[1] This concept of freedom was a passion for him which he would and could not see compromised "for bread, for power, for security, for prosperity, for the glory of the state or for anything else".

During the 1920's JP emphasized equality and fraternity but later on, turned to be a votary of individual freedom and liberty. He had once stated that "human freedom could be fully and wholly realized only in a stateless society", i.e. in a communitarian society. JP's concern thus combines the concerns of both the young and the matured Marx. Marx's early writings wanted end of man's alienation and his matured writings emphasized freedom from exploitation in communism. JP shares both concerns but JP is more humanist than Marx and comes closer to Sartre. A little later, JP expounded the concept of the minimalist state. He said that a handful of people, an oligarchy concentrates economic and political power in their hands and are in league with profiteers. In the words of JP "the democratic socialist state remains a Leviathan that will sit heavily on the freedom of the people".

Distrust of political parties became the essence of JP's philosophy. Later Democracies treat individuals as atoms or pebbles, he said, the turned to be a harsh critic of the voting system in which the individual casts his vote as an atom of society, not "as a living cell in an organic relationship with other living cells." It is not living together that is expressed and represented in the institutions and processes of democracy but an abstract individual. "The present party system, like the elections, finders the growth of an organic or participatory democracy. The party manipulates to impose its own will instead of translating people's will in to proposals and schemes of the government. The party members and even people are not free to think, their thoughts are bargained and manufactured.

No self government can exist without people's initiative and strong will to participate. People are to be really made to feel the pulse of freedom (He echoes Hayek's concept of freedom as power) and that is possible only in an organic and participatory democracy. In this kind of democracy people act and feel as a group which is like an individual by common sharing of views and actions. For this, the polity is to be decentralized. Power would move upwards and not downwards as happens in parliamentary democracies which are inorganic. The smaller units are to be autonomous in their respective domains. JP is all in favour of ensuring regional autonomy. Local or village communities are the "key" or "optimum" communities. By an organic process of growth, these communities have to be integrated to the district, the provincial, and the national community. Lower tiers, however, have to have more powers; the higher tiers have only such powers as are delegated to them.

In organic democracy, there will be neither parties. In place of electoral contests broad consensus will be evolved to choose candidates for the village councils. These "nominated" best servants of the society will by near unanimity, choose best persons for the higher tiers. JP favours indirect democracy and no imposition from above or from higher organs on the lower organs in decision making.

JP is aware that the king of polity he is recommending requires a high moral character on the part of every individual (which may not be possible) and "an ability to live in amity, justice and cooperation with his fellowmen". Freedom requires nine moral qualities — (i) concern for truth; (ii) aversion to violence; (iii) love of liberty and courage to resist oppression and tyranny (iv) the spirit of cooperation; (v) preparedness to adjust self interest to the larger interests; (vi) respect for others' opinions and tolerance; (vii) readiness to take responsibility (viii) the fundamental equality of men; and (ix) faith in the educacability of human nature.

JP bases his philosophy on the assumption that freedom implies particpation in governance (a point he shares with Hayek and Rawls. But many may he forced or condemned to be free in this meaning of freedom because many including intellectuals are apathetic towards and alienated from politics and anomic or deviant criminality is rampant. Hence the plea for replacing the present inorganic democracy by the participatory or organic democracy may appear rather utopian. But JP's concept of economic democracy emphasizing simplicity, plain living and rusticity may make democracy dependent upon a communitarian style of living. JP shares Macpherson's concern that democracy should not rest on the shoulders of a possessive and consumerist individuals but be based soundly on the concept of a moral man. JP shares Gandhi's prescription of "voluntary poverty" or limited wants. Democracy is essentially a moral system, concerned with making men human. Materialism robs man of the means to be truly human. Hence, materialism and democracy become incompatible JP's thesis undermines theses of scholars like Lipset who find positive correlation between democracy and industrialization, urbanization, exposure to mass media, educational attainment and high rate of consumption. Instead, JP pins his hope on blending of man's nature and culture. Since this blending is not possible in cities the process of urbanization needs to be halted and the present cities decentralized and reorganized. JP's education comes closer to Macpherson's denunciation of possessive, materialist and consumerist individual and JP makes a tireless effort for moral spiritual and educational revolution along with social, economic, cultural and ideological revolutions. He made a partial attempt to get such a revolution through. Like Mao's, JP's revolution was to be a permanent one. It is a pity that JP's disciples made no worthwhile effort to continue the "permanent" revolution.

NOTE

1. JP's Plea for the Reconstruction of the Indian Polity.

2

JP and His Experiments with Indian Democracy

Jitendra Narayan

Loknayak Jayaprakash Narayan, popularly known as JP, a commanding figure in Indian public life as a tribune of the nation, has drawn the serious attention of all those who particularly have remained interested in the working of democracy world-wide besides the common people of India who helped JP in his experiments with Indian democracy at different stages of his philosophical as well as political journey. However, JP was also mocked at by some social scientists in India as well as in other countries for his policy, and for living in a wonderland, a "prophet blinded by his" light." Some praised him for producing a precious and rare "piece a of systematic social theory".[1] His biographers Allan and Wendy claim that JP belonged to the long tradition of radical utopians. They further observe that JP has put all his mental and emotional resources into trying to devise a society in which people could live in permanent peace with one another. Although the political doctrines he has embraced for attaining this end have changed, his ultimate vision of a peaceful, free and just society never changed, nor has the method by which he hopes to attain it.[2]

Vision of a peaceful, free and just society was responsible for all his experiments, which JP carried out throughout his life. From Marxism to Democratic

Socialism to Sarvodaya of Vinoba Bhave to Gandhism was just a journey which was undertaken by him to reach the destination of a social, economic and political democracy. In this context JP's clarification is worth considering.

He said:

> I have often been accused of changing my views, and my field of activities. I claim that though all apparent changes, I have been pursuing a single goal, seeking to answer to a single question; how to make India Independent, and help to establish a social, economic and political democracy. This search took me to several ideologies and political paths, until I arrived at the conclusion that Gandhiji hold the answer; not a mindless application of Gandhiji's ideas, but their dynamic and revolutionary adaptation.[3]

Madhu Limaye also explained that JP throughout his career remained consistent so far as the details or the tactics employed were concerned but he always remained inconsistent so far as adherence to certain fundamental principles was concerned.[4] JP himself has observed:

> The past course of my life might appear to the outsider as a zig-zag and tortuous chart of unsteadiness and blind groping. But as I look back I discern it in a uniform line of development. The groping undeniably was there, but it was certainly not bling; there were clear beacons of light that remained undimmed and unaltered from the beginning and that led me on to my apparent torturous path. I, at least, am not sorry for having made this zig-zag journey, for, it has made me the surer path that I have decided to tread.[5]

No doubt, JP changed his routes time and again/ many times but he remained consistent so far as the goal of equality, freedom and peace was concerned. JP was ultimately convinced that the ideals could be achieved only through the democratic process. So his faith in democracy was without question and he never compromised with the ideals of freedom and democratic way of life. Once he revealed that "Freedom has become a passion of his life and I shall not see it compromised for bread, for power, for security, for prosperity, for the glory of the state, or for any thing else.[6]

JP once reminded that "The struggle for freedom was not fought simply for national independence. The establishment of democracy in free India was also an important goal that the Constituent. Assembly has drawn up a Constitution for democratic India and adopted it on 26th November 1949 on behalf of the Indian people.[7] JP noted it with sense of profound satisfaction that the constituent Assembly of India adopted the ideal of constituting India into a sovereign, democratic, republic and resolved to grant to the citizens "Justice-social, economic and political, liberty of thought, expression, belief, faith and worship; equality of status and opportunity and to promote among them all fraternity assuring the dignity of the individual and unity of the nation. These aims and purposes together, he writes, do make upon inspiring and challenging image of democracy. In order to help render that image into concrete reality, the Assembly adopted and enacted the present Constitution of India, which as amended from time to time, stands as a bulwark of freedom and democracy. Again, the people of this country may justly be proud of the fact that they have deliberately chosen the democratic way of life, despite the example of many neighbouring countries having embraced dictatorship of one kind or another. It is an evidence of people's cultural and spiritual maturity that they have done so.[8] JP in his Prison Diary also has emphatically said that "the Indian democracy will rise even from the grave", such was JP's faith in his people.[9]

JP had been in the thick of party politics when the priority was the glorious struggle for freedom. At that time all the selfishness, weakness, factionalism were covered, pushed under the carpet and did not appear a big hurdle. However, when after independence, it became a struggle for economic development had political power all diseases of politics, petty jealousies and strife do come to surface. Though a convinced democrat he experimented with Indian democracy throughout his life but he developed a moral revulsion against the ills of party politics, Gandhiji and like him JP considered struggle for political power as a corrupting influence. In fact JP had no taste for any public office, he was a moralist driven into politics. Many before him had viewed party-politics as the last refuse of a scoundrel. When that struggle showed its ugly face he tried to reason out why should be so. That led bim to question the fundamental assumption of parliamentary democracy.[10]

As Jayaprakash sees it, the politics of the western World, and of all countries who have based their government on the party structure, has become a battle for power. The moral beliefs and attitudes of the individual become merged in the power group. The individual all too often submerges his personal views in the cause of the group coming to power....Men have great urges to power and since it can not be done away with, that society is best which spreads power equally among the people".[11] Increasingly corruption in parliamentary democracy due to the present form of working of party system in India has taken an ugly turn due to parochial situation, was one of the reasons of JP's anger and anguish explained by Romesh Thaper, editor of Seminar is one of his articles.[12] Reasons of revulsion against working of Party System was observed by JP himself in the year 1957 itself. He said:

> I saw how parties backed by finance organization and the means of progaganda would impose themselves on the people; how people's rule became infact party rule, how party rule in turn became the rule of a caucus or coterie; how democracy was reduced to mere casting of votes; how even their right to vote was

restricted severely by the system of powerful parties setting up their candidates from whom alone, for all practical purposes, the voters had to made their choice, how even this limited choice was made unreal by the fact that the issues posed before the electorate were by and large incomprehensible to it.[13]

Since than situation was becoming bad to worse so far as the working of democracy in India was concerned according to JP. Commenting on the situation once JP said that "the way political funds had have been collected in recent years, the huge election expenditure incurred, the large scale impersonation, the "capturing" of polling booth–these and other similar practices threaten to reduce elections to a mere formality.[14] JP further explained that "the large source of corruption is the collection of party funds mainly by the ruling party bosses which remains unaccounted and unaudited and are used for personal gratification, selectively financing the election of sycophants buying up defectors and toppling governments.[15] JP was deeply disturbed with the fact that floor crossing was a contagious political disease and political indiscipline was the order of the day. Selfishness and lust of power was rampant, legislators were not above board and were drawn in the market for sale and purchase and degradation and devaluation of ideologies was a persistent reality.[16]

Whole atmosphere has got polluted because of dominant politics in the whole system. JP has observed that "the galloping corruption is affecting and degrading because of the predominant position politics occupies in an underdeveloped society, the entire gamut of national life; business, whether it is private or public, administration; the professions; education; even customs, manners and personal relations.[17] JP further said that the political corruption ultimately leads to a black money economy, bureaucratic corruption, cynicism among the electorate and demoralization and frustration among opposition parties.[18]

JP was convinced that the most serious fault of parliamentary democracy, was its inherent tendency towards centralism. The sovereign individuals became helpless. He wrote, "The sovereign people being dispersed over the length the breadth of the country like particles of sand over the desert and having no other organized political force than the national state itself to interpose between themselves and that state, the latter naturally becomes all powerful. The issue of power in such state is decided not by the fictitious people but by a balance between political parties and such organized interests as industrialists and bankers and powerful labour unions.[19]

Since 1953 JP had been convinced that the pattern of democracy prevalent in Europe as inappropriate to India because of her feudal backwardness.[20] Furthermore, appallingly expensive and wasteful mass elections, manipulated by powerful, centrally controlled parties, with the aid of high finance and diabolically clever methods and highly efficient means of communication, amounted not to be a representation of the electorate, but a rape of the masses by the interests backing the parties. The need to win votes created an opportunity for indulging in lies and half truths and for arousing base passions or false hopes with dishonest. So democracy became another serious defect of parliamentary democracy. An election created unnecessary passion and dissension instead of education and enlightening the people on the real interests of the nation.[21]

Political parties, JP said, had became a state within the state run by caucuses that were beyond the control of the voters and even the enrolled members of the parties. Bureaucracy became the natural outcome of the centralization of power and administration, because overworked cabinet members left more and more to permanent officials who worked in secret, were unresponsive to the people and became a dangerous autocracy.[22]

JP, however, believed that the real guarantee of democracy was the faith of the people in democracy, the strength of the people, the capacity of the people to manage their affairs themselves.[23] But the above description of the working of Indian democracy suggested that the JP was much dissatisfied with the working of parliamentary democracy as was being practised in India because it has resulted incorruption and the ideals of social, economic and political democracy enshrined under the Constitution have remained a dream betrayed of. In this system the role of the people has reduced to a mere voter during elections. Since JP had faith in true democracy he was restless and also suggested a system in which the role of political parties could be minimized on the one hand and the role of the people could be extended to the maximum limit on the other hand. This was the essence of his participatory democracy. What JP suggest in form of party less democracy and Panchayati Raj system, his objective to make the people of the country conscious of their sovereign right to have a government of their choice and to change, it when it acted otherwise, Gandhiji had also believed essentially in the sovereignty of people based on pure moral authority.[24]

Throughout JP's life, starting from the childhood, there was a single factor underlying his thought process, his concern for the humankind and his growth and he tried to place man in the centre of the picture.[25] JP says "I happen to be an individual who believes in man as the measure of all things, who believes in deeply in the human philosophy...based on the belief in the universality and the supremacy of the human spirit".[26]

Since, individual always remained a primary concern of JP, his philosophical exercise was also directed to have a good society for him. For JP, the good society is that which helps men to achieve a higher standard of morality; to be free, to be responsible and self-reliant politically and economically, to be creative and just. Thus, in JP's new society, democracy rests upon consensus not upon the will of majority. Majority rule in western type societies has become associated with democracy, but in reality the concept of the will of the majority which is not the same thing at all.[27]

For JP, real democracy lies in economic, social and political equity in the true sense of the term, while delivering one of his speeches, JP said that "We have to make democracy real and strong for true rule of the people, we have to put an end to injustice and exploitation."[28] And for this JP had suggested a system of participatory democracy—a system in which even the people at the grass-root should have their say and also their participation in policy decision and policy implementation process. In other words, he was interested to devise a method to ensure the maximum participation of the people in governance and for that he favoured the concept of decentralisation of power. He was opposed to the centralisation of power because it ultimately might lead to dictatorship of all kinds.

And, JP's ideals of this kind of system or governance were responsible for his departure from Marxism. When JP observed the working of Marxism in Russia and role of communist parties in India, he realized that communists could never think of sharing power with anyone except as a makeshift with convenient stages.[29] Since JP was deeply influenced by Gandhian theory and practice, he was keen to formulate political strategy and tactics rooted in the indigenous soil of India with primary emphasis on peaceful transformation.[30] JP also parted with party politics when he realized that the party system had developed a tendency to reduce the people to a voter only during elections. These real masters have become mere spectators of the day to day events due to the increasing role of political parties under the strong and deep shadow of strict party discipline. So he experimented with the concept and ideals of Socialism and Sarvodaya to achieve the goal-economic, social and political, however, he was conscious of the fact that it would not be possible to do away with political parties completely. So, keeping importance and inevitability of the political parties in mind he tried to devise a means to minimize the role of political parties on the one hand and to maximize the role of people on the other hand in the working of political system.

JP's thought culminated in a brilliant synthesis of Gandhian and traditional Indian practices into proposals for the reconstruction of Indian Polity. This eightynine page booklet was published by the Gandhian Movement and in it he has used a variety of thinkers from all over the world to fill out Gandhi's concepts of self sufficient villages and the thoughts about indirect elections that Gandhi had voiced at 1930 Round Table conference in London. Jayaprakash saw mankind confronted with a choice between robotism in large centralized capitalist or communist states or else freedom in small communities in a communitarian state. To his mind, his proposal to invert the power pyramid was rational, scientific and most suited to India's immediate political needs, because parliamentary democracy had shown serious and major defects and had an inherent tendency towards centralism.[31]

JP, therefore, outlined the form he wished to see Panchayati Raj take on the basis of political consensus in small communitarian village societies, cooperative economic enterprise, abolition of representative assemblies, and the withering away of the finest intellectual achievement of the lifetime an one of the twentieth century's most critically perceptive and pragmatically visionary pieces of political philosophy. For it he was subsequently awarded a share in the Magsaysay prize for prominent Asians.[32]

Under his philosophical scheme of political structure all adults in a village, JP maintained, should meet regularly as members of their general assembly (Gram Sabha), the highest political institution of their primary community. There should be no candidates or parties, but selection of a village council (Gram Panchayat) should be carried out by general consensus of opinion or by drawing lots, procedures that were already common practices in the villages. The responsibility of the assembly and council would be to ensure that no one in the village went without food, clothing or shelter; that all children received primary education; that everyone received primary medical care; that there was no unemployment; that a minimum standard of living for all was achieved; that serious inequalities of wealth were prevented; and that the village became self sufficient. These two bodies might provide primary schools, wells, dams and handicraft industries. Achieving the integration of cities in the hierarchical structure would be difficult but possible by re-constituting them as federations of communities.[33]

The next level of political structure would he that of regional community, with the Gram Panchayat integrated into Panchayat Samitis. Similarly, the Panchayat Samities of a district would be integrated into state assembly and state assemblies integrated into national parliament. Thus, a political institution at each level would be an integration of institutions at the lower level. There would be indirect instead of direct elections.[34]

JP made it very clear that if "local bodies" were given more powers and direct system of election was replaced by an indirect one, while the rest of the social organization were left as it was, there could be any worthwhile change. The policy suggested, was not a "graft" on the existing body of society but an organic part of a radically transformed social order.[35]

However, JP was conscious of the fact that such a polity could not be built in a day and there would be a period of transition also. Thus, to begin with elections should be so conducted that Political parties did not play any role in them up to district level. Een at the State and National level, the candidates must be selected by the people themselves and not by the parties, which during the period of transition might be allowed to support particular candidates after their selection by the people. JP proposed in a speech to the Members of Parliament on September 23, 1958 that instead of political parties setting out candidates, the community, the voters themselves, should be enabled to do so. Meetings of voters could be enabled to do so. Meetings of voters could be held in each booth area of all the constituencies. Each meeting, of perhaps two thousand, could be held in each booth area of all the constituencies. Each meeting, of perhaps two thousand, could elect two delegates by a majority vote. All these delegates from the booth areas, perhaps six hundred in all, would then hold a conference at which the nomination of candidates could take place. By law any one should be entitled to propose and second the name of prospective candidate and the nominee could become a candidate upon receiving a certain percentage, perhaps twenty five to thirty percent or more, of the votes of the delegates at their conference. The delegates who formed a kind of electoral college would then do the campaigning. The existing political parties should not propose names for nomination, but should perform only educative functions, explaining issues. After the nomination of candidates, the political parties-could decides to give their support to one or other of the candidates of the people's choice.[36] In this way gradually the role of the political parties would be decreased in the political process and that of the people would increase leading eventually to the establishment of "Partyless Democracy" or "Communitarian Society."[37]

JP, however, suggested a procedure slightly different from one suggested in his "Reconstruction of Indian Polity", mentioned above in his "Swaraj for the People". JP feared that indirect election might encourage parochialism and retard the growth of national outlook among all citizens. It was also more liable to be corrupted by moneyed interests, as the number of electorates, would be small except at the lowest level. He, thus recommended a method of election which would be direct, yet so organized as to give the institutions of Panchayati Raj at every level a definite role in it. Thus, it may be possible to have advantages of direct election without affecting the organic nature of the new polity. He further argued that the role of political parties should be restricted as far as possible and people be enabled to select their own candidates for election through popular constituted electoral councils. Every constitutional and educational device should be adopted to encourage councils to set up not more than one candidate for every seat thus avoiding contest. JP considered all this essential for fulfillment of democracy–"no matter what be its kind" so that its processes are little divisive as possible, or to put it positively as cohesive".[38]

JP was conscious of the fact that the desired reconstruction of polity might perhaps be idealistic even utopian. He would not however, consider that to be a disqualification. The achievement of that ideal would be a colossal task. Thousands, perhaps hundreds a number of years to accomplish it. Since the task was one of "social engineering", this would require the help of the state, of scientists, of experts, educationists, businessmen, experiments of men and women, of young and old. It would be a "task of dedication of creation of self-discovery".[39]

The details as analysed above suggest that JP's philosophical exercise was directed to devise a method to ensure the maximum participation of the people in governance of the state and for that he favoured the concept of decentralization of power. He was opposed to concentration of power, because it ultimately lead to dictatorship of all kinds. JP found dictatorship against the concept of good society.[40]

JP was applying his ideals to concrete situations all the time during his life. The store of his ideas and their practical implications which he has left behind him could serve generation of seekers to interpret and improve upon by practical application. Like Gandhiji, JP too spent his whole time trying to figure out an ideology which could serve as an alternative to Marxism and one which could suit the Indian ethos. During his time JP field-experimented his ideas, wherever his hectic journey through Marxism, Communism, Socialism, Sarvodaya, and Bhoodan took him. This brought him into close touch with fellow men of all kinds. With their cooperation he set up organizations to give shape to his ideas. Voluntary organizations like AVARD (Association of Voluntary Agencies for Rural Development), Trusteeship Foundation, Gandhi Peace Foundation, Civil Liberties Movement, Committees for Electoral Reforms, Constitutional Amendment, Educational Reforms, Rural Development and many other came into being.[41]

Field experiments of JP made his belief and commitment deep and strong in masses to the extent that he allowed himself even at the fag end of his life to lead a world wide known and much debated agitation of Bihar termed as JP agitation against the accumulated evils of party politics resulted into the dictatorial attitude of the then ruling power in 1974. JP reiterated his stand once again in his Prison Diary when he said:

> I had written and spoken powerfully against political corruption (Party, government, administration) suggesting means to check it as well as the need to reform the electoral law and procedure. I had met the PM twice in 1973 specially to discuss these points; and had come away sorely disappointed. It was then that I had written the article in which I had declared that the people of the country themselves must fight, in peaceful ways, of course, for deliverance from the corrupt system under which they were suffering. Apart from corruption, they must also fight hunger,

unemployment, inflation, social and economic injustice of many kinds, the futile class system of education, which in the first place left most of their children uneducated and in the second place mis educated the rest. It was in this background, of calls for people's and students, action to tackle their problem themselves that both the Gujarat and Bihar students' movement took place.[42]

All talk of man's primary, morally based laws and democracy, however, could turn futile under conditions of exploitation of man by man himself. One form of this exploitation according to JP was political dictatorship. When this actually happened in this country in 1975, JP advocated a simultaneous resistance movement to this evil through struggle, even while developing a movement for strengthening people's power through self education, self development. Such ideology, JP felt would help to implement the national ideals stated in the Indian Constitution.[43]

JP purposely reminded us about celebrating January 26 as Republic Day every years since 1950. But this celebration has an earlier history he emphasized. It was in 1930 that the nation first decided to celebrate January 26 as Independence Day. On that memorable day hundreds of thousands of men and women all over the country took a Pledge which became famous as Independence pledge. The pledge affirmed "the inalienable right of the people "not only to have freedom" but also "to enjoy the fruits of their toil and have the necessities of life so that they may have full opportunities of growth". The pledge also asserted that "if any government deprives people of these rights and oppresses them, the people have a further right to alter it or to abolish it. Indeed, using the words of the independence Day Pledge, it can be asserted that it has ruined Bihar "economically, politically and spiriturally.[44]

In the days of Bihar Movement. JP repeatedly stressed the supremacy of the people against the government and called those enemies of democracy who were opposed to the peaceful demonstration and protests of the people.[45] JP believed that in the absence of right of electorate to recall deviant representative, people's political participation is reduced to mere casting of votes.[46] As the repository of all powers, people must have the right to recall its rulers when they forfeit its confidence. The struggle in Bihar was an assertion of the principles of continuous and continuing accountability of the representatives of the people to the people. It stands for a dynamic doctrine of democratic correctives. To borrow a phrase from Burke, it asserts that democratic institutions are not a control upon the people but a control for the people.[47] The system of recall demanded by JP should be understood in the spirit in which he and many others have demanded it. Under the present system, the elected representatives of the people soon become unrepresentative. They fail to keep their promises, not because too many of them succumb to corruption–in the Gandhian as well as in the more mundane sense.[48]

A.N. Das has observed that the questions JP has forced on the attention of the Indian public are basically concerned with the nature of democratic political system and properties of the democratic mandate.[49] JP declared that if the people were not satisfied with the way the government was being carried on, they should not sit quiet till the next election came around. The right to recall should be given to the people and the Constitution should be amended for the purpose. He replied to those who charged him of weakening the democracy that a true democracy calls for the operation of people's power as against the power of the government. So, JP wanted to make *lok hakti* superior to the *danda* or *raj shakti*. But the politics of the people's power would not be imposed from above but would grow from below. It would be born from the womb of the people's power.[50]

However, it was alleged that the movement which JP led in Bihar was not based on the principle of lok shakti or people's power but on the contrary it was the game of few and also the handiwork/game of party politics. Therefore, it had nothing to do with the ideals of participatory democracy advocated and experimented with them earlier.

But JP asserted that it was based on the ideals to which he remained committed throughout his life and the movement was based on the people's power and it had nothing to do with the party politics. JP's own clarification is worth considering.

He wrote:

> Moreover, at its start while the Bihar students' movement was truly a non party affair and 80 to 90 per cent of the young men and women who participated in its programmes had no political party attachments, its leadership was surely made up of student and ex-student personnel who had strong party affiliations and who undoubtedly were guided by the party leaders outside. The parties involved were mainly four-Jana Sangha, Socialist Party, BLD and Congress (O). At several University Centres Jana Sangha was the strongest element and in some the BLD and the SP. The congress (O) leadership in the steering committee was quite mature and influential, though numerically weak. Now this was the situation when my association with the Bihar students' movement started. The political parties were there already. In fact, it will be admitted by all objective observers that my influence kept the party influences low, helped to evolve a consensus, and give the movement *at to* start the students' movement and then the people's movement a non party political character.[51]

JP further argued :

> After all, the parties that entered the movement in Bihar did not enter as parties, as their leaders, workers

and sympathizers came as individuals. These parties of course at their formal meetings outside the movement, passed resolutions and issues statements fully supporting the movement.[52]

Moreover, what JP said in this context is worth considering. He said "it is just not possible to keep political parties out from coming into an open mass movement".[53] JP Movement proved a biggest political event in which the awakening of the people was unprecedented in the last four-five decades in Indian democracy. This became responsible for uprooting a political party from seat of power having a history of more than hundred years. Never before world had experienced this kind of election. This was nothing but a miracle of democracy which world experienced in from of elections. Virtually election in the backdrop of JP movement proved a *Janata Party* (people's festival). However, this kind of experiment of JP with democracy was not aimed to change of the seat of power only but it had bigger objectives. The purpose was to assert the power of people and to make a realization that change could be and should be made possible by people and moreover this power also should remain continuous with the people.[54]

On the morrow of Jayaprakash Narayan's death on October 1979, The Times of India editorially commented: "He made his greatest contribution to the country in March 1977 when he helped the hastily put together Janata Party defeat Mrs. Gandhi's Congress which had during the 20 months of emergency fouled the great record as the party of India's independence and consolidation and thereby restore the rule of law and fundamental rights enshrined in the Constitution."[55] His is a philosophy that deserves careful consideration by all those who seriously question the success of the type of societies we have at present. No philosophy for political reconstruction is entire in all its details of implementation and it would be unjust to JP to assume that he is unaware of the human vices which may in the end make much less of his philosophy than he intended.[56]

The details as analysed above reveal that the issues raised by JP are still relevant, rather more relevant today. Participatory democracy in the true sense of the term requires maximum and continuous participation and control of masses in the working of political system. It might have been one of the reasons of the 73rd and 74th Constitutional Amendments in 1992 which recognizes the importance of Panchayati Raj Institutions in the true sense of the term. This development has added a new dimension to the working of Indian democracy. The concept and nature of elite has also taken a new dimension. And this was one of the important issues raised and discussed by JP in a systematic manner much earlier. Even the act of nationalization of banks and abolition of Privy purses by the Government of India in the year 1971 might have proved a matter of satisfaction for JP as these issues also figured in his 14 points raised as pre-conditions for joining the government by JP in response to the request of Prime Minister Jawaharlal Nehru in the year 1958."[57] However, many more steps are needed to fulfill the dream of real democracy of JP. Many of the critical problems our democracy is facing today were addressed seriously by JP much earlier.

JP was highly critical of the functioning of party politics in the country and also found it responsible for corruption at all levels. The increasing tide of corruption at all level-MP bribery case, Tehelka episode and many more cases of corruption at high places has engulfed our system in a big way. It also exposes the working of our political parties. Moreover, the way political parties of the country have reacted to the poll-reforms process, suggested by the Election Commission and justified by the law court, have exposed every political party and the fear of JP has also come true about the working of political parties. There is no denying the fact that the political parties are essential part of the parliamentary democracy but at the same time it can also not be denied that the present working requires revolutionary changes in the light of basic premises of democracy about which JP has talked about in his long career of political experiments. Today further more experiments are needed to make democracy participatory and real, and JP has many important things to offer for further experiment.

It has rightly been analysed that the value of JP's polity lies not so much in its practically for a new society as in its hope and its essential morality. Without vision the people can make no progress. People have to be told in every generation that man needs to create a society in which all that is essential to him as a man is satisfied. Man's independence of social and political institutions and his right to expect them to help him achieve these needs has to be re-emphasized, so that we see the institutions we create not as permanent and immutable creations, but as fallible structure erected by fallible men subject to change and modification according to their need.[58]

REFERENCES

See Allan, et.al., JP: His Biography, Orient Longman, New Delhi, 1975, p. 353.

See, Ibid, p. 405.

See, Brahmanand (ed) Jayaprakash Narayan, Towards total Revolution; Search for an ideology, Vol. 1, Popular Prakashan, Bombay, 1978, p. 7.

See Madhu Limaye, "Last of the Foundation Fathers", Sunday, Vol. II, No. 19, Oct. 14, 1979, p. 36.

See Narayan, Jayaprakash, From Socialism to Sarvodaya, Akhil Bharat Sarva Seva Sangh Prakashan (ABSSSP), Kashi, 1959, p. 9.

See, Narayan, Jayaprakash, Swaraj for the People, ABSSSP, Varanasi, 1961, p. 2.

See, Narayan, Jayaprakash, Prison Diary 1975, Popular Prakashan, Bombay, 1977, p. 15.

See Brahmanand (ed.), Jayaprakash Narayan, Communitarian Society and Panchayati Raj, Navachetana Prakashan 1970, p. 70, also see Asha Sinha, Political Philosophy of Jayaprakash Narayna, Janaki Prakashan, New Delhi, 1997, p. 130.

See Nimbakar, Krishnabai, "JP's Ideas: Assessment", Gandhi Marg, Vol. III, No. 1, April 25, 1981, p. 17.

See, Bajwa, D.K., Jayaprakash Narayan and Indian Politics, Deep and Deep Publication, New Delhi, 1987, pp. 136-137.

See Allan et. al,. op. cit., pp. 410-11.

See Thaper, Romesh, "Salvaging the Passion...." In Mahadevan, T.K., JP and the Future of Indian Democracy, EPW, New Delhi, 1975, p. 127.

See Bajwa, D.K., op. cit., p. 117.

See Narayan, Jayaprakash, Towards Total Revolution: Total Revolution, Popular Prakashan, Bombay, 1979, p. 6.

See Singh, Mahendra Prasad, "Jayaprakash Narayan on Parliamentary Democracy and Electoral Reforms in India", Gandhi Marg, New Delhi, Vol. 1, No. 12, March, 1980, p. 761.

See Patil, V.T. et. al., JP: Sarvodaya Total Revolution, Deep and Deep Publication, New Delhi, 1989, pp. 58-59.

See Singh, Mahendra Prasad, op. cit.

See Ibid, p. 761.

See Narayan Jayaprakash, "A Plea for Reconstruction of Indian Polity", ABSSSP, Kashi, 1959, p. 68.

See Allan et. al. op. cit., p. 344.

See Ibid, pp. 348-49.

See Ibid, pp. 349.

See Bhattacharjee, Ajit, Jayaprakash Narayan : A Political Biography, Vikas Publishing House, 1975, p. 127.

See Harijan, Jan. 2, 1937, in Bhattacharya Buddhadeva, "Gandhi and Western Parliamentary Democracy", Gandhi Marg, Vol. 1, NO. 6, New Delhi, Sept. 1979, p. 327.

See Masani, Minoo R., JP Mission Partly Accomplished, Macmillan Company of India, Delhi, 1977.

See Raj, Sebasti, L. "A Man Centred Philosophy : Reflections on JP's concept of Man", The Indian Journal of Political Science (IJPS), Vol. 1, No. 1, Jan-March 1989, p. 75.

See Allan et. al. op. cit, p. 410.

See Dutta, Vijay Ranjan, "Continuing Revolution", The Hindustan Times, Patna, Oct. 11, 2002, p. 9.

See Gupta, R.C., Great Political Thinkers, Lakshmi Narayan Agrawal Educational Publishing, Agra, p. 168.

See Patil, V.T., op. cit., p. 52.

See Allan et. al., op. cit., p. 348.

See Ibid.

See Ibid, pp. 349-50.

See Ibid.

See Ibid.

See Allan et. al., op. cit., pp. 351-52.

See Narayan, Jayaprakash, A Plea for the Reconstruction of Indian Polity, op. cit. pp. 78-79.

See Narayan, Jayaprakash, Swaraj for the People, ABSSSP, Varanasi, 1961, p. 25.

See Narayan, Jayaprakash, A Plea for the Reconstruction of Indian Polity, op. cit., p. 81.

See Allan et. al., pp. 406-410.

See Nimbakar, Krishnabhai, op. cit., p. 17.

See Narayan, Jayaprakash, Prison Diary, op. cit., p. 24.

See Nimbakar, Krishnabhai, op. cit., p. 16.

See Narayan, Jayaprakash, Towards Total Revolution: Total Revolution, op. cit., p. 118.

See Sinha, Asha, op. cit., pp. 144-45.

See Singh, Mahendra Prasad, op. cit., p. 761.

See Dutta, Dev, "The Great Defreeze", in Mahadevan, T.K. (ed.), op. cit., p. 28.

See Ganguli, B.N., "Rotten Boroughs...", in Mahadevan T.K. (eds), op. cit., p. 28.

See Das, A.N., "In a Country of Thieves...", in Mahadevan, T.K. (ed) p. 43.

See Nargolkar, Vasant, JP Vindicated, S. Chand & Co. New Delhi 1977, pp. 35-36.

See Narayan, Jayaprakash, Prison Diary, op. cit., p. 56-57.

See Ibid, p. 58.

See Ibid, p. 56.

See Singh, Ramjee, Gandhi Vichar: Darshan, Dharm, Rajniti Aur Arthniti, Manak Publications, Delhi, 1995, pp. 255-56.

See The Times of India, New Delhi, Oct. 9, 1979, in Singh, Mahendra Prasad, op. cit., p. 577.

See Allan, et. al., op. cit., pp. 412-13.

See Patil, V.T., et. al., Jayaprakash Narayan: Dynamics of Socialism, Deep & Deep Publications, New Delhi, 1989, pp. 110-116.

See Allan et. al., op. cit., p. 418.

3

Challenges for Progress and Peace in Contemporary Economy Polity, and Society

D.M. Diwakar

Introduction

Speech of the General Secretary of United Nations Mr. Kofi Annan in a summit of the World Economic Forum on February 5, 2002, reflected the realisation of the hard fact: "The reality is that power and wealth in this world are very, very unequally shared and that far too many people are condemned to lives of extreme poverty and degradation."[1] (Krishnaswamy, Feb. 5, 2002). Challenges before the world in general need to be comprehended carefully in view of the history of progress that the world has witnessed. To take stock of the fact in the light of the practices across the countries on the globe is essential in this context. A quick look at the balance sheet of human development suggests that about 24 per cent of the population of the developing countries are living below the poverty line. If they are reduced to the halves by 2015 as per United Nations Declaration, there will still be 900 millions people living in extreme poverty, 826 million people undernourished and nearly one billion people will still lack access to improved water resources[2] (Human Development Report 2001: 22).

However, region wise poverty displayed in Table 1 suggests that 1199 millions people are below the income of less than US$ 1 per day. World Employment Report of the International Labour Office provides alarming picture of increasing unemployment rate of selected countries of the world economy as displayed in table 2. Addressing the delegates of World Economic Forum Mr. Kofi Annan warned a note of caution : "None of us, I suggest, can afford to ignore the condition of our fellow passengers on this little boat. If they are sick, all of us risk infection. If they are angry, all of us easily get hurt." This reminds me the speech of Vivekanand: "The upper classes will no longer be able to repress the lower, try they ever so much. The well being of the higher classes now lies in the helping the lower to get their legitimate rights. ...When the masses will wake, they will come to understand your oppression of them, and by a puff of their mouth you will be entirely blown away"[3] (1979, vol. 7: 149-50). There is general view among the development experts that globalisation has bypassed the poor. Human Development Report indicates: "many of the poorest countries are marginalised from the growing global opportunities. The income gap between the poorest and the richest countries are widening"[4] (HDP, 2000:82). Mr. Annan also shared his perception: "The general perception among many is that this is the fault of globalisation and that globalisation

Table 1 : Poverty and Number of People Living of Less Than US$ 1 Per Day

Region	*Percentage of Population*		*Number (Millions)*
	1990	*1998*	*1998*
East Asia and the Pacific	28	15	278
Europe and Central Asia	2	5	24
Latin America and the Caribbean	17	16	78
Middle East and North America	2	2	6
South Asia	44	40	522
Sub-Saharan Africa	48	46	291

Source : World Employment Report 2001, ILO, Zeneva, p. 22.

Table 2 : Rates of Unemployment & GDP (Growth in Different Regions of the World (1990-2000)

Region & Countries	*Unemployment*		*Annual Growth Rate (%) '90-99*	
	1990	*2000*	*G.D.P.*	*Employment*
Development Countries	6.1	6.2		
Austria	3.2	4.7	2.0	0.8
Belgium	7.2	8.6	1.7	1.1
Finland	3.2	10.2	2.5	0.2
Japan	2.1	4.7	1.4	0.1
France	9.2	11.8	1.7	0.3
Greece	7.0	10.8	1.9	0.8
Spain	16.0	15.8	2.2	1.2
Sweden	1.8	7.1	1.5	–1.1
U.K.	6.8	6.0	2.2	0.3
Europe	7.7	9.0		
USA	5.6	3.9	3.4	1.3
Latin America & the Caribbean	5.7	8.9		
Argentina	7.5	15.4	6.2	
Brazil	4.3	7.5	3.1	
Chile	7.4	9.2	8.3	
Colombia	10.5	20.4	4.1	
Ecuador	6.1	14.9	3.2	
Peru	8.3	10.3	6.0	
Ururguay	9.2	13.3	4.1	
Venezuela	11.0	14.6	3.2	
Asia and Pacific	4.0	4.6		
Singapur	1.7	4.6	8.0	2.5
China	2.5	3.1	10.7	–
Hong-Kong China	1.3	4.7	3.8	2.1
Taiwan China	1.7	3.1	6.1	1.4
Repub. of Korea	2.5	6.3	5.7	1.3
India	–	–	–	1.4
Pakistan	3.1	5.9	4.0	2.4
Bangladesh	1.9	2.5	4.8	1.4
Mid-East & N. Africa	7.1	10.9		
Algeria	19.8	28.7	1.6	4.4
Morocco	15.8	22.0	11.7	2.7
Repub. Macedonia	23.6	34.5	–	–
Albania	9.5	18.0	2.3	–
Russian Federation	9.5	11.4	–6.1	–2.4

Source : World Employment Report 2001, ILO, Zeneva, pp. 16,

is driven by a global elite, composed of at least represented by, the people who attend this gathering."[5] (Krishnaswamy, Feb. 5, 2002). In view of emerging global challenges and the results of practices, this paper is an attempt to participate in the debate of progress and peace in order to identify framework and institution towards an egalitarian non-violent society. This exercise includes brief accounts of (i) challenges (ii) civil society and progress (iii) process of transformation, (iv) democratic participation and development and finally (v) beyond bourgeois democracy.

Challenges : India Scenario

Dwelling with Indian scenario of progress, Human Development Index (HDI), gives an idea about the material progress that the world has made so far, India ranks 127 in terms of HDI. A quick look through Human Development Report 2003 suggests that 16 per cent population are yet to get access to safe drinking water, 25 per cent are waiting for the access of health services and 71 per cent population are without access to sanitation (Table 3). During last ten years (1987-98) poorest 20 per cent of the country could get on an average only 8.1 per cent share in the national income or consumption, whereas richest 20 per cent could enjoy 46.1 per cent of the national income and consumption. Population on an average below poverty line during 1989-98 stagger to 44.2 per cent. Thus, it is obvious that much are left to reach the desired level to attain social justice. When we say these, we do not intend to negate the level of achievements that the country has attained. But at the same time we can not deny the facts that we have spent more than five decades and the issues of dalits are yet to be addressed properly. Recent data from the Ministry of Rural Development suggests that number of family assisted under poverty alleviation programmes of self and wage employment schemes have significantly decreased. There is reduction in share of women as well[6] (IAMR, 1998-472).

Table 3 : Population without Access to Amenities and Share of Income/Consumption in India

	Indicators	*Percentage*
1.	Population Without Access to	
	(a) Safe Water	16
	(b) Health Services	25
	(c) Sanitation	72
2.	Share of Income or Consumption during 1987-98 for	
	(a) Poorest 20 per cent	8.1
	(b) Richest 20 per cent	46.1
3.	Population below Income Poverty Line during 1989-98	44.2

Source : 1. Human Development Report, 2003.
2. Gupta, S.P., Trickle Down Theory Revisited: The Role of Employment and Poverty, Lecture delivered in Annual Conference of the Indian Society of Le Butter Economic Society, December 1999.

Another set of data on poverty reveals that there has been significant fluctuation in poverty ratio (Table 4). It has increased at faster rate during last one decade. According to the Central Planning Commission, rural poverty ratio was 41.7 per cent in 1992, which could be reduced to 38.5 by 1995-96. But again the poverty ratio has increased to the higher level (i.e., 45.2 per cent) in 1998 that that of 1992. If the number of people below poverty line is considered, they were 348.0 millions in 1992, which increased to 348.8 millions in 1995-96 and further addition by 1998 made this volume to 406.3 millions. Thus, about 583 millions poor people were added to the volume of poverty in India. However, there is sudden decline significantly in the poverty ratio and number of persons below poverty line in 1999-2000. These figures however, attracted many methodological criticisms. Some of the experts have suggested a fresh estimation to remove these shortcomings[7] (Sen, 2000, EPW). There is also another consideration that only the physical access to two end meet, minimum clothing and housing are not enough to understand the quality of life. Other essentials regarding health, drinking water and education, which are still beyond the safety nets should be brought under considerations[8] (Vaidynathan, 2001: EPW, May 26; Radhakrishna, 2002, January).

Table 4 : Population Below Poverty Line in Rural Areas

Period	Bihar		India	
	Number (lakh)	Percentage	Number (lakh)	Percentage
1973-74	336.52	62.99	2612.90	56.44
1977-78	354.48	63.25	2642.47	53.07
1983	417.70	64.37	2519.57	45.65
1987-88	370.23	52.63	2315.79	38.09
1993-94	450.56	56.21	2440.31	37.27
1999-2000 (30-day recall)	376.51	44.30	1932.43	27.09
(7-day recall)	322.96	38.00	1713.35	24.02

Source : The Planning Commission, Government of India, Press Release, 1997 & 2001.

Gaps between deprived and privileged have been widening at a faster rate. Income gap between agriculture and non-agriculture has increased from 1:2 to 1:6. If we take stock of the recent situation, particularly of about two decades, which are pertinent in terms of inter decade comparison of pre and post liberalisation, it may through up some light in understating the issues and level of social justice. Data for the two decades, i.e., 1981-82 to 1990-91 and 1991-92 to 1999-2000, as given in table 5, suggest that the growth rates of GDP were almost constant but there was significant decline in production of agriculture and manufacturing industry, per capita rural income, and employment in organised sector. Agricultural production decreased from 3.9 per cent during first period to 2.9 per cent. Manufacturing sector recorded 7.8 per cent during pre liberlisation and subsequently declined to 5.7 per cent in the post liberalisation years. Per capita income of the rural area has decreased from 3.1 per cent to 1.8 per cent and employment in organised sector. Increase in the rates of change was registered for tertiary sectors, i.e., from 6.2 per cent to 7.5 per cent and poverty, i.e., 33 to +23 per cent. There was marginal increase in total per capita income from 3.2 per cent to 3.7 per cent. Flow of foreign capital as a percentage of national income decreased from 2.63 to 1.6 but the ratio of outflow of interest and profit to national income increased from 0.93 to 1.72 (85%) and 0.89 to 2.18 (145%) respectively. Altogether increase in the ratio of total outflow was from 1.82 to 3.9, i.e., 114 per cent. Ratio of domestic saving and investment to national income decreased from 21.0 to 18.4 (–12.4%) and 23.4 to 21.0 (i.e., –10.3%) respectively. Thus, there has been over all deterioration in the economic condition of the country.

Table 5 : Performance of Indian Economy During Last Two Decades of Pre and Post Liberalisation

Indicators	*Average Annual Rate of Change*	
	1981-82 to 1990-91	*1991-92 to 1999-2000*
1. Agricultural Production	3.9	2.8
2. Industrial Production	7.8	5.7
3. Employment in Organised Sector	2.56	0.75
4. Total Employment	2.7	1.3
5. Production of Services	6.2	7.5
6. Gross Domestic Product at Factor Cost	5.7	5.8
7. Per Capita Rural Income	3.1	1.8
8. Total Income	3.2	3.7
9. As a Percentage of National Income		
(a) Flow of Foreign Capital	2.63	1.6
(b) Payment of Interest	0.93	1.72
(c) Profit and other Outflow	0.89	2.18
(d) Total Outflow (b+c)	1.82	3.90
(e) Domestic Saving	21.0	18.40
(f) Total Investment	23.4	21.00

Source : Economic Survey, Ministry of Finance, Government of India, various Issues.

Social discrimination and atrocities are at the lowest ebb. Now even fundamental rights to live are denied. They are killed indiscriminately by the private armies and the State has been ineffective to check such recurrences.

Dalits have been killed in their home states and at place of works as migrant labourers outside their states. They hardly enjoy the constitutional guarantee to safeguard their lives. Untouchability although has been reduced in urban setting to a certain extent but t still persists in its bad shape and the situation is worse in rural areas. These facts also raise the question as to whether the present set of ruling class is really interested in solving this hardship at all, which may turn against his interest. It is precisely because they have sufficient insights of progress, issues therein and the strategies. In such a miserable situation it is hard to believe that the growth with justice have been promoted to attain the goal of progress. The factual position regarding global economy and quality of life particularly in developing nations like India provide scope for second thought for the development process that can achieve the goal of progress with justice. This also gives an opportunity to reflect and examine the concept of progress that emerged in the process of development of society.

Civil Society and Progress

Civil society has been perceived in many ways and with many meanings. It has been perceived as an obligatory adherence to existing legal order or changes instituted in system. It has been considered as an opposite to military, uncivil, private, etc.[9] (Johnson; 473). Tester (1992)[10] considers civil society as a possibility of a society with modernity and voluntary association of contractual arrangements, free from the dead weights of tradition and authority.[11] Seligman (1992) takes it as an ethical harmonization that makes a social order possible. This concept may have consonance with flexible modernity of post industrialisation, but it will be a difficult match with market and globalisation. Hegel considers civil society as the set of institutions that look after the needs of economic life and regulate people's pursuit of their private affairs. Unlikely to traditional theorists Hegel combines the values of civil society with those of families and transcended both of them.[12] (Britanica, 959). Marx does not treat civil society as a concept other than a socialist egalitarian society, i.e., stateless and classless society with peace and harmony. Departing from the tradition of Marx,[13] Gramsci (1972) considers civil society as a form of struggle for hegemony of cultural and ideological sphere rather than economic domain. According to him the state is uniquely bound to civil society in the developed capitalist world for 'active consent' of the public is secured not through democracy but through hegemony. Civil society, therefore is the site of constant struggle for power as different classes and social groups seek to define popular aspirations in their own terms. Falling in this line of argument Walzer[14] (1992), writing on contemporary relevance of civil society, explains that 'good life' and conflict free social order is not a possibility. Whereas Kene argues in favour of reviving civil society as an integral part of democratic socialism and emphasise that state should be accountable to civil society. But, with the emergence of market and collapse of state socialist experiment how far one can depend on state is a debatable question. At the end, however, he pins his hope on civil society to check the power of the state. Here he seems close to Mahatama Gandhi, who advocates for the supremacy of civil power over state power.

Vision for social progress itself reflects the level of development that a society has attained in its process of continuous advancement towards a desirable direction[15] (Bury, 1955:2) in order to achieve its perceived ideals. Such ideals are perceived by the society and articulated by its visionary depending upon the state of consciousness that a society has acquired. In early history of mankind such ideals were perceived by philosophers mostly influenced by the state of religion that society enjoyed. The ideals for different societies until the middle ages were what were described in their religious documents. Since most of the religions were taking compassionate approach to humanism, at least on record if not in practice, they have strong influence over the ideals. Bury has maintained that the progress is "a condition of society in which all the inhabitants of the planet would enjoy a perfectly happy existence"[16] (Bury, 1955). One can trace this ideal in the work of Encyclopaedists[17] (Encyclopaedia, 1957: 495-99). Similar examples are also available, for instance in the literature of the Greek and the Jews and also in Hebraic-Christian interpretation of messianic intervention and salvation. Regeneration of glorious past, i.e., inspiration from Pericles and Augustus, renaissance of classical learning of Lucurgus and Solan, ideals of Christianity, etc., were conceived as the ideals in the period of degeneration.

Significant changes took place in the world, particularly in Europe, during fourteenth to nineteenth centuries. A few noticeable among them were: development of towns, expansion of commerce, exploration of new geographical regions, emergence of modern state, scientific invention and discoveries, industrial revolution, revolt of educated middle class, etc. These events weakened the hold of religious overtone over societal ideals. All these made room for more materialistic emphasis of ideals in the society. This also brought transformation and reform in religious philosophies. In this process faith in goodness of man and efficiency of conscious reason to create earthy utopia was also an emerging feature. Thus, progress was viewed as "an increase in adaptation of man to his environment that is of his internal power and wishes to his external lot and life"[18] (Bedgehot, 1956: 152). Further delineation of verifiable progress was noticeable in terms of new indicators of control and skill. Greater command of power over nature, external and internal power to command 'better' skill and knowledge for the health and comfort of present body and mind, etc., were acquired for better life styles. Hence, the progress was explained as a march of history of human being from savage to civilised one. "The difference between the savage and the civilised man may be explained on the basis of the theory that the former is yet so imperfectly developed that the progress is hardly apparent"[19] (George, 1956: 482). Thus, Euro-centric progress was considered as a historical continuity, implicit in historical evolution of national and civilization reflected in Hegalian formation of early nineteenth century influenced by material.

Euro-centric progress dominated the world after emergence of capitalist mode of production, although, this found expression in the craze for gold and gold as such. Even much before the advent of Mercantilism and Physiocrats, efforts to convert baser metal to gold has been the pre-occupation of the alchemist through out the middle ages, as gold was an ideal indicator of the wealth which was further emphasised by Mercantilism. During the age of Mercantilism the idea for the State was to facilitate the inflow of gold in the nation. Adam Smith's contribution of *Wealth of Nation* and the idea before the societies were deep rooted in the capitalist tradition of profit and accumulation, which also led to colonial expansion. However, materialistic implication of progress continued to find further support in the Darwinian theory of the struggle for the existence and survival of the fittest along with Schopenhaner's Doctrine of the will as an aspect of universal blind force. This led to a search for a colony and its exploitation, which resulted, into aggravated misery for a section of world population. Emergence of condition of industrial labour and barbaric exploitation of colonies led middle class intelligentsia to shift over emphasis on profit and accumulation as was being advocated by the capitalist Philosophy. They modified the capitalist piteous philosophy of profit and accumulation through the slogan of the values of humanity, equality, liberty, fraternity, etc. Their approach was to divulge and mellow down the harshness of capitalist culture by such reforms as would make it agreeable and appear humane. The earliest names in this context were of, Saint-Simon, Ferlinend Lassale. Wilhem Liebkneeh and Robert Owen. Others, who joined this camp with marginal deviations, were Fourrier, August Bebel, Pierre Loroux, Lamartine, Balzac, Sainte-Beuve, Durkheim, Lammenais, George I, Plekhanov Tocque Ville, Thoreau, Tolstoy, etc. Later they began to be known as socialist of different verities such as 1. Reactionary Socialism-expression of which was (a) Feudal Socialism (b) Petty Bourgeois Socialism (c) German; True' Socialism 2. Conservative or Bourgeois Socialism and 3. Critical-Utopian Socialism, etc.

Marx, using Hegel's dialectics of historical materialism, interpreted history of progress in terms of class struggle related to material interest as the determining factor for social progress in his doctrine of scientific socialism. His analysis of the dialectical and historical materialism brought forth the facts that it is the class struggle, which has replaced the institution of feudalism with a modern competitive capitalism and will further replace capitalism with communism in the background of much higher level to be achieved by the forces of production then what is obtained in capitalism. Marx described the ideal society as: "In a higher phase of Communist Society, after the enslaving subordination of the individual to the division of labour and therewith also the antithesis between mental and physical labour has vanished, after labour has become not only a means of life but life's prime want; after the productive forces have also increased with the all round development of the individual, and all the springs of co-operative wealth flow more abundantly-only then can the narrow horizon of bourgeois right be crossed in its entirety and society inscribed on its banner: "From each according to his ability, to each according to his needs"[20] (Marx & Engels, 1962: Vol. II, p. 24). To achieve this ideal he was convinced of the superstructure, i.e., Dictatorship of

Proletariat and for which he cited an example of the Paris Commune[21] (Marx & Engels, 1962: Vol. I, p. 485). With the progress of capitalism and bourgeois democracy many political parties took the socialist ideal in their fold. Notable among them was German Social Democratic Party, French Socialist Party, British Labour Party, German Workers Party, SEIO in France, Socialist Party of India, etc.

Indian Perception

The concept of progress in Indian context may be traced back as early as in the literature of the post-Vedic period of not earlier, where it was idealised through religious overtone. In India also right from the Vedic period religion had a role in maintaining peace on the earth. Well-articulated couplet in *Shukla Yojurveda* emphasises on restoring peace on the planet earth, ocean, forest and everywhere in the environment.[1] In the post-vedic period the ideals were translated into more articulated and concrete material forms in order to achieve 'happiness, health and welfare for all and sorrow for none. Manifestation of such ideal can be traced in *Smriti (Purana)* composed by Vyasa in terms of *punya* (good) and *papa* (evils) and translated in real life concretising into two formulas, i.e., to help others is good and to torture is an evil.[4] Another interpretation may be seen in the concept of universe as a family away from the discrimination of own and others at least at the level of perception[5] leading towards identification of the knowledge of self in others.[6] One of the best forms of the perceptions of social justice may be seen in another couplet in which material consciousness is reflected. Every one was desired to be happy in that construct free from disease with an articulated proposition for general well being to all and sorrow for none.[7] But the concept of happiness was still to be delinked from the deeds of last birth and its resultant continuity of the cycle of the good and evil performance in the present life span. Thus, the existence of sorrow in this life was exaggerated to the extent of interpreting as incurable as a fate of last birth. The facts therefore remained unchanged so far discrimination; injustice and exploitation in the brahminical order of society were concerned. Position of the people at the lower rung of the society, i.e., shudras was justified as a result of their evildoings of their last birth. The question of social discrimination and injustice although secularised and reduced to at perception level away from this framework in the medieval era of Kabir but it was not much away from the religious overtone when he made his request to God to provide him only so much of material privileges that he would be able to maintain subsistence of this family and guest.[8]

But there was another school of thought also, which challenged the proposition of rebirth and continuity of resultant distress. Charvak was one of the main proponents of this school.[9] Buddha's interpretation of the causes of miseries and their remedies in this material world itself gave a new dimension to the consciousness of the society and therefore to the perception of social Justice. He identified accumulation at the root of all the exploitation, discrimination and other social evils and therefore suggested measures for dispossession through inner transformation of individual, forming *Sangh* and adherence of truth, non-violence, and celibacy. Vivekananda diagnosed the evils of monopolising of the whole education and intelligence of the land by dint of pride and royal authority among a handful of man as the chief causes that ruined India (Vivekananada, 1972: Vol. IV; 482)[22] and therefore self assertion of shudras is necessary for their liberation.

It has been the irony of the facts that although Indian tradition has been ingrained with very rich perceptions of social justice and its measures, the society remained fragmented because of inner contradiction and weaknesses. One can hardly deny that on the one hand, we had a concept of universe as our family and on the other hand we were divided into numerous fragments of castes loaded with parochial identities and social evils like untouchability. We had teachings of non-violence and peace along with inherited sense of sacrifice but we had also the arch reality of discrimination, violence and hatred in the society. Consequently, we were conquered, robbed, enslaved and ruled by many rulers including the British colonisers who gradually took India into their strong grip. When the British reached to its further lowest ebb of exploitation, the context of social justice emerged again in the foray of national movement. But this time the perception and ideal of social justice was at the higher plain and also with finer articulation, equipped with the experience of French Revolution, Paris Commune and Socialist Revolution in European countries. This was very much reflected in the writings and speeches of our national leaders, which they used as powerful weapons to mobilise masses during freedom struggle. Gandhi was basically in this tradition, which adhered to non-violent social order, which was rooted in the teaching of Buddha. In his ideal of non-violent society 'no one is supposed to be first and none the last'. Gandhian ideals of a non-violent social order outlines the dream of India in his following words:

> "I shall work for an India in which the poorest shall feel that it is their country in whose making they have an effective voice; an India in which there shall b no high class and low class of people; an India in which all communities shall live in perfect harmony. There can be no room in such an India for the curse of untouchability or the course of the intoxicating drinks and drugs. Women will enjoy the same rights as men. Since we shall be at peace with all the rest of the world, neither exploiting nor being exploited, we should have the smallest army imaginable. All interests but not in conflict with the interest of dumb millions will be scrupulously respected, whether foreign and indigenous. This is the India of my

dreams... I shall be satisfied with nothing less." (Gandhi, 1931).[23]

Thus Gandhi shaped his ideals and dreams to bring the last man of the society into the mainstream of development process. He appears in the continuity of the transformation process of the society translated into Indian social context. All the ideals are sounding good and harmonious to the society. But the basic issues are to translate them into the ground reality in terms of living conditions of the common masses. The level of progress of a society, thus, should be seen in the context of the realisation of the set goals for the society. Development of productive forces as a result of closer interaction between man and nature has undoubtedly invented and developed significant technology to reduce the hardship of the life of human being to a certain extent but the facts still remain as to whether the benefit of the same has percolated down to the deprived societies and nations.

Among national leaders, it would be pertinent of refer Gandhi in this context, who was considered as an uncrowned leader of the national freedom movement for almost three decadės until his assassination. Gandhian perception of social justice can be seen in one of his writings, when he writes: "Everybody should be able to get sufficient work to make the two ends meet. And this ideal can be universally realised only if the means of production of elementary necessaries of life remain under the control of masses....they should not be made a vehicle of traffic for exploitation of others. Their monopolisation by any country, nation or group of group of persons would be unjust" (Gandhi, 1928).[24] Adding economic dimension to his concept of non-violent social order he emphasised: "Economic equality is the master key of non-violent independence, working for economic equality means the levelling down of the few rich in whose hands is concentrated the bulk of the nations wealth on the one hand and leveling up of the semi-starvd naked millions on the other" (Gandhi, 1994:20).[25] Nehru, as early as in 1929, was convinced of the argument that generating employment as the only effective solution to get rid of wide spread poverty with a vision of socialist order. When Nehru was with power Gandhi suggested his talisman to Nehru in August 1947 for clarity of his perceptions and removing his doubts while making decisions about the last man:

> "I will give you a talisman. Whenever you are in doubt, or when the self become too much with you, apply the following test. Recall the face of the poorest and the weakest man whom you may have seen, and ask yourself if the step you contemplate in going to be of any use of him. Will he gain anything by it? Will it restore him to a control over his own life and destiny? In other words, will it lead to swaraj for the hungry and spiritually starving millions? Then you will find your doubts and your self melting away." (Gandhi: CWMG, Vol. 96: 311, 427, Note).[26]

Running through pages in his *Village Swaraj,* i.e. poor man's swaraj where 'non one is to be the first and none the last' (Gandhi, 1959:76, 73, 9 & 100)[27] and elsewhere also Gandhi articulated his ideals of just social order in terms of removal of poverty, and unemployment, providing proper food, clothes, education and creative healthy condition of living for every human being so that common masses can work and earn easily to meet their needs (Gandhi, CWMG, Vol. 87, p. 463).[28] Gandhi emphasised on equitable distribution of land to eradicate poverty." No man should have more land than he needs for dignified sustenance. Who can dispute the fact that the grinding poverty of the masses is due to their having no land that they can call their own?"[29] (Gandhi, 1940:97). These ideals appear closer to the proposition of Marx, i.e., "from each according to his ability to each according to his needs"[30] (Marx, 1962: Vol. II, 24). However, the debates on approaches put them poles apart. Many scholar have tried to find out common ground and flow of thoughts. Needless to mention that resemblance of words and phrases may not necessarily reflect the proximity of perspectives. Ambedkar was restlessly worried about deep-rooted injustice in the society and therefore he argued for social democracy. His concept of social justice was firmly rooted in the synthesis of social equality, i.e., dignity, involving freedom and liberty with economic equality[31] (Guru, 1997: 237-46). Integrating all these concerns of the national leaders that they made for a concerted efforts to frame a comprehensive constitutional provision with greater enthusiasm and expectation after transfer of power from the British to the Indian ruling class.

Process of Transformation

Process of transformation for the progress of a society may broadly have two aspects: (a) basis and (b) superstructure. Former may consist of the material conditions of living of a society and latter may have two dimensions. One, transformation in institutions may be socio-economic, political, etc., at a given stage of productive organisation and development and two technological progress and its impacts on material conditions of living and institutions in the corresponding time and space. An exercise is required to identify and evaluate the process of development consequent upon changes in its forms, content, and operative mechanism of base and superstructures along with changing productive forces, which start transforming themselves within existing productive organisations. We learn from history that so long these factors are compatible among themselves process of transformation may progress smoothly. Incompatibility, on the contrary, among these factors create contradictions, challenges the continuity of outmoded institutions and replaces the outdated technology in the historical process of social transformation.

In this context of transformation, emergence of State *inter alia* is one of the most important phenomena, which has overpowered these superstructures through effective control and welfare mechanism. Modern welfare state has come forward and taken some policy measures through which the state has been labelled as a dominant force of the changing agent. Besides assuming the key role of transformation by the welfare state, internal dynamics of class relations in production and appropriation of surpluses and external dynamics of accumulation and formation of capital decide the course of transformation and development. 'When we speak of production, we always have in mind production at a definite stage of social development, production by individuals in a society, i.e., various phases in the historical process of development. All stages of production however, have certain common features, elements and categories without which production is inconceivable. For example, no production is possible without an instrument of production (simplest form may be hand), without past accumulated and materialised labour (may be the skill acquired by repeated practice and concentrated in the hand of savage). Thus, capital is a universal and eternal relation, which turns the instrument of production or accumulated labour into capital. Production is always appropriation of nature by individual within and with the help of a definite social organisation'.[32] (Marx, 1970, 189-90).

At the level of organised thought if one attempts to deal with the process of transformation through history of economic thought if not earlier than mercantilism, one could trace that the trade was considered as the most important factor to acquire precious metals as wealth for which state was the powerful mechanism to exploit colonies, promote factor to acquire precious metals as wealth for which state was the powerful mechanism to exploit colonies, promote export and restrict import during sixteenth and late seventeenth centuries. But it was the era of Physiocrats from last quarter of seventeenth century to three fourth of the eighteenth century when agriculture was advocated as the only main source of surplus (net *product*) generation for social transformation. Manufacturing and trade according to physiocrats were unproductive activities. Non-Marxist classical school led by Adam Smith considered self-interest as the guiding principle added with division of labour as the key to transformation at the age of industrial revolution. However, Ricardo emphasised the niggardliness of nature and falling tendency of the rate of profit whereas Malthus believed that it was population, which remained instrumental for transformation. Classical school was mainly concerned with the supply side of economics. Neo-classical economist introduced demand side, but functional distribution was assumed to its spontaneity, which ignored the complications created by the interest groups. In other words they depended on market forces to take care of all these things, Hence, the problems of dynamising market condition remained the basic issues. In this context, Keynes advocated role of effective demand where state was considered as prime mover in order to get aid of great depression.

The school of thought which veer around the post Keynesian dynamics has associated growth with increasing per capita Gross Domestic Product (GDP), consumption of steel, power, etc., in per capita terms and similar indicators of material progress. The most talked of the proponent of this thesis, W.W. Rostow has described five stages of growth in historical perspectives: i.e., (a) traditional society (b) Pre-conditions of take-off, (c) take-off, (d) drive to maturity and (e) High Mass consumption [33] (Rostow, 1961: 4-16). It presumed natural course of trickle down as an operative mechanism, which has failed almost, in the context of Indian economy at least. Moreover it ignores about any deliberate effort to promote distributive justice and therefore the stage of high mass consumption remains segmented for a certain privileged class and oblivion to general masses.

Although those, who followed Marxist tools of analysis, are concerned with material prosperity and have described development of society in terms of moving ahead from one mode of production to another mode of production. For example, a primitive society moves into a slave mode of production followed by feudal, capitalist and communist modes of production. In other words, this process of transformation results, first in primitive communism and then, passing through the stage of feudalism, steps into the degradation of class society. They divisions inherent in a class society based on indigence and rooted in the realm of necessity, and can overcome once men achieve mastery over nature and socialize property by a revolution. With it generic man will return to himself in his own embodiment, will enter a realm of freedom that is integral expression, one which will belong indivisibly to the whole society in which man will be reconciled to man. "The total product of our community is a social product. One portion serves as fresh means of production and remains social. But another portion is consumed by the members as means of subsistence. A distribution of this portion amongst them is consequently necessary. The mode of this distribution will vary with the productive organisation of the community and the degree of historical development attained by the producers" (Maix, 1986; 83), Thus, epochs of development are so much associated with the institutional and structural set up that any analysis of transformation in isolation from modes of production is an exercise in futility (Prasad, 1986; 3). Because "it is not the article made, but how they are made and by what instrument, that enables us to distinguish different economic epochs."[34] (Marx, 1975; 175). Thus, historical process of movement of a society from one mode of production to another makes a recourse of transformation towards an egalitarian society.

Society has transformed its basis and superstructure through practices. History of society may be seen through its evolutionary process from primitive-slave-feudal-capitalist to state less egalitarian, i.e., communist society. Egalitarian Society as an ideal society has been conceptualised by Hegel as a Civil Society and Marx as a stateless and classess society free from exploitation and Gandhi as a Non-violent Society. States of transformation towards an egalitarian society in its ultimate analysis in which questions of inequality and exploitation do not exist, however, varies and depends on the level of consciousness that a society has acquired in its historical process of development of productive organisations[35] (Marx, 1970:20). Forms of materialistic control and senses of deprivation are directly linked with the nature and forms of productive organisation and inherent contradiction in the process of accumulation therein. In primitive society since material accumulation was yet to be a part of social consciousness, questions of inequality, exploitation and therefore of justice did not arise until accumulation came in its way as a resultant obstacle. Material consciousness of accumulation in due course of its historical development process stretched over its control over productive organisation operating through productive forces relations of production. The level of development of productive forces and the stages of relations of production thus, reflects the level of consciousness of the masses of that society to interpret and analyse its material conditions and contradiction therein, which in turn decides the level of consciousness for justice in that society.

A society may have more than one set of productive organisations operating simultaneously; Dominant set prevails over other social orders through its institutions that emerged in its historical process of development to serve its interest as a substantial and integral part of the relations of production (Byres, 1986: 90). However, other sets of productive organisation emerge and develop simultaneously within the existing system, which would have the potential to replace the existing system of productive organisation but the emerging dominant set of productive organisation can only replace when it is matured[36] (Marx, 1970, 1970: 21). Thus, the concept of social justice has both micro and macro dimensions regarding exploitation and justice, i.e., question of exploitation of one country and society by the other.

Democracy: Participation and Development

Democracy-political, social economic-has been evolving with many dimensions since fifth century B.C. when it was used as demokretia. Although 'democracy has never been identified with a specific doctrinal source-it is rather a by-product of the earlier development of Western civilisation (p.112). In Marxian sense democracy is a higher form of superstructure that a society could develop over one or the other set of political superstructure corresponding to a changing productive organisation and therefore provides more space in public sphere. However it emerged within feudal structure and later overpowered it and destroyed outdated productive organisation. This has provided significant space of direct oligarchic participation of the people in decision making. But this was not the results of the generosity of historically backward productive organisation rather a victory of the people's movement against exploitation in the respective productive organisation. History of expansion of public sphere in India can be seen in the writing of ancient history. *Ganrajya* of Lichhavi is often quoted as ancient institution of democratic republic. It appears clear from the researched document that *ganrajya* was not the synonyms of republic. *Ganrajya* was a form of oligarchy of tribal lord or king. The *gan* was essentially a warrior and not a common man or slave or worker. They used to fight and collect wealth, which was deposited before the *ganan anpati,* who used to distribute equally among them.

Their oligarchy was based on slavery and bondage (Sharma, 1989: 351, 156-60).[37] Thus *ganrajya* appears different than the democracy of today's capitalism in the name of civil society and welfare state.

Liberty equality and fraternity emerged from French Revolution. Technological breakthrough was witnessed in industrial revolution. Emergence of welfare state was a logical culmination of bourgeois capitalist development to contend the resentments of the people of the home country and colonial expansion as hinterland. Colonial exploitation provoked nationalists to consolidate their struggle against imperialist forces. Meanwhile there was clash of interest among the capitalist forces, which led to World War. The World witnessed two world wars, losses of lives and property of the people. USA captured the leadership of the capitalist government after the Second World War. A cartel of capitalist countries was formed in the Bretton Woods Conference, which laid the foundation of International Financial Institutions-International Monetary Fund (IMF), International Bank for Reconstruction and Development (IBRD), which popularly known as The World Bank, etc., as a platform to pursue the agenda of capitalist power. Concerted mobilisations against colonial exploitation resulted into gradual liberation of the countries followed by installation of democratic government, which could create more space than every before for public sphere. Thus, people's movement could achieve a certain degree of civil rights through legislation, parts of which were implemented and others were kept on the backseat. Interests of the capitalist agenda got space through legislation at the costs of people's interest. Roles of state as welfare state were minimised and Finance Capital came in a big way through globalisation, liberalisation and privatisation. New carted emerged as World Trade Organisation (WTO) to care for Multinationals and Trans National Capital.

Spillover Effects

Spill over effects of development in general and technological development in particular played an important role in reducing the hardship of society. However, it has created challenges before the humanity as well. This is precisely because the technology has never been class neutral in history. If the society is governed by the bourgeois democracy initially through welfare state and later through Trans National Capital the benefit of technology is bound to be harvested by the capitalist agencies and society. Competition to harvest profit has been undermining the interest of the common masses of the world and resulted into wider unemployment, poverty and misery of the humanity. Labour saving technologies and jobless growth dominated the society of the world at large irrespective of region specific requirements and transitory exceptions.

Access to democratic institutions to certain extent could of course be possible for the common people. Many constitutional provisions were achieved for their welfare and parts of them were implemented also. However, the democracy is still functioning as oligarchic institution and yet to become meaningfully participatory. The use of the word 'participatory democracy' emerged as an efficient sailing coin suggested from every nook and corner of the political sphere. But order to participate remains the spirit of participation (Blanchet, 2001).[38] Participation has been co-opted by the capital controlled states and their agencies. Hence there is need to take care of state sponsored slogans of participation. One can take participatory rural appraisal and development by development agencies across the country of the world and Panchayat Raj Institution (PRI) for an example for people's participation in India. PRI has been achieved after continuous efforts and mobilisation of the people towards participatory democracy. Insight and vision of Buddha, Gandhi, Vinoba, Jayaprakash Narayan (JP) and commitment of revolutionaries of the country and the world at large for collective thinking and action with collective vision has contributed significantly in this context. But it has always been forgotten that if the society is divided into castes, religion and other parochial identities, it would inevitably be reflected in fractured representation in consonance of the social character in the political superstructure as well. Therefore, if there is an urge of good governance for a peaceful society, a compromise between state and civil society in transition for an active sense of togetherness is essential. But it is needless to mention that compromise is an apparatus, which works between two powerful or equal entities. So far my little knowledge goes about history, there is not other way but to help them to be organised for their struggle, if they have to wield power. This process has inverse relation between powers of state and the people. If the people are more organised, the state is reduced to less power. Hence, the tendency of the state has been to evolve symbols and labelling to keep the people in various sacks. Therefore, the efforts to transform superstructure of bourgeois democracy in order to have egalitarian or non-violent social order does not appear compatible suggestions unless the property relations are changed accordingly. It may be worth noting here that state controlled capital was not as aggressive as capital controlled state would be. Therefore, repression against any resistance today is expected to be more ruthless and insensitive than ever before. Thus, struggle against imperialism today requires more preparation and better networking than national liberation struggle.

Beyond Bourgeois Democracy

The basis of progress ensures distributive justice of material production and has inherent character of social justice, but so long the process of misappropriation of surplus by non-producer castes and class continues, condition of common masses may not be improved. Expecting any miracle within this given system especially, in the syndrome of gradually intensifying economic reforms at the dictate of imperial power in which state intervention has been weakening day by day and privatisation an market orientation is at ever increasing scale, no let up is visualised to generate sustainable employment opportunities and progress. Democratic institutions have been captured and used by capital in the interest of the market, which has the only motive that is to maximise and accumulate profits, the situation ahead is going to be worse. In last fifty years, means of production could hardly be transferred effectively to the direct producers in order to remove injustice for which, Gandhi expressed his deep concern. Exception apart, no sharp polarisation of masses has been witnessed for sustainable resistance against exploitation either. The question of liberating masses impoverished by this very system, thus, appears merely hoping against hope unless masses themselves come forward to resist their exploitation.

Parliamentary democracy in the hands of bourgeois political parties has been generating false hopes in order to blunt their consciousness of understanding about their material condition. This form of democracy has been creating hurdles against the process, though weak one, of consolidating as class in themselves to transform as class for themselves. The rightist parties are not in a position to maintain the welfare state character of the democracy and gradually surrendering before the capital. The role of the most of the left parties in parliamentary politics, which should have geared up struggle for social change, equity and justice, is not significantly different from others. So is the case of liberal socialist. Mobilisation on caste and communal lines, irrespective of the provisions made in the Constitution of India, which a segmented approach in this caste ridden society has been counter productive which has been reinforcing outdated reactionary element in the society further. It may result into infighting between social groups under different banners which may lead to hatreds among inter and intra castes. The question of land reforms has almost lost its ground in their agenda of struggle irrespective of ideologies. However, sometimes they discuss in their meetings. It has become difficult to differentiate them substantially from other political parties, who serve as good servant of imperial masters which survives through exploitation of Neo-colonial countries of the world (Prasad, 1996). Implications of democracy controlled by the capital in such situation, needs to be analysed carefully. Unless economic democracy is ensured merely political democracy as an oligarchic control on democratic institutions may not provide space for progress (JP: 1977:30-34).[39] JP was convinced of the effects of eeonomic decentralisation and therefore he argued for decentralised agro-industrial community, i.e., organic blending of agriculture and industry (JP, 1977:33)[40] as an alternative social order in the present context of social reconstruction.

Non-violent mobilisations have success stories and lessons from failure also but the tasks for replication are yet to be confirmed at larger scale. Participation of the people in democratic mobilisation against exploitation is yet to be seen effective. Lessons derived from mobilisation of students in particular and masses in general against fascist government in seventies by JP need to be analysed carefully. Although JP was then different than that of the colonial period, it is pertinent to put here the views of Gandhiji about JP regarding non-violence. While writing a letter to Khursheed Behn Naroji on July 15, 1946, Gandhi wrote: "I see that your ahimsa and mine are poles apart as under. I have great regard for Jayaprakash but not for his views," (CWMG, Vol. 91: 280).[41] It shows that Gandhian line of non-violence has comprehensive vision in totality loaded with constructive programmes and cadres with social commitment. Unless independent cadre is developed and protest movement is transformed to social movement, merely change in set of rulers in one government to another could not work for social change any longer and could not change the character of bourgeois democratic superstructure significantly. However, the space for intervention has increased and there has been change in contents of participation to a certain extent. Undoubtedly, mobilisation of people from local to global level is an uphill task for people's power and government. There is simmering reaction right from local levels to national and international level against undemocratic move in the name of democratic concern, which is now spread across the countries against globalisation of capital (Dubhashi, 2002:537-43).[42] Recommendation of Bonn conference known as Kyoto protocol has been ignored by many of the G-7 countries except France. This shows how oligarchic democratic institutions are. Protest against globalisation was seen at Genoa, Doha, and Cancun meets of WTO. This shows concern of the people against tightening rope of capitalism. There are a few brilliant examples in the history, which suggest that only masses have strength, insight and idea to resolve the contradictions. The question is to listen, comprehend and practice them with necessary modification in the light of experiments in due course of needed (Mao, 1975: 119). "The only remedy seems to be for the people to take their fate in their own hands and shape it according to their will." (JP, 1977:52).[43]

This reminds Gandhi and Marx who repose faith in people to change and overthrow the existing exploitative oligarchic order in the name of democracy. If at all there is social commitment for a non-violent social order, it requires sincere efforts towards effective decentralisation of economy and polity from the below unlike of today, that is from the above. Effective land reforms and water management added with co-operative venture and collective ownership of the means of production supplemented with agro based cottage and small industries for generating sustainable employment to improve the economic conditions of the masses on priority basis appear necessary steps to start with. There is also an imperative need to mobilise common masses to resist against exploitation at the grassroots and macro levels as well. This is a hard task, which capitalists aligned ruling class, would hardly permit, as this would raise question against their existence. Therefore, no option other than mass struggle seems left as an alternative (Prasad, 1995:208-11).[44] This question however, remains as to how mobilisation of masses can be made faster in order to involve them towards building a just society. This needs proper understanding about the masses to develop an efficient skill of communication in terms of constructive works and expand grassroots network so that mass involvement is possible. There may not be a tight compartment. Strategy may vary according to adaptability of the region but in broader sense the practices to be carried out may work as complementary to each other. Lessons from Gandhian as well as Marxian practices from the history of society including India need to be understood and analysed for evolving dynamic strategies for mobilisation. Needless to mention that strategies would be such, which reorient democracy for the people and not the people for the democracy and therefore democracy should work as an apparatus to achieve the goal of progressive non-violent egalitarian social order. In order words, the need of the hour is to go beyond this bourgeois democracy, i.e., the rule of the capital, limitation of which was articulated painfully by JP himself, when he was put behind the bar in so-called independent India of largest democracy. Now the so-called democratic allies of JP movement against fascism are sincerely demolishing democratic institutions in which JP deposed his confidence for creating democratic forces against fascist forces and structures. The world is deliberating on the issues of democracy and development. None of these two can be separated. If there is non-development syndrome it will be difficult to operate through democratic institutions. It is always to be underlined that democracy is not an end in itself but is one of the means to achieve the goal of egalitarian society and progress through development and distributive justice and people are the real agents and ultimate master to hold the power.

NOTES

1. The couplet is expressed as: "*Prithvi Shantih, aapah shantih, aushadhyah shantih, Vanaspatayah shantih.... Shantih, shantih, shantih.*"
2. See Rajgopalachari, C., (1931): Magnacharta, *Young India*, 10.9.1931.
3. Marx wrote: "In the social production of their existence, men inevitably enter into definite relations, which are independent of their will, namely relations of production appropriate to a given stage in the development of their material forces of production. The totality of these relations of production constitutes the economic structure of society, the real foundation, on which arises a legal and political superstructure and to which correspond definite forms of social consciousness."
4. Writing about the essence of entire eighteen puranas of Vyasa it has been said:

   Ashtadas puraneshu Vyasasya vachanadwayam
   Paropakaray punyay, papay par pidnam.

   (i.e., in eighteen puranas of Vyasa there are two statements–to work for the wellbeing of others is good and to torture others is bad.)
5. It is a famous couplet from post vedic literature often quoted for generous gesture:

   Ayam nijah paroveti ganana laghu chetsam
   Udar charitanantu basudhaiv kutumbkam.

   (i.e., people of narrow mind do calculate about his own and others, generous persons consider the whole earth planet as his family.)
6. Sensitiveness as self for all living creatures is reflected and identified as knowledge of the society, (i.e., *atmvat sarva bhuteshu yah pashyati sah panditah.*)

7. *Sarve bhavantu sukhinah sarve santu niramayah*
   sarve bhadrani pashyanti ma kashchit dukhbahag bhavet.

   (i.e., be all happy and in good health, we wish wellbeing to all and sorrow to none.

8. Kabir says:

   Sayeen itna dijie jame kutum samay
   Main bhi bhukha na rahun sadhu na bhukha jay

9. Charvak was one of the main proponents of the school of thought who maintained:
   Bhasmi bhutasya dehasya puaragamanam kutah.

REFERENCES

Bedgehot, W., (1956): Physics and Politics, Bescon Press, Boston.

Blanchet, K., (2001): Participatory development: between hopes and reality, *Indian Social Science Journal,* 170.

December, Blackwell, UNESCO.

Bury, J.B., (1955): The Idea of Progress, Dover Edition, New York.

Byre, T.J. (1986): Agrarian Transition and the Agrarian Question in John Harris (ed.): *Rural Development,* ELBS.

Dubhashi, P.R. (2002): People's Movement against Global Capital, *Economic and Political Weekly,* February 9.

Gandhi, M.K., (1928): Economic Constitution of India, *Young India,* November 15.

Gandhi, M.K., (1931): Young India, 10.9.1931.

Gandhi, M.K., (1940): Harijan, 20.4.1940.

Gandhi, M.K., (1959): *India of My Dreams,* Navajivan Publishing House, Ahmedabad.

Gandhi, M.K., *Collected Works,* Vol. 87.

Gandhi, M.K., *Collected Works,* Vol. 96.

Gandhi, M.K., (1994): Constructive Programmes, Navajivan Publishing House, Ahmedabad. Reprint.

Guru, G., (1997): Ambedkar's Ideas of Social Justice in Bhattachrjee, A., (ed.): *Social Justice and the Constitution,*

Indian Institute of Advance Study, Rashtrapati Nivas Shimla.

George, H., (1956): Progress and Poverty, Robert Schalknbach Foundation, New York.

Gramsci, A., (1972): Selection from the Prison Notebooks ed. By Geoffrey Nowell Smith and Quintin Hoare, London.

Lawrence and Wishart, 1971, New York: International Publishers.

Human Development Report 2001. UNDP, Oxford University Press.

Institute of Applied Manpower Research (1998): Year Book of Manpower Profile, India.

JP (1977): Swaraj for the People, Sarva Seva Sangh, Varanasi.

Krishnaswamy, Sridhar, (2002), Power, Wealth, Shared Unequally, The World Economic Forum, New York, The Hindu.

06.02.2002.

MaoTse Tung (1975): *Collected Works,* Foreign Language Publishing House Pecking, Vol. 3.

Marx, K., (1975).

Marx, K., (1970): *A Contribution to the Critique of Political Economy,* Progress Publishers, Moscow.

Marx, K., & Engels, F., (1962) : *Selected Works,* Foreign Language Publishing House, Moscow, Vol. II.

Muralidharan, V., (1997): *Educational Priorities and Dalit Society,* Kanishka, New Delhi.

Prasad, P.H., (1986).

Prasad, P.H., (1995): Mass Struggle: The Only Option, *Economic and Political Weekly,* Jan. 28.

Prasad, P.H., Dynamics of Neo-Colonial Exploitation, *Economic and Political Weekly,* March 23.

Seligmen, A., (1992): The Idea of Civil Society, New York, Free Press.

Sharma, B.D., (1994): *Dalit Betrayed,* Haranand Publications, New Delhi.

Sharma, R.S., (1993): Political Theory and Institutions in Ancient India (Hindi), Rajkamal.

Tester, K., (1992): Civil Society, London and New York, Routledge.

Vivekananda, : The Complete Works of Swami Vivekananda, Advait Ashrama, Kolkata.

Walzer, M., The Civil Society Argument in Chantal Mouffe (ed.): Dimensions of Radical Democracy: Pluralism.

Citizenship, Community, London, Verso.

Wood, G.D., (1981) : State Intervention and Agrarian Class Formation: Dimensions of the Access Problem in the Koshi.

Development Region of NE Bihar, India, *Public Administration and Development*, Vol. 4.

4

Total Revolution and Developing Countries : Validity of the Concept in the Era of Globalisation

Vijay Kumar

> It is impossible to withdraw from the world, and associate with birds and beasts that have no affinity with us. With whom should I associate but with suffering men? The disorder that prevails is that requires my efforts. If right principles ruled through the kingdom, there would be no necessity for me to change the state.
>
> **– Confucius.**[1]

Loknayak Jayaprakash Narayan, the soul-mate of Apostle of Peace, Mahatma Gandhi, affectionately called JP by his contemporaries and followers, was a great visionary, a strong 'moral force' and a 'conscience keeper' of the national politics of India in the post-Independence era. An enigma in Indian politics, JP, gave up the comforts of a normal life and throughout his lifetime worked for the betterment of the community. A valiant fighter during the Freedom Struggle, JP started his political career as a Marxist. In 1942, when Mahatma Gandhi gave the call of 'Do or Die' to the Indian people in their struggle against colonial rule, JP scaled the high prison walls of Hazaribagh jail[2] and led an underground movement which made him the 'hero' of the Quit India Movement. He was a beacon of strength and courage to the young, a person of strong will and commitment. Like Gandhi he was in constant search for a new ideology. He went on making ideological experiments of his life searching for the best for the Indian society and its people.[3] His constant search for best standards, his changing moods and shades of his political thoughts, not usually in tune with the stalwarts of the Congress and the socialists, made lesser mortals think of him as a man of vacillating attitudes. But such a mistake leads to wrong conclusions and beliefs about JP's personality. On basic issues, his vision was crystal clear.[4]

JP was for the establishment of a new and better social order based on human equality free from all indignities. He declared that nothing but a Total Revolution-a peaceful one-can transform India, build an India of his dreams, in which freedom and bread go together.[5] In fact, Gandhi and Vinoba had preceded him in providing us the glimpses of India they had visualised but JP led a life long peaceful struggle with faith and courage for a Total Revolution. He has shown a path, left a legacy, not only for India but to the humanity at large and Human Rights in the present context of liberalisation and globalisation.

This paper aims to delineate the concept of Total Revolution as visualised by Jayaprakash Narayan and emphasise its relevance to the Indian society in particular and developing world in general. The thesis that the society must change first and the change in individual would automatically follow was rejected both by Gandhi and JP. They believed that the society and the individual must simultaneously transform. All sub-revolutions of the Total Revolution-social, economic, political, cultural, ideological or intellectual educational and spiritual must occur simultaneously because they are not held together in a casual sequence or are a conglomerate of dissonent variables but are intimately and systematically related to individual and social life and are all interdependent.

Thus a holistic approach to development is needed. Piecemeal efforts are futile and generate dissatisfaction. The whole debate on 'development' in countries now focuses on this approach throwing to the wind the 'trickle down effect' and other peace meal approaches.[6] Development thinkers and agencies now talk in terms of 'sustainable development'[7] which reminds us of Gandhi and JP. As indicated earlier in this paragraph, this paper aims to examine the concept of 'Total Revolution' envisaging extensive and qualitative change in both the social structure and human attitude and behaviour and prove its relevance in the context of developing countries.

The Concept of Revolution According to JP

'Revolution' as a concept has been defined in a number of ways in socio-political literature. Although revolutions are associated with the modern world, the meaning of the term has kept changing over time. In *The Politics,* Aristotle was concerned with 'revolution' in the city-states of Ancient Greece. But when Aristotle spoke about revolution, he was merely referring to a transfer of power that involved a change in either the individual in power or the constitution.[8] Such a definition would not be acceptable to a contemporary student of revolution. A revolution entails much broader and deeper alteration within society. Such changes may include the alteration of social values, social structures and political institutions, as well as changes in the personnel of the ruling elite or its class composition.[9] Many authors emphasise value change as focal issue in revolution while others lay emphasis on structural and institutional transformation in the existing social relationship and institutional bases of the society. The Marxists believe that a change in social structure is basically a change in the component of the ownership of property. As such revolution in the Marxian tradition means the replacement of the propertied class by the toiling classes because it is ultimately the property relations that a revolution aims at changing.[10] Any of the above dimensions of change may means a revolutionary change, but a revolution is somewhat more specific and can be broadly defined as:

> an acute, prolonged crisis in one or more of the traditional systems of stratification (class, status, power) of a political community, which involves a purposive, elite directed attempt to abolish or to reconstruct one or more of said systems by means of an intensification of political power and recourse to violence.[11]

Revolution, therefore, signifies drastic and fundamental transformation in socio-economic or political order. According to Dunn:

> Revolutions are a form of massive, violent and rapid social change. They are also attempts to embody a set of values in a new or at least a renovated social order.[12]

Revolutions are complex events essentially involving three aspects-state breakdown or transformation, competition among claimants for central authority and building new constitutions which need not occur in 'clearly separated stages or in a consistent order'. They need not always be violent and may silently over the world, as did the Industrial Revolution or the present Info-tech Revolution.

For JP, the Total Revolution is 'basic change in all aspects of life. "It would not only be a social revolution which would merely bring out a change in the structure of society, but would aim at improvement in the character of the individuals comprising it.[13] Total Revolution for JP meant, in essence, an all comprehensive social revolution. Like Gandhi, JP believed that mere value changes or changes in ideas and ideals are not enough. They just sound empty in the absence of practice. Gandhi did not consider the individual as independent of his social context. Hence, together with a revolution in "ideas" and "spirit" of the individual, society must also change. To quote Nageshwar Prasad:

> The Gandhian revolution, as such, is a much deeper and a more radical process. It is not concerned with a revolution in only one aspect of either the individual or the social order. It spans the entire continuum along which values as well as social and institutional structures are ranged.[14]

However, when Gandhi talked of revolution, he conceived of far reaching and novel changes in the entire social organisation which consisted of the economy, polity, technique of production, recruitment system of both the economy and polity, and above all, the means to be adopted for effecting the change. It is in these areas of his revolutionary programme that he becomes an "unconventional" revolutionary-a "pacific anarchist" a revolutionary Sui generis.

JP's concept of revolution is very similar and as comprehensive as that of Gandhi. It consists of a wide variety of socio-economic political and educational programmes. It is also non-conformist in so far as it departs from the usual meaning attached to revolution. To quote his own words:

> "I believe only in two kinds of militancy. There is the Gandhian non-violent militancy and there is the violent militancy.....I started out by advocating violent revolution after my return from the US in 1929 and continued to be a revolutionary in that sense until I saw that Independence was achieved by Gandhian way. I then told Gandhi that there was no room in Independent India for violent change because we now had our own and not a colonial government. I haven't changed since then.... The only way to achieve permanent social change is through nonviolence".[15]

Describing the objective of the Sarvodaya movement in India and referring to the Bhoodan and Gramdan programmes he talked of Total Revolution. To him there was no differences between Sarvodaya and Total Revolution because if Sarvodaya is the goal, Total Revolution is the means. It is basic and comprehensive change in all aspects of life. However, the term became a recurrent theme of JP's speeches and writings only since 1974 and assumed hereafter a central place in Indian political discourse.[16]

Unfolding his plan of struggle on behalf of the students' Struggle Committee of Bihar at a mammoth public meeting at Patna on 5 June 1974, JP declared that the struggle was not going to be limited to securing the demands of the students alone, including the demand for the resignation of the Ministry and dissolution of the Assembly in Bihar, but would aim higher at bringing about a Total Revolution or Sampoorna Kranti,[17] which was the need of the hour to solve the urgent problems of the country and usher in a new society based on Gandhian principles from which the country has totally deviated.

The idea of Total Revolution was not totally JP's own. He had borrowed it from Marx, Gandhi and Vinoba.[18] Marx used the concept in his work, the *Poverty of Philosophy* (1847). Gandhi's writings implicitly talk of Total Revolution through reconstructive programmes and Vinoba too aims at bringing about a three-fold revolution: 'First I want a change in people's hearts; secondly. I want to create a change in their lives; and thirdly, I want to change the social structure. A Socialist comrade of JP, Lohia, too talked of Saptkranti-seven revolutions rolled in one. But it was JP who popularised the term, gave a blue print for its implementation and led an agitation to bring about a social transformation as envisioned. The term, therefore, is genuinely his coinage. Without using the term, he had been talking of a social revolution since late 1940's which would bring about a change in the structure of society as well as an improvement in the character of the individuals.

The Components of the Total Revolution

The total revolution visualised "fundamental changes in the social, economic, political, cultural, educational and moral spheres" of the present society and aimed at creating a "new society totally different from the existing one" with a "minimum of undesirable features". Its aim was to fulfill a longing" for a new India in which each and every one of its inhabitants will lead a happy life and in which the extreme disparity between the rich and the poor that we see toady will be a thing of the past. Exploitation will disappear....social evils will cease to exist and justice will prevail in this new order."[19]

The Total Revolution would involve the "revolutionisation of the whole life-style of the people...the entire social system....down to even its inner essence of spirit."[20] The struggle for Total Revolution would not be for limited objective. Its goal would be far reaching. To quote JP himself :

> It aims at making the democratic system of India real and strong at establishment of real people's Raj, at eradicating injustice and exploitation, at bringing about a cultural and educational revolution, at creating a new Bihar and ultimately a new India.[21]

Touching all aspects of life, the Total Revolution will be comprehensive and all-inclusive. According to JP the Total Revolution will be a combination of seven revolutions: "Social, economic, political, cultural, ideological or intellectual, educational and spiritual". He is not fastidious about this number and these can be increased or regrouped for convenience. What is important is a holistic emphasis on changes in all aspects of life. JP has not spelled out these changes in detail while talking on Total Revolution, but picture of the same can be found in some of the tracts he penned in late 1950s and early 1960s, particularly in *A Plea for Reconstruction of India*[22] (1959) and *Swaraj for the People*[23]

(1961). The same ideas have been reaffirmed in *Prison Diary*[24] (1975).

The problem of reconstruction of the new polity would be a part of the larger problem of social reconstruction. Modern industrialism has resulted in a disintegration of the human society and made man an alien among his fellowmen. He wanted to remedy the situation and 'put man in touch with man', so that they may live together in meaningful, understandable, controllable relationships. In short, the problem is to 'recreate the human community'. The new socio-political system must be so devised as to promote and provide a congenial environment for a true community based on sharing, participation and fellowship.[25]

The base of the new social order will be local or primary communities which would neither be so small that a balanced development of communal life and culture becomes difficult, nor so large that life in them becomes impersonalized. They will be neither rural nor urban, but agro-industrial, based on a balance between agriculture and industry. Just as a number of families come together to form the primary community, likewise the primary communities would come together and cooperate among themselves to tackle common problems and build the regional community. A number or regional communities in their turn will join together to form the district community which would federate to form provincial communities and these provincial commu-nities will join hands to form the national community. People would address their problems from base upwards and as such there would be less and less for the bigger communities to do. Consequently, at the national community level there would be only such matters to deal with as defence, foreign relations, currency and inter-state coordination. Thus, the system would consist ultimately of "self-governing, self-sufficient, agro-industrial, urbo-rural local communities."

Such a political structure as sketched above would require for its base a new kind of economic structure. Satisfying the material needs of man would definitely be its main objective, it would, however, not endeavour to satisfy the insatiable hunger for more and yet more of materialist demands which the present capitalists, socialists and communists had created. Like a true Gandhian, JP would expect people in this system to voluntarily limit their wants. He believed that "agreed for more and yet more would lead to mutual conflict, coercion, spoilation, war; and also to a system of production that would be so complex as to bind democracy hand and foot and deliver it to a bureaucratic oligarchy."[26] He pleads for a decentralised economy on the pattern of the polity not only because it would be democratic, but also because it would bring immediate benefit to the masses by offering employment on a mass scale and producing wealth in a manner that would ensure its wide distribution and make 'wage goods' immediately available to ordinary consumers.

In this short paper it is not possible to provide the details of this decentralised economy but it would be worthwhile to point out that this would be a viable modern economy, sustainable in the true sense, though the like of which does not exist and has neither existed. The economic relationship in this decentralised economy "includes technological, industrial and agricultural revolutions, accompanied by a radical change in the pattern of ownership and management."[27]

Apart from these, JP had in the past suggested far-reaching and comprehensive recommendations with a view to reforming the present democratic structure of India. Like Gandhi, JP was opposed to the western democratic system and though he favoured a partyless democracy, he did not make it a plank of his Total Revolution. He left open to the people to decide upon the perspective of the movement as it went into progression. But he expected to purge the political system of defection and corruption and handover the control of legislators to the people and always to see the legislators on the straight and narrow path of ethical conduct. He expected the movement "not (to) destroy the country itself" but to purify it "just as five frees gold of its dress."[28] The movement had four demands-checking of corruption and high prices, solution of the unemployment problem and changes in the existing system of mis-education.

Need for Total Revolution in India

It was on 5th June 1974, at a public meeting at Patna, that the call for Sampoorna Kranti or Total Revolution was given by JP. Why did he choose to give this call at the old and advanced age when he was approaching the fag end of his life? To find an answer to this question, let up look into what this hero of the nationalist movement believed and remained committed to. In his own words:

> till my body and mind keep functioning I shall continue to serve my country and the world.[30]

In December 1972 itself he had called upon the youth of India to come forward to save democracy, which was being eroded by "money-falsehood, corruption and physical force." Prompting them, he said:

> Will our youth continue to look on idly at this strangulation of the democratic process? Surely, there can't be a more important issue which should move the youth to action.[31]

According to JP, the moral foundations of the existing political system had collapsed because of the growth of corruption in public life, erosion of legitimacy of the electoral process, expenditure of huge sums of money in the elections, and the unresponsiveness of public representatives after they got elected. With moral anguish in his heart, JP wanted to restore the value of integrity, legitimacy of the electoral process and responsiveness of the people's representatives. He believed that these political objectives, coupled with other social, cultural, educational and ideological goals could be achieved by organising and mobilising the people, making them conscious of the basic ills of the polity in time otherwise, the country would plunge in a violent revolution whose outcome would be difficult to fathom. The whole situation was such that he was reminded of 1942.

> I observe that the situation that obtained in 1942 is taking shape today....revolutionary situation.... is developing all over the country from Kanya-kumari to Kashmir. The masses are on the move and the reins of power are fast slipping from the hands of our rulers. The people are grimming under the hardships they have had to undergo during these twentyeight years of Swaraj. There is hunger. There are high prices and corruption.... Our people are ground down by all kinds of injustice. Even the educational institutions are becoming corrupt. The future of millions of youth is uncertain and dark....The number of the unemployed among the poor and uneducated is increasing day by day...today there are more landless agricultural workers than ever before.... (The society is) already divided into the exploiter and the exploited, the rich and the poor....A handful of people are reaping rich dividends as never before....Today we are witness to a very unholy alliance of dishonest and corrupt politicians, officials and businessmen."[32] (the words in bracket mine).

The symptom of the malaise in India may seem economic superficially showing itself in price rise, shortages, black marketing and industrial disputes but underlying the symptoms was a disease which had destroyed democracies in the past and the basic causes of the disease are not economic. They are moral and political and constitutional, and in order to cure it, they had to be recognised as such. This was what JP did. He found that malaise and attacked not the symptom but the roots of the disease itself.

In support of what JP observed, it would be worthwhile quoting portions of David Selbourne's comments from his book. *An Eye to India: The Unmasking of a Tyranny"*:

> India is a rich country, which is poor. It is rich in minerals and power, in coal and iron; rich in oil resources; rich in its rivers. It has the most extensive cultivated alluvial plain in the world, and the potentially highly productive volcanic soils of the Deccan; it has 'vast ground water-resources'.... India is actually capable of economic self-sufficiency. But India's rural millions-more than 450 million live in the countryside, dependent upon its impoverished agriculture-are universally known to be poor and indigent... 75 per cent of the land under crops is without irrigating; under-fertilized the net area of rural India sown and cropped barely rising in a decade.... At last 40 per cent of rural fock are entirely landless.... A figure which is rising rural bankruptcy increases....a stagnant rural economy... of mountainous inequalities.
>
> There is a growing and unquantifiable number of rural and urban unemployed and under-employed, a long-run stagnation....[33]

He further holds that the history of post-Independence India has not only been a stagnant and unstable one, but also a humiliating and bloody one, belonging both its 'independence' and its non-violent character. Its political economy has held the poor in a vice-like grip[34] perpetrating a system of inequality and injustice from which they have no respite. The situation was very much rife for political violence.

Probably, the leadership provided by JP to the movements in Bihar and Gujarat saved the situation which remained largely peaceful and democratic.

Relevance for the Third World Today

When JP talked of Total Revolution, he meant to build up a strong Indian society-free of corruption, injustice, inequality-based on dignity of the common Indian who could meet his basic needs of food, shelter, clothing and education. He visualises a decentralised political society "based on 'people's participation' and an economy which can be self-sustaining on the one hand, and employment generating on the other. Apart from these he wanted to build-up a powerful cultural, social, ideological, intellectual and spiritual foundation for the socio-economic order be envisioned. Because without changing the values and spirit of the individuals in the society, no transformation can be lasting, no revolution can succeed. It is in this sense that we can call his Total Revolution a continuing revolution. Though JP did not survive to see the results of his labour, the suggestions that he made to reform the electoral system, check political defections, control corruption, develop a code of conduct for political parties and people's representatives, make education relevant to society, reform the agrarian economy and relations, etc. have haunted the decision-makers in India ever since. No doubt, very little has changed, but an alternative to the Congress system emerged slowly and gradually. The themes of his revolution that he put forward have been championed by international development agencies like World Bank, UNDP, Human Rights Organisations and above all Non-Governmental Agencies not only in India but in most of the developing countries of the world facing problems similar in India.

The world, however, walked over into a new era of 'globalisation' and 'liberalisation' within less than a decade of his passing away. India too joined the bandwagon of liberalised states to reap the fruits of globalisation. Forces of "turbo-capitalism" or "predatory-capitalism" have been let loose on the unsuspecting masses in developing countries where "profits are exploding" for the rich, but the poor are losing out. There are winners and losers, both at state level and within the society, in North as well as South. The Human Development Report 1999 produced by UNDP contains plentiful evidence of the fact that globalisation is "without a human face." It has created "global apartheid" by creating huge social disparities between the richest and poorest fifths of the world population. What Ulrich Beck calls, "global social Darwinism", is in full swing which is increasing the wealth of the few and leading to the magnetisation and impoverishment of the many.[35] According to the 2001 annual report of Amnesty International, the growing economic pressure brought about by globalisation in all societies poses a systematic threat to human rights.[36] Though western scholars plead that democracy, the market economy and human rights belong together like equal sides of a triangle, experiences in developing countries, tell a different story.

The common man has lost his freedom. The promised era of equality, liberty, justice and freedom have proved elusive visions. Corruption, jobbery, money power and misuse of political authority are a common feature of the developing countries world over. The reconstruction of society at the bottom as self-reliant and classless units of administration can alone safeguard the people from the onslaught of new imperialism of multinational corporations and oppressive state. What is needed is a fully democratic society on the lines suggested by Gandhi and JP which would be a guarantee against political power becoming oppressive and against inequality of status and capabilities in society growing wild.

JP has invoked Community Power (Lokshakti), People's Power (Janshakti) and Youth Power (Yuvashakti) for the success of his revolution. He, like Gandhi, believed in the goodness of man and people's participation for a cause. People have a dream; they have a vision for themselves as well as their children. They want to build up an utopia and they are willing to sacrifice for it. If scholars like Adi M. Doctor call JP's attempt at reconstructing the Indian polity as an "exercise in utopia building", they must not forget that the word 'utopia' is inseparably united with effort, dedication to the task, unconditional commitment to the job. It is indispensable that the people themselves participate and fight their own battles leaving little to the state. That is why JP seeks to build the new polity neither on power nor material prosperity but on 'the spiritual regeneration of man'. Ideas are strong, as Lenin said, only if they are put in action by the masses. Revolutions will take place wherever impoverished people become instruments of change towards a better future. JP's movement for Total Revolution was what we, today, in our social science, terminology call 'popular education' and 'popular mobilisation' of the masses. It is not an assistance-oriented or paternalistic approach, but rather an attempt, through mass-involvement, to enable people to become subjects of their own history by giving them an opportunity to acquire a high degree of consciousness and knowledge about the present condition so that they would be able to design their own models of social organisation that will permit them to assert their power in society. His whole approach was adjusted to the people and geared to serving those who ought to structure society with a vision. JP knew and had seen that the basic asset of the country was its people, their conscience, their effort and their participation and not the power hungry, mammon worshipping politicians.

REFERENCES

Quoted in H.M. Tichenor, *Chinese Philosophy of Life* (Givard, Kansas: Haldeman-Julius Co, 1922) Little Blue Book No. 153, p. 3. This passage truly conveys the anguish of Late Shri Jayaprakash Narayan before and after imposition of Emergency in 1974.

R.R. Diwakar, Editorial, *Gandhi Marg,* Vol. 11 No. 8, (Nov. 1979), p. 488.

See for details, Bimla Prasad (ed.) *Socialism, Sarvodaya and Democracy: Selected Works of Jayapakash Narayan* (Bombay, Asia Publishing House, 1964), pp. 138-171.

JP was aware of this criticism and responded to it way back in 1957 in the following words: "The past course of my life might well appear to the outsider as a zigzag and tortuous chart of unsteadiness and blind groping.... I discern in it a uniform line of devlopment. The groping undeniably was there, but it was certainly no blind..." See for details, Jayaprakash Narayan, *From Socialism to Sarvodaya* (Kashi: Akhil Bharat Sarva Seva Sangh Prakashan, 1958), p. 4.

This phenomenon has been called "synthesis of socialist revolutionary dynamism and agrarian rural realism" by V.P. Verma, "Total Revolution Phase of JP," in *Special Conference Number in Economics of Total Revolution,* published by Economic Association of Bihar (Patna: Jigyasa Prakashan, 2002), p. 24.

See Gustavo Esteva, 'Development', in Wolfgang Sachs (ed.) *The Development Dictionary* (London : Zed Books Ltd., 1992), pp. 6-25.

Colia Leys, *The Rise and Fall of Development Theory* (London, Nairobi, Bloomington, 1996) especially in the introduction.

Aristotle, *The Politics* (Harmondswarth: Penguin, 1967) bk. 3, ch. 5.

A. Cohan, *Theories of Revolution* (London: Nelson, 1975) p. 31.

See for details, Samuel P. Huntington, *Political Order in Changing Societies* (New Haven: Yale Univ. Press, 1968), p. 264, Thomas S. Kuhn, *The Structure of Scientific Revolution* (Chicago : University of Chicago, 1970), p. 93,Wilbert E. Moore, *Social Change* (New Jersey: Englewood Cliffs, 1963), K. Marx and F. Engles, *The Communist Manifesto* (Moscow: Foreign Languages Publishing House, 1848, many editions), and Ted Gurr, *Why Men Rebel* (New Jersey; Princeton University Press, 1980).

Mark N. Hagapian, *The Phenomenon of Revolution* (New York: Dodd, Mead, 1974), p. 1.

J. Dunn, *Modern Revolution* (London; Clarendon Press, 1989), p. 12.

See for details, Jayaprakash Narayan, *Prison Diary* (Papular Prakashan, Bomay, 1977, pp. 33-34.

Nageshwar Prasad, "The Meaning of Total Revolution", *Gandhi Marg,* Vol. 1, No. 8, November 1979, p. 494.

Indian Express (New Delhi), July 13, 1974.

Bimal Prasad, "JP's Concept of Total Revolution", in No. 5, p. 33.

Jayaprakash Narayan, *Total Revolution* (Varanasi: Sarva Seva Sangh Prakashan, 1992), pp. 15-20.

No. 16, p. 32.

No. 17, p. 64.

Ibid, p. 64.

Ibid, p. 70.

Jayaprakash Narayan, *Plea* for *Reconstruction of Indian Polity,* Varanasi, Sarva Seva Sangh Prakashan, 1959).

Jayaprakash Narayan, *Swaraj for the People* (Varanasi : Sarva Seva Sangh Prakashan, 1961).

Jayaprakash Narayan, *Prison Diary* (Bombay : Popular Prakashan, 1975).

See for details No. 22, pp. 23-24.

Quoted in No. 16, p. 42.

No. 24, pp. 95-96.

No. 17, p. 11.

Ibid., p. 20.

Quoted in Ram Ugrah, 'Homage', *Young Indian,* October 13-19, 2001, p. 3.

Ibid.

Collected from No. 17, pp. 1-7.

David Selbourne, *An Eye to India: The Unmasking of a Tyranny* (Harmond sworth, Penguine, 1977), Collected from pp. 1-7.

Ibid., p. 11.

See for details, Fernando Cardenal, "The validity of Utopias", *Adult Education and Development* (Germany), Vol. 44, 1995, pp. 153-179. Frenz Nuscheler,

"Globalisation: is the South Losing Touch?" *Ibid.*, Vol. 58, 2002, pp. 117-132. See also the issue of *Seminar,* 507, Nov. 2001. The Issue deals with Economic Turmoil.

Nusheler, No. 35, quoted on p. 129.

Adi H. Doctor, *JP's Total Revolution* (Delhi: Seema Publications, 1987), pp. 81-92.

5

People's Power in JP's Thought

Ravindra Kumar Verma

Jayaprakash Narayan has outstanding place in Indian history as statesman, social and political thinker and believer of people's power. His contributions in remaking Indian nation and social change cannot be ignored. We find no other leader equal to JP who sacrificed his whole life right from freedom struggle to re-achieving the civic liberties of Indian citizenary. Power and authority could not lure him because he believed in sovereignty of the people, not in the power positions. His belief in democracy of people's supremacy made him to fight for Total Revolution. His thought was inspired by values like equality, social justice, communal harmony and decentralization of power. Here it must be reminded that JP's thought was not the result simply of belief or commitment but grown from his acquisition of knowledge, experiences and understanding of socio-economic conditions of various other countries like USA, Germany, England etc. His thoughts gradually took shape by growing accomplishment of his understanding about social, economic and political conditions in the contemporary societies. He always kept people in the centre of his thought. The journey of his thought starts from belief in Marxism and ends with Total Revolution through socialism and tenets of socialism required for Indian populace. However, the ultimate goal of his ideas has been strengthening the people's power.

In the back–drop of this hypothesis the present paper examines JP's political thought and underlines his quest for people's power.

Genesis of JP's Ideas

Born in a middle class kayasth family on 11 October, 1902 AD, Jayaprakash Narayan did not lead a luxurious childhood, not compelled by economic conditions but by nature and temperament. He opted a responsible life right from childhood by nature. He studied historical novels at the age of ten. The imprint of ideals of national and international great men of his time had been deepening in his mind since school days. The value like 'nationalism' was inculcated in him by stories of Britishers' atrocities over slave India. After completion of his school education, JP shifted to Patna for his studies as I.Sc. student. He got more exposed to nationalist ideas and leaders as well as 'Satyagrah' experiment of Gandhiji in Africa. JP was impressed by lectures of the leaders like Abul Kalam Azad and call of Mahatma Gandhi. On Gandhi's call to students in 1921, JP jumped into the freedom struggle just a month before the I.Sc examination. His guardians wanted him to continue his studies and decided to send him England for the purpose. Initially JP refused but having been persuaded by parents he left India for United States of America. It is said that he was influenced by the history of American freedom struggle that attracted him to USA. He got admission in California University in 1922 as a Science student and later he studied in other univer-sities like Ioa University, Wisconsin University and Burkley University. During his stay in America, he did not depend on his parents for meeting the needs. He moved from one university to other in view of availability of job prospects. JP earned by working in grape fields during his stay in California, and it was job prospects that made him to shift from one university to other. He secured 'A' grades in all the universities wherever he studied. It was Wisconsin

University where he started congealing his political ideas.[1]

His Belief and Anomie in Marxism

JP studied political ideas and European literature deeply in Wisconsin University where he had the opportunity to discuss the ideas with likeminded fellow students. Robert Marion La Follete used to fight for the cause of poor and against the corruption in government at Wisconsin. Follete's revolutionary ideas influenced JP's approach to form political ideas.[2] There he met some American communists who inspired him to study communist literature including Marx's 'Das Capital'. JP was attracted by communist literature which attacked over American capitalism. JP dreamt to rebuild India with Marxian ideas. He came to a belief that 'Marxism was not only key to freedom but it contained the goals of social equality and individual liberty'. Saul Dozer, one of his fellow students, has written about JP "He was profoundly aware of and understood the Marxism that he had studied it that he had observed it"[3] JP had himself expressed belief in Marxism and said that Marxism had provided him the second torch of equality and fraternity; liberty was not enough as real liberty laid in liberty of lowest of the lower and freedom from poverty, hunger and exploitation.[4] The first provided to him was the ideas of Mahatma Gandhi.

But later JP turned critical to Marxism as he saw that even communism did not ensure power to the people. He was hurt by the Communintern's decision to keep communists away from Indian freedom struggle. Besides, the communist rulers did not transfer political power to the common people. In JP's view, power shifted from one exploitative Czar to few communist leaders who were just keeping common people away from political power. He rejected the dogma of 'Democratic Centralism' and said that people were not free from exploitative influence of new communist rulers. JP believed only in popular decentralization of power that communists did not ensure.

Search of People's Power in Socialism

Although socialism is the product of protection of interests of proletariate of industrial societies, yet JP was impressed by contents of people's power in Socialism. Emergence of Socialism as protector of interest of proletariate against the capitalist friendly rulers was hailed by him. Like Communists, Socialism believes in nationalization of resources but both differ on mode of change of power. What attracted JP towards Socialism was belief of socialists in democratic modes of change of power.

JP met the socialist leaders like Ashok Mehta, Minu Masani, Achyut Patbardhan etc in the Nasik Jail where it held a great deal of discussion on conditions in India and the ideology of Socialism. JP congealed his belief in socialism and freedom struggle with socialist objectives. He decided to form Socialist Congress Party. JP was of the view that nationalism and economic movement should go together. After being released from Nasik jail in 1934, JP formed a relief organization for quake victims and by that time Ganga Sharan Singh had formed Pradesik Socialist Party. JP attended the conference of the Party in Patna and accepted the responsibilities of Secretary of Congress Socialist Party. He prepared the ideology of the party beginning with "power to be transferred to the producing masses". He emphasized cooperative and community agriculture besides other objectives. JP desired the transfer of power to the people through Socialism.

He argued that political parties, ballot boxes electorate and candidates do not constitute real democracy. The disparities among people would have to be eliminated. He was against the exploitative institution of zamindars, therefore, he advocated for equal distribution of land. In short, JP wanted the extension of economic and political power to thc people and found Socialism the most potent ideology. Later he propounded the idea of 'Socialist Nationalism' about which he told that it was not code of individual conduct but a goal of social reconstruction which can eliminate coercion.[5]

People's Power Through Sarvodaya, Lokniti and Total Revolution

In course of time JP started that the root of Indian problems do not lay in economic and material aspects. It is required to establish spiritual and humanistic values in our society. He felt that political party system encouraged corruption in our society and degeneration of ethical and human values. Thus he suggested to adopt *Lokniti* instead of *Rajniti.*[6] He has argued that there are two kinds of social values–first inspired by environment and second by spontaneous culture. He has preferred to have strengthened spontaneous values and suggested to adopt *yam* and *niyam* of Pnatajali yoga philosophy for an ordered society.

Sarvodaya, as the term suggests, is upliftment of all including lowest of the lower class people. Sarvodaya is not based on only materialistic upliftment but believed in equal apportionment of social and economic resources among all. Again to JP, Sarvodaya and Socialism have similar goals but the difference lies in modes of achieving the goal. He argued that Socialism's belief in nationaliza-tion of resources would lead to a new kind of State-Capitalism (as Ambedkar had also argued) paving way to the dominance of bureaucracy over the common man. Thus, he suggested to curtail the state's control over resources. In his view state ownership over land is less fruitful than to villagers' ownership which enhances the economic viability of the land. In order words, ownership of rural community over land resources is better than state's ownership. He believed that "Bhoodan" was more effective that governmental measures of land reforms. Sarvodaya philosophy advocates for partyless democracy. Political parties have fierce and desperate competition for power and dominant parties develop grip over society, as a result exploitation continues and people are depowered. The people lose capacity to political initiative and opportunity to express 'general will'. The use of propaganda techniques, information sources, media and wealth by political parties frusrtrate the expression of people's political will and thereby making them weak. Therefore, JP suggested *Lokniti* and partyless democracy. He has clearly written. "The device of the democratic elections can not equate 500 representatives to eighteen crores looking after their affairs directly, to that extent the powers and functions of the state are restricted and real democracy is practised."[8]

To JP and Sarvodaya, there are four ways to achieve this goal—

(i) Group of social workers be formed unanimously at village level, who will select such groups for Panchayat level and Panchayat level will select for Thana level, Thana level will select for District level and so on. By this way national level body will be formed. As such a party less democracy will be established with 'Community consensus'.[9]

(ii) Sarvodaya worker will not fight elections and vote by his own conscience.

(iii) Existing political parties be made to join Sarvodaya and their ideology would be for upliftment of all.

(iv) The members of Parliament and state legislature would not be committed to any party but represent their constituents only. Council of Ministers will not be formed from members of parties but members themselves should suggest the names for ministerial position.

The state power will be exercised by people from village to district levels and their fate will not be decided by their MPs and MLAs but by their own, JP enumerated following fruits out of this arrangement—

(i) There will be no class struggle unlike Marx.

(ii) Majoritism will be replaced by consensusism.

(iii) There will be community-based-politics instead to power-based-politcs.

Although the above ideas seem to be utopia, yet JP's belief in people's power is reflected through these ideas.

JP at last saw that the present system of governance could not provide real power to the people and so he advocated for a total revolution in the society. He advocated for a governance on the basis of Gandhian '*Gram Swaraj*' and '*Janata Sarkar*'. He suggested to the formation of a '*Parishad*' at constituency level of five representatives, represented by Panchayat Jana-Sabha and Chhatra Sangarsh Wahini. The Parishad will elect a representative from among its members for Parliament or state legislature. He has adopted the seven point revolution as conceived by Lohia for total revolution. But so far people's power is concerned in JP's thought, we can conclude with the views of JP expressed in his Prison Diary—

"Here was I trying to widen the horizon of our democracy. Trying to do it mainly by involving the people more intimately and continuously in the process of democracy. This in two ways-one by creating some kind of machinery through which there could be a measure of consultation with people in the setting up of candidates; two by providing a machinery-through which the people could keep a watch on the representatives and demand good and honest performance from them".

REFERENCES

Based on Ajit Bhattacharya, *JP: A Political Biography,* Vikash Pub. New Delhi, 1978.

Ibid.

As quoted in Ajit Bhattacharya, *op. cit,* p. 48.

V.P. Varma, *Political Philosophy of Mahatma Gandhi and Sarvodaya,* Lakshmi Narain Agrawal, Agra.

Jayaprakash Narayan, *Towards A New Society,* p. 161.

Akhil Bharat Sarva Seva Sangh, *JP: Socialism to Sarvodaya,* 1955.

Ibid.

Jayaprakash Narayan, *op. cit.*

Akhil Bharat Sarva Seva Sangh, *op. cit.*

SECTION - II

JP and Rural Development

6
JP and Rural Development

Sachchidananda

JP's Vision of the Village

JP found that Indian villages at the present day were 'atomised, backward and listless'.[1] Even though panchayats have been established they were like empty shells.[2] Whatever authority they have, has come from above. Thus they represent more the intrusion of centralized power into the village than the flowering of Gandhiji's Ram Rajya.[3] In this context, it will be good to explore JP's own vision of the ideal village.

There could be three different views about the future of Indian village. The first looks upon it as an outdated institution condemned to extinction. The second views its retention as necessary for the existence of the urban industrial civilization which depends on the village for the supply of food and other essential raw materials. The votaries of this view are for the development of the village so that it may be able to play its role as a junior partner in a better way. JP believes in the third view which regards the village as a natural and sensible habitat of man and the primary unit of social organisation.[4] For the full development of human nature, the primary community is necessary so that the individual is able to establish personal relationships and meaningful association with others. This is not to be found in towns.

Certain values of life like cooperation can better be worked out in the villages. Cooperative living is only possible in small communities. Even democracy can better be learnt and practised in a small community.

JP firmly held that the trend of urbanization should be checked and for this villages had to be transformed and made more attractive for living.[5] This view of the village fitted very well with his concept of communitarian society in which he conceived of a hierarchy of communities from the primary or the village level to the national level. In his view, the territorial contiguity of a number of families does not make it a community and as such, the present day Indian villages are not proper communites.[6] Life in them is individualistic rather than communal, mineral rather than organic. People are divided by caste, class, race, religion and politics. Division, he believed, is poison for the community.[7]

In communitarian society there is no dichotomy between urban and rural.[8] The primary community should not be so small that a balanced development of communal life and culture becomes difficult and not so large that life in them becomes impersonalised. The community will have self-imposed discipline and common culture. There is understanding participation by all members of the community in its communal affairs. Cooperation in the community embraces all walks of life. The general will of the community is expressed by the Gram Sabha which consists of all adult villagers. The Panchayat is its executive body. JP does not conceive of election for Panchayat. All the decisions would be by consensus or by drawing lots.[9] The Gram Sabha must ensure that no one in village went without food, clothing and shelter and that no child went without primary education. Medical care must be made available to every one. In short, the Gram Sabha was an institution for giving training to the people in self-government.

The Question of Land and Bhoodan

From his early days JP firmly held that land should belong only to the tiller and that there should be no absentee owners.[10] In addition to this no one should have more land than necessary to support his family on a fair standard of living. He pleaded not only for the scrapping of the Zamindari system but also for freedom from farm bondage.

On his release from prison in 1946 he presented his own vision of socialist agriculture which meant the breaking up of big landholdings. He felt that no one should have more than thirty acres. The legal ownership of land in his picture of socialism was to vest with the village.[11] The Panchayat would settle the land with individual peasants but the property right would be limited to receiving the produce from the village lands in accordance with the size of his holding. No one could sell land except to the Gram Panchayat. Each Gram Panchayat was to act as farmer's cooperative and would conduct buying, selling and borrowing operations on behalf of the entire village community. All those who labour in the field would receive wages in cash or kind and the produce would be distributed among the peasants after deducting cost according to the size of holding. This was his vision of cooperative agriculture.

Ideally the next stage would be collectivisation. However, conditions in India were not ripe for this purpose as it would need coercion for seventy percent of the peasants even though it might be for their own good.[12]

The question of land figured prominently in his 'fourteen points' letter to Nehru in 1953.[13] He pleaded for the reduction of large land holdings to remove economic inequality and end exploitation. He was keen to give all preference to schemes meant for the uplift of landless labour and poor peasant. He was for the immediate stoppage of all evictions from land. He pleaded for suitable legislation to prevent fragmentation of holdings beyond a particular limit and also to bring about consolidation of holdings. He was for the abolition of the remaining forms of landlordism. The rural economy was to be transformed into a cooperative economy through building up multipurpose societies whose membership would be mandatory for all peasants. The state according to him shall not deal with individual peasants as far as possible. It shall deal with them only through an organisation like Panchayat or cooperative. He made a plea for the reclamation of wastelands and for settling landless labourers on them organised as village collectives. No wastelands were to be allotted for cooperative farming.

When the Sanjukta Social Party, Praja Socialist Party and the Communist Party launched a movement for mobilising landless people to occupy vested land under Benami and fictitious settlement, JP welcomed the move as it would help government in dispensing justice to those who had been wronged.[14] Land which would be salvaged could be redistributed among the landless through the Gram Sabha. The Sarvodaya workers were advised to locate government land occupied by landlords so that it would be available for distribution to the landless.

In February 1973, JP called upon the opposition parties, particularly the left opposition to cooperate with the state government in implementing land reforms from the state to the village level.[15] He suggested the formation of village committees consisting of all sections of society with adequate representation of the weaker sections to help the government implement the land laws. Land disputes arising from the enforcement of the laws should be settled in consultation with this committee. The government should also make arrangement to help beneficiaries to develop their land. He suggested to the state government to seek the cooperation of Sarvodaya workers in implementing land reforms laws.

In December 1973, JP visited two villages in the Thanjavur district in Tamil Nadu where injustices were heaped on Harijan landless labourers by landlords who had usurped temple land. He endorsed the struggle being waged there under the leadership of Sri Jagannathan and his wife. When sweet reasonableness had failed Satyagrah had been resorted to. JP interceded with the then Chief Minister to solve immediate difficulties and to make necessary legislation for long term changes.[16]

JP met Vinoba for the first time in 1951 and was at once drawn towards the Bhoodan movement. In the Pachmarhi Conference of the Socialist Party in 1952 he saw in it the 'revolutionary force of Gandhism' which 'could shake up the whole country and start a big conflagration against injustice'.[17] Some time before the beginning of his Poona fast he met Vinoba again and thereafter plunged himself completely in Bhoodan work and collected 7000 acres of land in Gaya district. He referred to it in his speech at the Asian Socialist Conference at Rangoon in 1953 as a solution to the country's biggest problem—the land problem. However, he held that Bhoodan was not asking for charity, but a demand for realization of rights in an experiment in non-violent revolution. JP devoted himself to Bhoodan with the proverbial zeal of a convert. He looked upon it not only as a method of peaceful distribution of land but also to lay the foundation of a partyless form of democracy in which decisions were taken by consensus on the model of the village panchayat. It was also an instrument for creating mass awareness.

After a few years Bhoodan flowered into the Gramdan movement which paved the way for Gram Samaj, JP was deeply impressed with the results in Mangrot, a Gramdan village in U.P.[18] The Gram Sabha, the Gram Kosh, the Village Cooperative and the Shanti Sena laid the foundation for the Sarvodaya Society after Gandhiji's vision. It was the beginning of the process in the change of values, not an instant revolution.

JP Tried to build bridges between government efforts in rural development and the Gramdan movement. In 1957 the Yeluril Conference of the Sarva Seva Sangh a number of political leaders like Nehru and Morarji Desai were present. Community Development was to be kept above party politics and the Sarva Seva Sangh and Community Development were to try to coordinate their work. However, JP was not happy[19] with the kind of Panchayat Raj sought to be established by the government since his advice that all public lands should be vested with the Gram Panchayat and they should exercise real authority, over civil servants in their charge was unacceptable to the government. 'The real guarantee of democracy is the faith of the people in democracy, the strength of the people, the capacity of the people to run democracy, the capacity of the people to manage their affairs themselves!' JP did not see this happening in our country.[20]

Rural Reconstruction in Sokhodeora

In April 1954, some months after his famous 'jiwan dan' declaration at Gaya, JP decided to launch his ideas of rural reconstruction in the field. The area selected was in the Kawakol police station in Nawada district, JP had realized that the Bhoodan movement should not be confined only to getting and distributing land among the rural poor. It was indeed only the first step towards a non-violent revolution whose ultimate aim was Sarvodaya. It was therefore necessary to help the peasants in building up the new economic order. Agricultural development, livestock development, village industries, educational programmes and promotion of self-dependence had to be conducted with the help of new local people trained for the purpose.

At that time Vinobaji was not in favour of establishing ashramas. In fact he even wanted to close down the old ashramas.[21] This was because of the feeling that the old ashramas were largely inner-directed and contact with outside world was extremely limited. However, the new experiment that JP was launching was to make the ashramas outer-directed, its basic purpose was to make it rooted in Bhoodan and it was also meant to disseminate rays of change in the area around through spread of new ideas, distribution of land and multi-faceted constructive programmes.[22] The ashrama was to concentrate on training and education of constructive workers drawn for the same area. The trainees would have a readymade field to test their innovative ideas. Its activities in agriculture, animal husbandry, village industries, health and educational fields were meant to serve as instruments of training and also as the basis of all round constructive work in the intensive area. It would also help make the area self-sufficient to a large extent.

The work is started at Sokhodeora with the putting up of the ashram. The population comprised largely of Harijans who were settled on Bhoodan lands in new villages like Gandhidham and Jayanagar Kasturbagram. The land was all barren and rocky and with hard work and faith in their ability to change the land and their life, things began to change. People showed their readiness to adopt new ideas without losing their anchor in their own social values. A number of landless labourers who were lowly serfs of their feudal masters by the dint of hard labour have emerged as proud landowners and painstaking master craftsmen. The barren rocky terrain is now covered with lush green crops. A number of wells, pumping sets and small dams, new agricultural techniques and fertilizers have raised the agricultural productivity fourfold. This has not only brought economic betterment but a new confidence and dignity among the Harijans. The opposition of the caste Hindus to the new life style of the Harijans has been blunted. A large number of children are going to school. The Khadi and village Industries Training-cum-Production Centre has proved to be boon to the area. Through JP's personal efforts a number of foreign experts in agriculture and village industries not only visited the area but stayed in it for long periods to give training to the people. In the field of health provision has been made for both preventive and curative aspects. For the eradication of leprosy, a hospital has been started at Kapasia. A number of cooperative societies, some multipurpose and other craft based were also started. Steps were also taken to organise and train the village youth as Gram Seva Dal. The All India Khadi and Village Commission constituted this area as an intensive area for all round development. Pottery, printing, dyeing and printing of cloth, carpentry, leather works, cycle repair and a number of other crafts have provided gainful employment to the villagers and made available to the people things of their daily need. 1500 people from the four nearby C.D. Blocks have been trained as artisans and given technical and financial assistance to set up their own trades.

Gram Sahbas have been established in a number of villages. Distribution of land collected through Bhoodan has been done in the neighbouring villages. Gram Kosh has been created in many villages. Through scientific agriculture the 60 acre plot yields annual revenue of Rs. 1,60,000 with which the Ashram supports a large number of workers.

The Musahri Interlude

In June 1970 the Musahri Block, which is adjacent to Muzaffarpur town was in the grip of Naxalite violence. In that district the gramdan campaign had been rapidly losing its momentum. The condition of the villages was very miserable. JP found that even after more than two decades of independence and government efforts to ameliorate the situation in the countryside 'what ultimately met the eye are utter poverty, misery, inequality, exploitation, backwardness, stagnation and loss of hope'.[23] The socio-economic reality in the village was ugly and distressing in the extreme. Even the existing laws concerning homestead, share cropping, land ceiling, minimum wages and money lending were not implemented efficiently. The main reason for this was that the village community was not organised and run democratically. There has been no change in people's attitudes and values of life. The result was that the balance of power in the community continued to be tilted in favour of the rural elite who had built up oppressive structures. The institutions and processes of democracy were found to be woefully lacking. In such a state of affairs it was no wonder that frustration and anger had turned the people towards violence.

At this point of time JP wanted to try Gandhian methods for meeting the challenge. Constructive work was to be stepped up. Conversion by gentle persuasion was the method adopted but when the situation so required, non-violent non-cooperation or resistance might be resorted to. Bhoodan, gramdan and ultimately gramswaraj were the paths to this non-violent change in the village. Through this a voluntary process of individual and social change was initiated leading to community self-government or gramswaraj. It involves attitudinal and value changes as well as changes in socio-ecönomic and personal relations.

More specifically JP's programme related to the implementation of gramdan pledges[24] obtained earlier, such as the establishment of *Gramsabha* in each village, redistribution of one twentieth of land covered by Gramdan, setting up of *Gramkosh* and organisation of the *Gram Shanti Sena,* Efforts were also to be made to secure legal confirmation of gramdan through government agencies. Stress was laid on distributing undistributed Bhoodan lands along with correcting mistakes discovered in respect of previously distributed land, to see that every Harijan received the homestead *parcha,* to look into the problems of the landless labourers with a view to solving them, and to take up specific cases of injustice and oppression brought up by people for redressal.

The programme was to be implemented by door to door[25] visit to the houses of landless people and taking up and ventilating the question of wages. JP used to camp in each village for a number of days trying to meet people and help in the solution of their problems. It was his resolve to stay in that area for as long as traces of violence did not disappear. It was intended to make the Gramdan movement intensive and deep going. He was, however, clear in his mind that Gramdan will only prepare the necessary socio-psychological climate for direct democracy of the village to function properly. The *Gramsabhas* will have to gain both strength and moral resources to resolve conflicts in the community and to prevent injustice to the weaker section. The *Gramkosh* was to be collected regularly and utilized for the purposes laid down. The Sabhas will have to learn to prepare their own plans for development, to husband their own resources for their execution and to obtain help from government and credit institutions. However, JP could not stay in Musahari beyond six months, as other national concerns claimed his attention from time to time. In 1971 he became so involved in the Bangladesh agitation that the Musahari programme had to be left to others.

JP's work lifted the spirits of Sarvodaya workers. At a meeting in Sevagram in October 1970, the Sarva Seva Sangh decided to follow his lead by de-emphasising the collection of gramdan pledges and starting centers to work for the implementation of gramdan.[26]

With JP's departure from the field the campaign could not be sustained by other leaders. Gram Sabhas could not be formed in all the villages of the Block. In some villages they existed only on paper. Even in those where they were functioning, they were divided into the haves and have-nots. The interests of the weaker sections continued to suffer. Changes in people's attitudes and values did not occur to the desired extent. The poor coverage of the villages by Sarvodaya workers, paucity or resources, lack of people's initiative, inarticulate collective conscience and inadequate mechanisms of tension management continued to set at naught the spirit generated by JP's intervention in Musahari.[27] The process of internalisation of Sarvodaya's values by the peasantry in Musahari was far from complete.

The Musahari experience led to JP's disillusionment with gramdan work.[28] The changes effected in Musahari were not a manifestation of people's power. He felt that the results achieved were not commensurate to the efforts. In October 1971 at the Bhopal session of the Sarva Seva Sangh, JP suggested that the Sulabh gramdan had waterdowned the movement and lent support to Dada Dharmadhikari's view that landless and small peasants should be organised. In the summer of 1972 JP convened a Conference of Sarvodaya activists and concerned social scientists at Bangalore to discuss ways and means of broadening its canvas of the Gramdan movement. The problems encountered in the movement, it was suggested, should not be bypassed but taken up with Satyagrah, if necessary.[29] JP also suggested a sub-committee of the Gram Sabha composed of the disadvantaged sections of the community. There were other proposals to deal with political deterioration in the country.

JP pleaded for a massive programme of rural industrialisation.[30] He felt that the khadi and village industries hardly touched the fringe of the problem. Small scale industries had hardly entered rural areas. Large scale industries had done more harm than good. A balanced agro-industrial economy had to be built up so that urban exploitation structures do not get a foothold in the rural areas. Such a kind of rural development would produce a salutary effect even in the urban sector. For this he made the suggestion for the setting up of a Rural Industrialisation Commission as an apex decision making body.[31]

He believed that considering all the factors of the Indian situation such as huge population, terrific rate of population growth, heavy pressure on land, low productivity of agriculture, vast unemployment and under-employment etc., industrialisation of the rural area is the only remedy.[32] Rural industrialisation, however, does not mean setting up large industries in the rural areas, it must be an even spread of industries throughout the countryside. Rural industries need not necessarily be confined to agro-based industries.

There are two important considerations[33] for the establishment of rural industries:

(a) local resources, both human and material;
(b) local needs.

The raw materials for rural industries may be obtained from the neighbourhood but in part they might also come from the cities, such as iron and steel for agricultural and rural crafts implements. It should also be seen that the industries are so planned as to meet the needs of permanent as well as part-time and seasonal employment.

In regard to the use of power and technology in rural industry, he held that a balance should be maintained between employment and efficiency and certain social values such as those of self-management and social equality and avoidance of exploitation should be promoted.

Thus rural industrialization would be able to transform the lopsided agricultural communities into balanced agro-industrial communities. This would, however, require a dose of rural education suited to meet the needs of the emerging situation. It cannot be possible without far reaching educational planning. Thus rural industrialisation is a process of educational and cultural development. For this the entire process of planning has to be geared to the process of rural industrialisation. As far as possible private profit interest should not be allowed to exploit the field of rural industry. Necessary protection has to be provided for the products of rural industry to save them from competition of large scale urban industries. As far as possible these industries should be run by cooperative and panchayat institutions. For this purpose, it would be necessary to set up appropriate agencies at the district, state and central levels. This would do away with fragmented and peacemeal approach to rural industrialization.

He was highly critical of the efforts made in this direction, and made three very useful suggestions[34]:

(a) The Planning Commission should initiate studies into all such possible industries so that the operational blueprints are available for rural areas;

(b) Immediate research must be undertaken to improve the technology and manufacturing processes used in rural industries. He was thinking in terms of intermediate technology the application of which would make rural industries more productive and profitable;

(c) In view of the scarcity of electric power alternative non-conventional sources of energy should be actively explored. He deprecated the flight of enterprise from the villages to the towns leading to the dearth of entrepreneurial talent in the villages. It was necessary therefore to provide training in business organisation, promotion and management of educated rural youth in regional languages.

Taking the cue from JP in this direction, the Government of India started Pilot Projects in several states. In Bihar, the two Pilot Projects were entrusted to voluntary agencies, the Khadi Gramodyog Sangh at Muzaffarpur and to the Gram Nirman Mandal at Gaya.

Conclusions

Like Gandhi, JP believed that the soul of India lay in the village. If the village suffered decay the country as a whole would lose its identity. The village had to be restored to their old glory and was not to be developed as a poor relation of the city. It was to develop as a primary community, largely self-dependent and proud. The economy although largely agricultural would have an industrial facet also. It was to be run by the Gram Sabha with a great measure of autonomy to look after not only system maintenance but also after development. He wanted social values to change so that the weaker sections would not be neglected and would themselves gear up strength to face injustice or discrimination. JP was not against government action in respect of the villages but did not lay great store by it. Voluntary action could produce better and faster results if it was backed by resources both human and material. It was towards that end that he had founded the Association of Voluntary Agencies for Rural Development (AVARD).

REFERENCES

Building up from the village—Talk from the All-India Radio, April 1, 1959.

Op. cit.

Op. cit.

Op. cit.

Op. cit.

Jayaprakash Narayan : A plea for the Reconstruction of Indian Polity; quoted in Bimal Prasad (Ed.): A Revolutionary's Quest, O.U.P., 1980.

Op. cit. p. 219.

Op. cit. p. 221.

Op. cit. p. 235.

Draft resolution for the Ramgarh Congress, 1940.

My Picture of Socialism, Janata Vol. 3, No. 43, Nov. 24, 1946.

Op. cit.

Letter of March 22, 1993 to Pandit Nehru.

"The Land Grabbers' in Brahmanand (Ed.): Towards 'Total Revolution, Vol. III, Popular Prakashan, Bombay, 1978.

Inaugural address to the Eastern Regional Seminar on Land Reforms, Feb. 15, 1973, A.N. Sinha Institute of Social Studies, Patna.

People's Action, Vol. 8, No. 1, Jan. 1974.

Speech at the Socialist Party Conference at Pachmarhi, 1952, quoted in Ajit Bhattacharya: Jayaprakash Narayan.

Ajit Bhattacharya: Jayaprakash Narayan.

Ajit Bhattacharya: Jayaprakash Narayan, p. 127.

Op. cit.

JP's preface to the First Report of Gram Nirman Mandal 1956.

Op. cit.

Jayaprakash Narayan: Face to Face, Nachiketa Prakashan, Varanasi 1970, p. 12.

Op. cit. p. 9.

Op. cit. p. 24.

Roderick Church: Vinoba Bhave, Jayaprakash Narayan and Indian Democracy, Unpublished Seminar Paper 1978.

Sachchidananda and S.A. Kinchan: Sarvodaya and Development: Multidisciplinary Perspective from Musahari, The Sociological Perspective, *Journal of Science and Economic Studies,* March 1976.

Roderick Church, op. cit. p. 11.

Op. cit. p. 12.

Speech at 15th Sarvodaya Sammelan, April 1961.

Deplorable Progress in Rural Industrialization, Hindu, August 31, 1963.

Problems of Rural Industrialization in Brahamanand (Ed.): Towards Total Revolution, Vol. III.

Op. cit.

Deplorable Progress in Rural Industrialization, op. cit.

7

Gram Nirman Mandal : An Exercise in Social Reconstruction

Manohar Lal

I

After being disillusioned with party-politics during early fifties, JP started thinking more and more in terms of the Sarvodaya Movement. He decided to withdraw from party and power politics not due to disgust, but because of his belief that politics could not deliver the goods and that unless Socialism was transformed into Sarvodaya, the beacon-lights of freedom, equality, brotherhood, and peace would remain beyond its reach.

In 1954, JP left the Socialist Party and joined the Sarvodaya Movement. At the Bodh Gaya Sarvodaya Sammelan, held under the leadership of Vinoba in April 1954, he made a proclamation of Jeevandan (dedication of life) for the cause of Bhoodan Movement.

Soon after the Sarvodaya Sammelan, JP set up Sarvodaya Ashram in May 1954, in a remote and backward village Sokhodeora in Kawakole Block of Nawada district of Bihar. He began living in the Ashram, with his wife Prabhawati, leading an Ashram life. He started working with his full strength to popularize the Sarvodaya Movement in the country and disseminated the message of love and brotherhood, as a means of attaining the goal of social transformation.

In this paper the role of Gram Nirman Mandal, Sarvodaya Ashram Sokhodeora has been examined in the context of translation of JP's ideals of social reconstruction into reality during the last fifty years of its existence.

The Beginning

JP firmly believed that social transformation was not possible without the help of a committed, voluntary and non-violent revolutionary force. He thought about the shape of new villages, and the strategy for reconstruction and training for the workers (change agents). He also pondered over the form of new socialism required for desired change in the society. After giving serious thought over these issues, JP felt the need to establish a centre and an agency, to translate his ideas into action, on the pattern of Gandhi's Ashramas.

He wanted to establish such a centre in a remote and backward region in the country. After initial hesitation Vinoba approved JP's plans with a condition that such a centre (Ashram) would be opened only in an area where people donate five thousand acres of land in Bhoodan. Ugrahanarayan and his associates of Kawakole, a backward region of Nawada, Bihar came forward and put their claim to Vinoba promising the gift of required quantum of Bhoodan land. On their next visit they informed Vinoba that Budhauli and Madra Mahants of Kawakole area were ready to donate five thousand acres of land in Bhoodan, if JP promised to open his Ashram at village Sokhodeora and declare Kawakole as his area of operation. In addition, other landlords were also ready to donate their land to JP in Bhoodan.

Soon JP obtained the promised land in Bhoodan from the Mahanths through his emissary. As a follow-up, JP, along with other Sarvodaya workers, visited Khadsari,

Sokhodeora and Lalpur on 19-21 January 1954. He was convinced of starting the Ashram at the earliest so as to mitigate people's problems and mobilise them to fight against exploitation of the Mahanths.

After sometime, JP and his associates revisited the area and selected Kshirsagar, an upland site near Sokhodeora, to build the Sarvodaya Ashram.

The foundation of the Ashram at Sokhodeora was laid on May 5, 1954. The Ashram was inaugurated by JP on August 14, 1954 on the auspicious Shrawan Purnima day. JP, in his inaugural speech, made it clear that Ashram will act as a place of night halt for the Sarvodaya workers, who have to work in the village area during the day for mobilising the people. Gram Nirman Mandal was constituted as an agency to look after Ashram's activities. It was registered on October 1, 1954 under Societies Registration Act of 1861.

The twin purposes of the Mandal were to change the hearts of the people as well as to work for their material advancement.

II

Objectives, Organisation and Activities of Gram Nirman Mandal, Sarvodaya Ashram Sokhodeora

Objectives

1. To build a non-exploitative, stateless, non-violent society based on truth and non-violence, so as to make village life happy, healthy, self-governed, free and self -reliant.
2. To strive for changing human values in such a way that self-interest is replaced by social good and material uplift is guided by spiritual demands.

Organisation

There is a 15-member Niyamak Samiti of the Gram Nirman Mandal. The activities of the Mandal are organised under the following units:

1. Khadi Gramodyog Samiti.
2. Krishi Vigyan Kendra.
3. Minor Irrigation Project.
4. Kushtha Sewa Samiti.
5. Khadi Gramodyog Vidyalaya.
6. Nagrik Adhikar Evam Kartavya Parishad (Council for Rights and Duties of Citizens)

Programmes and Activities

Various programmes and activities taken up by the Mandal for uplift of all and creation of a better village society based on Sarvodaya philosophy are as follow:

• Economic Growth and Technological Development

Krishi Vigyan : Training in oil seeds and pulses, horticulture, animal husbandry, agricultural engineering, home science, soil testing, demonstration, production and sale of seeds.

Rural Industries : Production and marketing of khadi and village industries products such as silk, cotton, woolen and poly khadi, soap, agarbatti, furniture, bricks, repair of diesel engine & pump sets etc.

Irrigation Management : *Pyne* & *Ahar* construction, boring, tubewell and other related activities.

• Social Reconstruction

Gram-Swaraj and Panchayati Raj :

: Bhoodan, Gramdan and Gram Sabha.

: Education of citizens about their Rights and duties, self help, community building,

: Development of Dalits and Tribals.

Education :

: Adult and Non-formal education.

: Khadi & Village industries training.

: Appropriate technology, research & development.

Health :

Community Health

: Sanitation and drinking water management.

: Reproductive and child health (RCH).

: Cataract Clinics.

: Leprosy control.

: Health awareness and eduction

III

The Shaping of Life and Work at the Ashram

The philosophy on which JP founded Sokhodeora Ashram was both social and spiritual. The basic idea was the formation of the perfect community and the purification of the individual workers through the sweet fire of Gandhian living reborn in the spirit of Vinoba. As perfect human beings remade after living in the perfect community they would carry their spiritual uplift into the world and, fortified with spiritual strength and some practical training in social uplift work, would remake society according to the Gandhian ideal.

The Ashram was built on the basis of JP's map. Residential houses for the workers were built on single pattern in 10 acres of land. JP's residence and Jawahar Library were build near Karyakarta Niwas. On some distance were Udyog Bhawan, Office and Matri-Seva Sadan. The kutcha road inside the Ashram was flanked by flower and shady trees. Rajendra Bhawan was built for holding large-scale meetings and functions. A separate cow-shed was constructed for the cattle. In another 10 ares of land fruit trees were grown. The rest of 44 acres of Ashram land was set apart for cultivation. Three Dam Ahar were constructed to collect rain water from the adjoining hills.

Large number of Sarvodaya Workers and Volunteers came to work with JP from other parts of India and from abroad. Many of them left in between due to difficult and arduous life in the Ashram.

JP took up Bhoodan work as the first initiative for village reconstruction in Kawakole block. Big land owners, middle and small farmers came forward to donate their land under Bhoodan. This land was distributed to landless farmers in 50 villages of Kawakole. After accomplishing the work of land distribution, the Gram Nirman Mandal started reclaiming the wasteland and converting into cultivable fields. Simultaneously it started various other agriculture related activities such as soil testing, digging irrigation wells, imparting training of pumping sets to the people in village area, and initial support to poor formers in the form of seeds, fertilizer and diesel pumping sets for irrigation. Thus, Gram Nirman Mandal made its presence felt in the field as an agency for development of the people and not simply an agency for doing Bhoodan work.

In October 1955, Gram Nirman Mandal decided to implement the Intensive Area Plan of the All India Khadi Gramodyog in Kawakole Block. JP envisaged that under this plan, the villages should be developed in such a way that all the primary needs of the people in these villages were fulfilled. The six primary needs included food, clothing, housing, health, education and employment. In addition, agriculture, animal husbandry, khadi and village industries were to be developed side by side.

Thus, the workers took up the Bhoodan work and rural development activities together. Field centres were opened in many Bhoodani villages to coordinate both types of work. These centers were at Pavapur, Gobria, Lalpur, Badrawatari, Mahudar, Gaighat, Taratanr and Jhillar. The workers, known as Gram Sewaks, used to organise refresher course on rural industries for the villagers. Twenty four Vikas Mandals were established in the operational villages for strengthening field coordination. Dayanand Sahay and Tripurari Sharan were given the responsibility of looking after the whole programme. Though all the programmes were implemented with great vigour, the experiment did not yield desired results perhaps due to centralised planning at the Madal level with poor participation of field level Vikas Mandals.

JP was aware of the predicament of his Socialist turned Sarvodaya companions. In a big rally organized at Kawakole on January 1, 1957, JP reminded the people of the area about the Bhoodan work and various development works carried out by the Ashram workers for the last two years. It was beginning of the larger development and reconstruction work to be taken up in the villages in Kawakole area for creating a mini model of Sarvodaya Samaj. JP exerted the large rural work force to work united by for their own development rather than to look for outside help. He called them to first organise village development committees in each village unanimously before Ashram could initiate development work there.

There were two types of workers in the Ashram-Sarvodaya Socialists and pure Sarvodaya with distinct life styles and thoughts. However, JP was able to mobilise both types of workers to work together for rural reconstruction and development. Each worker was given monthly allowance of Rs. 65/- plus Rs. 10/- for each child in the family. Foreign worker was given Rs. 200/- per month. Life for them was austere. They were expected to wear Khadi clothes, use village handicraft products and avoid all luxuries. Alcohol, cigarettes and other intoxicants were prohibited.

To develop familial atmosphere among the workers and save cooking time, a community kitchen was started in the Ashram. It was compulsory for all the workers to become members of it. The experiment continued for about five years from 1955 to 1960. After this, the community kitchen was closed due to obvious reason of difference in the taste and food habits of workers coming from different parts of the country. A kitchen for guests has continued to function in the guest house since then.

IV

Experimenting With Training of Workers

One of the objectives of Sarvodaya Ashram was to act as a centre for training the Sarvodaya workers engaged in the work of Bhoodan and rural development. The first such training course was held on 12.5.1955 by JP himself at the prayer ground of the Ashram. He called for changing the society through change in attitudes and beliefs of the people on the basis of Sarvodaya ideology of Gandhi and Vinoba.

Aspired by JP's speech, the Gram Nirman Mandal opened Gram Nirman Mandal Vidyalaya for imparting regular training to the workers. Local and outside scholars were invited as resource persons in these training courses.

The Mandal opened Khadi Gramodyog Vidyalaya in April 1967, directly under the Khadi and Village Industries Commission (KVIC). Chandrika Prasad Singh was made its principal. The Vidyalaya functioned efficiently till emergency in 1975, when KVIC ordered its closure. The central government withdrew its support to Mandal and the Vidyalaya because of JP movement and JP's association with Mandal. However, the KVIC granted permission to reopen the Vidyalaya in 1978 after Janta Party government came to power at the centre. A new course of 'Naveen-Bunkar' was started in February 1978 with 22 trainees. Husband-wife teams were selected for this course to enable them to start some family based craft-industry for self reliance. Persons from dalit, tribal and backward communities were given preference for this training course. Quite a few of the trainees of the Khadi Gramodyog Vidyalaya joined and served Gram Nirman Mandal and held prestigious positions.

V

Rejuvenation

After dissolution of Kshetra Samiti, JP constituted a Samanvaya Samiti (Coordination Committee) of sixty selected persons of Kawakole block at Phuldih village. The Samanvaya Samiti held its first meeting on June 12, 1960 at Sarvodaya Ashram Sokhodeora. It created a deep impact on the people by taking two important decisions. It resolved to create irrigation facilities for the coming Kharif crop by constructing a dam through "sharmdan", and repair of existing irrigation ponds (Ahar) and drains. The area was divided into 15 circles, each in the charge of a member of the Samiti. A separate committee was formed to look into the problems of Bhoodan farmers. The Samanvaya Samiti appeared to be more efficient than the previous Kshetra Samiti. With a view to rejuvenate the Gram Nirman Mandal, the Executive Body (Niyamak Samiti) of the Mandal held its meeting at Nawada on 29-31 July, 1964 under the chairmanship of JP. In this meeting Tripurari Sharan was elected as General Secretary unanimously and JP once again to continue as the Chairman of the Mandal.

Once again the Gram Nirman Mandal became the hub of activities. There was tangible evidence of the progress made in the village area through concerted efforts of Mandal office bearers and workers.

The Gram Nirman Mandal has always believed in the creation of a casteless and classless society. It has considered religion as a matter of personal belief. Therefore Vinobaji had started the practice of silent prayer, which JP also accepted. Silent prayer continues to be in practice in the Mandal even today. Mandal workers have played active role to restore communal harmony and peace among the people affected by communal violence from time to time in various parts o Bihar such as Jamshedpur, Ranchi, Bhagalpur, Bihar-Sharif, Sasaram etc.

Problems of Bhoodan

Gram Nirman Mandal have done some good work in Bhoodan movement. Mandal distributed 1307 acres of land among farmers and agricultural labourers of Kawakole block and 26,000 acres of land among 16,000 landless families of Nawada district. It created a Gram Kosh of Rs. 4960 through formation of Gram Sabhas in its operational area and created irrigation potential for 67 thousand acres of land through land development work. However, the process of mutation, fixation of land rent could not be accomplished in a large number of cases due to vested interests in the government machinery, the landed community and inertness of the Bhoodan Yagya Committee.

The main objective, of Bhoodan-Gramdan, of bridging the gap between landlord and the landless, could not be achieved. However, some impact of Mandal's work through gram sabhas and distribution of land can be seen in backward and tribal villages of Kawakole area such as Jhillar, Badrawatari and Tisri. The Mandal has v.aged a successful struggle against exploitation of tribals by the local money lenders in these villages.

Leprosy Control

The Kawakole area can not be developed properly without eradication of two dreaded diseases-alcoholism and leprosy. Mandal recognized these two major problems of the area from the very beginning. Though Mandal could not do much to eliminate the former vice, it has done a good job towards leprosy eradication from its beginning in 1955. Initially leprosy patients were treated in the Matri-Seva Sadan at the Ashram by Dr. Ravi Shankar Sharma and his team. Soon the number of leprosy patients visiting the clinic swelled and the leprosy clinic was shifted to Kapasia. Leprosy centre was built on Bhoodan land at Kapasia and was inaugurated on April 6, 1959 by the then President of India, Dr. Rajendra Prasad.

Soon the patients from adjoining districts of Munger, Hazaribagh, Gaya and others started visiting the leprosy centre and get benefitted. The leprosy centre had created the capacity to treat 300 indoor patients till then. After getting government grant for leprosy control, Mandal extended its area of operation. It covered a population of 2 lakhs for distribution of leprosy medicine. Eight distribution centers were opened in the area. Weekly mobile clinics were held at these centers. Para medical workers and supervisors used to conduct survey along with distribution of medicine. Additional wards and residential quarters were constructed with public contribution to accommodate increasing number of patients and workers at the leprosy centre.

Since then, the Mandal has been serving the suffering people through its leprosy centre by carrying out various activities like survey, treatment and rehabilitation. Dr. Srikant Dwivedi gave his valuable services for 10 years between 1969-79. After him Dr. Mishra has been serving as Medical Officer of the leprosy centre. Large number of cured persons (ex-patients) have been rehabilitated as para medical workers in the leprosy centre. Many of them have got married and have children and were leading normal social life as a part of the mainstream society.

VI

Rural Industries Project

Initially JP presented his ideas about rural industries project in a Sarvodaya convention. He lamented that even after more than a decade of Swaraj and planned development, the rural areas had witnessed increase in poverty and unemployment. The large agencies like All India Handicraft Board, Silk Board, Khadi Commission etc., which were created for developing rural industries, have done least in this direction. Therefore, these organisations should be dissolved and a new organisation for rural industrialisation should be created in their place. As requested by the learned audience, JP Prepared a proposal and sent it to the Planning Commission. The Commission while agreeing to JP's proposal did not think it proper to dissolve these all India organisations. It suggested to the creation of an organisation at the implementation level to coordinate activities of all these national level organisations. JP agreed to this proposal and thus was born the Rural Industries Project. The Planning Commission requested JP to shoulder this responsibility on non-governmental basis. Thus, in 1962 49 Rural Industries Projects were initiated. The two projects run on voluntary basis were those which were managed by Gram Nirman Mandal and Bihar Khadi Gramodyog Sangh, Muzaffarpur.

The project at the Mandal was run under the guidance of JP. This project was adjudged the best of all by the Evaluation Team of the Planning Commission, set up for this purpose at a later date.

In 1977, after the Janata Party took over at the centre, the Rural Industries Project was transformed into District Industries Project. With the change in policies and priorities under the new dispensation, the performance of Mandal Project was effected adversely. The benefits were usurped by the industries located in the urban areas and the household and village industries were completely neglected. The District Industries Centre (DIC) lost its voluntary character and was completely bureaucratised. The Mandals Niyamak Samiti, therefore, resolved to hand over the charge of DIC to the government.

Commitment to Propagation of Khadi

Gram Nirman Mandal has contributed considerably towards propagation of Khadi in the state of Bihar. It is ahead of all other voluntary organisations engaged in popularising Khadi. Production, quality and ideology are interwoven in the khadi produced at the Mandal.

As per decentralisation policy for khadi work, the Bihar Khadi Gramodyog Sangh handed over the Khadi activities of Gaya district to Gram Nirman Mandal in January 1958. Mandal, in turn, formed Khadi Gramodyog Samiti for planned development and extension of khadi work with its headquarter at Gaya. At that time khadi activities were carried out through 8 centres, 13 sub-centres and 50 khadi workers in 16 community development blocks in Gaya district.

The Mandal has always emphasised development of rural industries and handicraft along with Khadi. For this purpose the Gramodyog Samiti was constituted in 1978-79. Later on it was merged with the Khadi Gramodyog Samiti. Khadi and village industries were expanded in all the new districts of the Magadh division. The Mandal has played significant role in getting the new pay scale implemented for khadi workers in Bihar. It has resulted in raising the motivation and commitment of khadi workers resulting in expansion of khadi activities under the Gram Nirman Mandal as well as other agencies in other parts of Bihar.

The Mandal has specialised in production of thick khadi 'chadar', which used to be imported from Haryana and Punjab till 1965-66. In addition, Mandal also started producing 'Dari' and carpet at Obra in Aurangabad district. Black coloured blanket and woolen chadar produced at Obra have become very popular even in other states. The modern finishing plant for woolen clothes and blanket established at Obra has been catering to the needs of the state as well as Sikkim and north-eastern states.

VII

Krishi Vigyan Kendra

In 1979, Krishi Vigyan Kendra (KVK) was established in the Ashram campus with grant from ICAR, New Delhi. The objective of KVK was to impart modern scientific knowledge to the farmers about agriculture and allied fields. KVK has been organising vocational training programmes for farmers-men and women as per their interests, and priority needs of the area in agriculture and allied activities. The training is given through "Do and Learn" methodology. Rural women are given training in home science, health, nutrition, horticulture, animal husbandry, bakery, fruit preservation etc. In addition, the KVK has been organising training for extension workers, demonstration programme etc., to help to raise production and economic self-reliance of the farmers. The KVK field tests the quality of seeds on its own demonstration plot of 76 acres before distributing it to the farmers on fair price.

VIII

Taking Care of Health Needs of the People

The Mandal has been making all efforts to provide preventive, promotive and curative medical care, health services and health education to the people in the Kawakole area. Matri-Seva Sadan was established in 1956 at the Ashram to provide health care services to the people. The Mandal started a primary treatment centre in 1972, which afterwards became the main centre for extension education on health and disease. Thus, under the community health programme of the Mandal various activities have been carried out such as Action Research on Health and Family Welfare, Reproductive and Child health (RCH), eye camp, health awareness programme and leprosy control programme.

IX

Antyodaya

More than one third of Kawakole's population is of dalits. Among them fifty percent are Musahars. They are the most backward dalit community in the block. They make their living through wage labour. Mandal has made considerable efforts to improve their socio-economic conditions through distribution of Bhoodan land among them and creation of employment through labour intensive works. The Mandal in collaboration with the Government of Bihar has rehabilitated large number of Musahar families by settling them in Prabha Nagar, Kasturba Nagar, Vinoba Nagar and Jayaprakash Nagar located in the vicinity of the Sarvodaya Ashram.

Tribal Development

For the development of traibals in Kawakole area, Mandal has been making concerted efforts from the very beginning. For example Santhals of Jhillar village have been linked with programmes of silk cocoon rearing, growing of fruit trees and spinning of silk thread. Fruit orchard has been developed in 3.50 acres of land in the village. Arjun trees have been planted in 26 acres of land for rearing of silk cocoons.

Similarly 16 families of Birhor tribe have been permanently settled in Pachambha village of Kawakole block. Houses for them have been built under Indira Awas Yojana (IAY). Mandal has been regularly generating employment for them in agriculture and spinning of silk. Non-formal education centers have been started for Birhor children in the village.

Recently the Mandal has taken up watershed programmes in Kawakole area to meet the drinking water and irrigation needs for agriculture. Similarly poly Katia Weaving programmes of CAPART and Self-Help Group (SHG) programmes have been taken up to provide employment and self-employment to both men and women in large number of villages.

X

Gram Nirman Mandal as SVO of CAPART

Based on its efficient management structure, resource base and ability of functionaries and workers in the Mandal, CAPART has chosen it to act as a Supporting Voluntary Organisation (SVO). Under this programme, Mandal assists small voluntary organisations in various activities-project planning, staff development, guidance and direction in implementing CAPART sponsored projects. Mandal has been organising workshops, from time to time, to impart knowledge about plans and projects to all those voluntary organisations which are linked to CAPART under micro-finance programme.

XI

Mobilising the People for Rebuilding the Society

Under the Nagrik Adhikar Evam Kartavya Parishad (Council for Citizen's Rights and Duties) various activities have been carried out for social awareness, participatory democracry, gram-swaraj and gram panchayat. The Parishad has worked together with similar organisations, for eradication of the traditional method of carrying human excreta on head by the scavengers. It has succeeded in creating some awareness about this issue among the society, politicians and the government.

It has taken the initiative to create suitable environment for propagation of philosophy of Khadi and its role in nation building.

The Parishad has also worked for socio-economic and political empowerment of women through various programmes like awareness campaign, self-help group etc. It has planned to create awareness about citizen's rights in collaboration with Bihar State Gandhi Smark

Nidhi, Patna and other agencies through building a clean and conducive social environment in the state.

XII

Whither Gram Nirman Mandal?—Retrospect and Prospect

The establishment of Gram Niman Mandal, Sarvodaya Ashram at Sokhodeora in 1954 opened up new vistas of rural reconstruction and development based on Sarvodaya philosophy. As a consequence the people in this region have become more conscious. They have adopted innovations in agriculture, silk rearing and allied activities. There has been increase in employment opportunities for the people in various development activities taken up by the Ashram. The people of this area have experienced expansion in their identity. They feel proud to refer to belong to the area of JPs Sokhodeora Ashram.

JP considered Sokhodeora Ashram as a central point from where he desired to channelise his work in Kawakole area as well as in other parts of Bihar and even outside the state. However, some sections of the people in Kawakole area could not rise above regional feelings even during JP's life time. They wanted all the benefits, even employment in the Ashram, for the local people only. This tendency based on the concept of 'Sons-of the Soil', has increased over the years, with local people claiming their special right on Mandal management and its resources. It is a great challenge to the existence and effective functioning of the Mandal.

Gram Nirman Mandal has established its identity as a mother (nodal) agency for undertaking participatory development programmes for the downtrodden in partnership with government and non-government agencies. It is functioning as a supporting voluntary organisation (SVO) of CAPART for other partner voluntary agencies. It supports other small voluntary agencies in formulating their project proposals, imparting training to their workers monitoring their work and networking them with governmental and non-governmental sponsoring agencies.

The Mandal has extended its operational area from Kawakole to the districts of Nawada, Gaya and Aurangabad over the last fifty years. It has also expanded scope of its activities. It started with the work of building the community through propagation of Gram Swaraj. It added other programmes of economic and technological development, education, research and training, community health and disease and conscientisation of the people in the area.

JP founded the Ashram to build a band of trained Sarvodaya workers (to act as the agents of change) fully equipped to bring about holistic development of the people in the area. The experience has shown that such a dream was over with the retirement of first generation of workers, who worked with JP. Today's workers are not inspired by JP's ideals. They take the work as employment for remuneration rather than service to the society. This has resulted in hierarchical and bureaucratic style of functioning in the organisation. The feeling of working for a great ideal has diminished over the years.

Human development cannot be divided into sectors. It has to be seen in a holistic perspective with efforts for the all round development including social, economic, cultural, political and spiritual upliftment of all human beings. JP's goal of holistic development for rural reconstruction has not been accomplished because the Mandal all along seemed to have engaged in such activities which tilt towards sectoral development rather than holistic development.

Respect for voluntary worker and voluntary agencies have diminished over the years. They also suffer from distrust of government officers. Voluntary agencies have become more of Project Implementation Agencies (PIA) of the government programmes and consequently their dependence on government has increased with the time. Moreover, some of them have been using the funds, meant for the people, for their selfish ends. Thus, they have misused people's trust. They function as B-team of the administration.

Voluntary agencies have to face challenges from the extremist groups in their operational areas. Taking advantage of the weakness of the voluntary agencies and the government, these groups have created pockets of influence here and there in the state. However, some anti-social and criminal elements masquerade as extremists.

If we look at the social life in the Ashram, there seems to exist a sense of social equality among the Ashramites. A sense of we-feelings, belongingness and togetherness is also visible at a time of any threat to their solidarity. The Ashram has produced a good number of Sarvodaya workers, who have established voluntary agencies of their own and are doing good work.

In the beginning, the Khadi Samiti as created with the purpose of providing financial support to the Mandal for undertaking development work in the villages. The idea was to become self-reliant rather then dependant on outside support for pursuing its goal of holistic development. However, support from Khadi Samiti could become reality a decade back when it decided to meet the deficit of funds in the Ashram. Today, Khadi Samiti is itself suffering from financial crisis and seem to be unable to meet its commitment to support the Ashram.

Efforts were being made towards achieving self-reliance in the Krishi Vigyan Kendra functioning in the Ashram for more than two decades. With the gradual diminishing of government grant, efforts were made to make it self-sustained.

It was observed that Bhoodan-Gramdan movement could not sustain fully in the Kawakole region where caste and land ownership issues continued to play crucial role in the village power structure. The work of organising and building a force of marginal and landless farmers could not be accomplished except for building general awareness about their predicament in the society. Thus, the goal of community building on the basis of holistic development and self-reliance could not be fully attained.

NOTES

1. I have served at Gram Nirman Mandal, Sarvodaya Ashram Sokhodeora for some time as a Social Scientist in a Community Health Project during 1973-74. My stay in the Ashram gave me an opportunity to have close insight into the life in the Ashram and various other activities.
2. I am indebted to Professor Sachchidananda, Chairman of Gram Nirman Mandal and former Director of A.N. Sinha Institute of Social Studies, who guided and advised me at every stage of writing of this paper. Discussion with Sh. Tripurari Sharan, Marg-Darshak of Gram Nirman Mandal provided me an insider's view of Mandal's contribution towards rural transformation. I am very thankful to him.

REFERENCES

Bharati Raveendra, 1995, *Gram Nirman Ki Prakriya: JP Aur Unke Baad,* Gram Nirman Mandal, Sarvodaya Ashram Sokohdeora (Hindi).

——1980, *JP Zameen Par* (Hindi), Sarva Seva Sangh, Prakashan, Varanasi.

Gupta, R.C., 1981, *JP: From Marxism to Total Revolution,* Chapter IV., Sterling Publisher, Jullundur.

Sarvodaya Ashram Sokhodeora, 2003, *Gram Nirman Mandal – Annual Report:* 2002-2003.

Scarfe, Allen and Wendy, 1975, *JP : This Biography,* Chapter 16. Orient Longman, New Delhi.

SECTION - III
JP and Land Reform

8

Jayaprakash Narayan and Land Reforms

B.B. Mandal

I

Jayaprakash Narayan had a deep concern for the vast majority of the rural population who had been suffering from social and economic injustices and exploitation. He thought that their condition should be remedied immediately after independence. But that did not happen. On the contrary, it further deteriorated. In his writings during 1960s and 1970s, he had relentlessly and repeatedly talked of their miserable plight. According to him, "millions of small farmers, in the absence of resources–cheap and timely credit, irrigation etc.–and in view of recurring droughts, scarcities, floods, fluctuating prices, adverse market mechanism, usurious interests, etc., have been forced to sell their land at buyers' prices to repay arrears of rent, loans and other dues. Under tenants and sharecroppers, in the absence of even a chit to establish their possession, have been systematically evicted. Countless others, from the weaker sections of the community, have been eased out of their holdings, including homesteads, simply by force or devious frauds".[1]

The growing rural violence and Naxalite activities in Bihar, West Bangal and other parts of the country had been very agonising for him. Although he was aware of the futility of violence, he did not make the Naxalite responsible for it. He held landowners, moneylenders, politicians and administrators who had persistently defied and defeated the powerful people had cheated the ceiling laws through benami and fictitious settlement, grabbed village common land and government land, denied the legal rights of their sharecroppers and evicted them from their holdings, underpaid their labourers and threw them out from their homestead, took away the lands by fraud. Their life was made all the more miserable by the moneylenders who charged usurious interest rates and seized the land of the poor and the weak. The upper castes looked down upon the Harijans and kept them deprived of their role in social life.

According to JP, the Courts of Law because of the lengthy procedures and heavy cost of justice, had denied a fair deal to the weak. The system of education had been producing an ever expanding army of ill-educated, frustrated and unemployed youth, and the kind of planning pursued by the governments was accentuating economic disparity.[2]

II

JP had succinctly described the land situation in the ex-zamindari states including Bihar. In these states, to quote him, "the government does not yet have up to date and reliable land records, hundreds of thousands of acres of 'vested' lands-uncultivated and unsettled lands previously owned by Zamindars and now vested in Government have been just grabbed by the stronger sections of the rural society."[3]

The situation in Bihar, according to him, was no better. The government "does not know how much vested land it had and what is the extent of encroachment upon it. Government policy and orders have also been such that encroachment though stealthy and illegal, has been given the appearance of legality. The administration has been so remiss and so permissive in this matter, that should the government make a serious attempt to recover its lands, in most cases it will have to go to court where the fraudulent are more likely to win. Even where government lands have been settled with landless persons, lands have been grabbed in one way or another by the stronger people in villages."[4]

JP had the firm conviction that effective and expeditious implementation of the tenancy and other reform laws could have partially mitigated the injustices and transformed the rural society of Bihar socially, economically and psychologically. He strongly advocated for the implementation of land reform laws, specially laws relating to (a) Homestead, (b) Ceiling, (c) Share-cropping, both respect of title to land and share of produce, (d) money lending and (e) agricultural wages.[5]

For non-implementation of land reform laws, he blamed the Congress governments which had enacted these laws but allowed to remain them on paper. The helplessness of the Congress governments arose from the following reasons[6]—

1. Lack of conviction on the part of the party and active sabotage by dominating landed interests within the party,
2. Lack of conviction on the part of the administrative machinery and sabotage by administrative personnel connected with such interests,
3. Widespread corruption in the administration which works to the advantage of vested interests, and
4. Social-economic weakness of those whom the reforms were meant to benefit.

However, JP did not expect that these laws could be implemented by any government so long any of the conditions stated above would exists.

For speedy and effective implementation of the land reform laws, according to JP, the government should have to take up two necessary measures. First, it would be necessary to bar the jurisdiction of the Civil Courts from such cases as title suits and to empower revenue courts to decide upon the benami settlements, encroachment upon government lands and enforcement of the legal rights of sharecroppers. Secondly, it should set up Conciliation-cum-Arbitration Board, comprising equal representatives of under tenants and landless labourers on the one hand and land owners on the other. It should be presided over by official chairman appointed by state government. But in selecting official chairman, care should be taken to choose honest officers who are sympathetic to the cause of the poor.[7]

JP was of the view that political parties could have rendered assistance to the governments in retrieving its property and dispensing justice to the sufferers. But for this they would be required to follow certain restrain in their approach and action. First of all, they would have to keep "politicking....out of their Land for the Landless Movement". If they could do it, there would be no difficulty in co-ordinating their efforts and conducting a joint campaign. Second, since the political parties are in close touch with villagers and there is hardly any thing that remains secret in village community, it is possible for them to discover government lands illegally occupied by landlords and also to discover benami lands. Thirdly, before launching any action, the parties should give a chance to the concerned landlords to correct the wrongs done by them. Party leaders should "meet the landlords, reason with them, appeal to them and persuade them to give up their unjustly occupied lands". It is only when persuasion fails, people's action be launched but only after giving due notice to the landlords and the administration. Finally, while distributing land, political parties should not try to favour their supporters and the whole process of distribution should be conducted peacefully. Even when landlords indulge in violence, political parties and the concerned people should face that violence with order and discipline.[8]

III

Mahatma Gandhi who envisaged a non-violent integrated society governed by moral laws, could not live to persure his mission of what he described as "India of my dream". However, after his sudden demise, Rajendra Frasad, Vinoba Bhave and others formed a Sarvodaya Samaj to realise the Mahatma's cherished mission. A programme of seventeen types of activities for the Samaj and a code of conduct for the sevaks (social workers) were drawn up and the Akhil Bharat Sarva Seva Samaj with its headquarters at Varanasi, was formed to carry on the task of the Samaj.

On his way back to Wardha from Sarvodaya conference held in Hyderabad in 1951. Vinoba Bhave visited Telengana where he received one hundred acres of land from one Mr. V.R. Reddy for redistribution among the landless at Pochampalli village. This made him convinced of the essential goodness of man and of the immense potentiality in the method of persuasion. This took shape in the form of Bhoodan movement. After one year, Bhoodan which was the campaign to persuade landowners to donate voluntarily a part of their land for redistribution to the landless, became Gramdan-movement and since 1963 it came to be termed as the Gramdan-Gram Swaraj movement so as to work towards the achievement of village republic. Vinoba Bhave had the mission of three-fold revolution, viz, to change people's hearts, to create a change in their lives and finally, to change the social structure. While Bhoodan was non-violent, persuasive programme for social transformation, Gramdan-Gram Swaraj movement sought to establish village republic.[9]

The basic components of Gramdan movement are the following:

1. At least 75% of the landowners in the village should sign the declaration form to donate their lands to the village assembly (Gram Sabha).
2. The total land donated in Gramdan should be at least 51% of the land in the village.
3. At least 75% of all families living in the village should agree to join Gramdan.
4. A Gramdan village may or may not be a revenue village.

On the fulfilment of these conditions, a village is considered a "pledged" Gramdan. After its registration, it becomes a "declared" Gramdan village. When the land donated is redistributed it becomes an "active" Gramdan village.

The major features of a Gramdan Village are that:

1. $1/20^{th}$ of the land donated to the Gram Sabha is redistributed to those landless who do not have any other occupation and will cultivate the land themselves. Redistribution of land is done with the concurrence of the doners.
2. Donors would be in possession of $19/20^{th}$ of the land with heritable right but they cannot sell or mortgage it without prior permission of the Gram Sabha, and it can be done to those who reside in the village.
3. Landowners are required to contribute $1/40^{th}$ of the total annual produce to the Gram Kosh or village funds. Landless persons and those who are in salaried jobs should contribute $1/30^{th}$ of the monthly income either in cash or in labour.
4. The villagers should abide by the decision of the Gram Sabha.

5. Gram Sabha is constituted either of all adult population or by drawing one adult member from every family in the village.
6. The Gram Sabha will function on the basis of consensus.

Beside securing donation of land and its redistribution to the landless, the programme of forming Shanti Sena and developing village industries would also be taken up for village reconstruction.

The Gramdan movement passed through three stages, namely, Prapti, Pusti and Nirman. In the first stage, a sense of belongingness or living together through persuasion is created among the landowners and they are prepared for dejure transfer of their land. This is carried forward through the formation of a single decision making body known as Gram Sabha. In the Pusti stage, land donated by landowners is redistributed to the landless with the concurrence of the donors and a Gram Kosh is formed to which every family is to contribute a portion of their income. At the Nirman stage, programme of social reconstruction is taken up for overall development of the village. Gram Kosh and such other resources that could be mobilised are utilised for this purpose.[10]

IV

JP was so much impressed by the Gramdan movement of Vinoba Bhave, he dedicated his life for the movement and to the cause of non-violent social change and social reconstruction. Under his leadership, the movement received phenomenal momentum in Bihar in respect of getting land donation from landowners.

It was only when there was emergence of Naxalite violence in the Musahari Block of Muzaffarpur district of Bihar, he took this threat as an "urgent call to demonstrate through positive action how the challenge of violence could be used to speed up the process of non-violent social change and reconstruction that Vinobaji had initiated through Gramdan-Gram Swaraj movement."[11] He went there with a modest programme of action with the determation of "either to succeed or perish in the effort". To fulfill his mission, a group of Sarvodaya workers, most of whom were from the Bihar Khadi Gramodyog Sangh, were also with him.

JP divided his programme of action into two parts. The first part which was related to the implementation of the Gramdan pledges obtained earlier in this Block, consisted of the following:

1. Establishment of Gram Sabha,
2. Redistribution of one-twentieth of the land covered by Gramdan,
3. Setting up of Gram Kosh,
4. Organisation of Gram Shanti Sena, and
5. Preparation of the necessary papers, village-wise, for submission to the Gramdan Confirmation Officer for legal confirmation of Gramdan.

The other part of the programme which was related to the distribution of land and to securing justice to the landless, comprised the following:

1. To distribute undistributed Bhoodan land and to correct mistakes and wrongs discovered in respect of previously distributed land,
2. To ensure that every "Privileged person" has received his Homestead Parchas and to rectify irregularities and wrongs in respect of previously distributed Parchas.
3. To look into the problem of landless labourers and try to do the needful, and
4. To take up specific cases of injustice and oppression to help in their redressal.

JP and his Sarvodaya workers took up intensive village work. They made house-to-house visit, often than once, addressed public meetings in every little hamlet and sometimes talked to small group of villagers at private houses. They organised youth meetings and camps. Villagers also used to meet JP at his camp, sometimes with their problems and complaints. In the process of programme implementation, they received the needed co-operation from the local Revenue and Development Officer, District and Divisional Officers.

V

JP camped in the Musahari Block for about a year from June, 1970. The flicker for violence was put out soon. He and his Sarvodaya workers made untiring efforts to raise the poor from the distressing condition with the programme of positive action. His experiment of Gramdan-Gram Swaraj movement in a volatile situtation, as was in the Musahari Block, received wide attention. Many saw in it the solution of the intractable problem of land and immense potentiality to restructure the rural social structure. Others doubted its revolutionary potential.

During 1973-75, a set of for studies were conducted in the Musahari Block. The first study was done by B.B.Mandal[12] to examine the potentiality of Gram Sabha to emerge as peasant organisation to protect and promote the group interest of the rural poor. The other studies by Sachchidananda and S. Akinchan, Jai B.P. Sinha and Pradhan H. Prasad were conducted to examine respectively sociological, psychological and economic perspective of the development efforts made in Musahari under the Gramdan-Gram Swaraj movement.[13]

The major findings of the studies were as follows:

1. Gram Sabha Comprising of landowners and landless were formed but the involve-ment of the weaker sections of the community in the decision making process was low.
2. In some villages Gram Kosh was formed but contribution to the Kosh was not regular and negligible.

3. Shanti Senas which were formed with three-fold objective, viz., Shramdan, helping village judiciary to clear off the local disputes and ensuring collective security, were not effective and lacked efficiency in their work. They were mainly drawn from the backward castes and Harijans.
4. Landless families had got Homestead Parchas and they were no longer evicted from their Homesteads.
5. Gross and crude exploitation had declined with increasing political awareness in people. Social distance between different caste groups was also on the deline.

Initial success of the movement could not be transformed into substantive change in social-economic life of the people because people's enthusiasm for the movement could not be sustained, stereotyped programmes were taken up, false hopes were raised and there was lack of active participation of the powerful people in the village. Besides, instead of equipping the people with knowledge and skill for better performance of their jobs, the workers promised them material benefits in the shape of gifts, incentives etc. The paucity of dedicated workers also weakened the movement to a great deal.

The situation that prevailed in the Musahari Block after the experiment can be summerised in the words of Sachchidananda : "A period of less than three years is too short a time to look for any fundamental change in attitudes and aspirations of people. There still remains a wide gap between the ideals of the movement and the social realities with which one is confronted within the Gramdan village. Acute paucity of redistributable land due to the indifference of the land-rich and the strain caused by the overwhelming number of the landless and land-poor looking for help, have already crippled many

Gram Sabhas. Half-hearted donations, discrimination in decision making, persistence of exploitation, and the revival of factionalism, etc., testify to the fact that the process of internalisation of the Sarvodaya values by the Gramdan population is yet a far cry. Devoid of charisma it seems to be imperilled by the revival of interest group politics, and reversion to old ways."[14]

VI

Although the movement in Musahari succeeded in bringing about a partial change in agrarian relations, JP's experience and his advice provide an invaluable guidance to all those who are engaged in rural reconstruction with the principle of "Conversion by gentle persuasion". When he and his team went to Musahari they did not receive the needed acceptance of the people, rather they were "looked down upon by the people as an annoying intrusion into their accustomed ways of life."[15] In the beginning he received help from one or two persons from every panchayat but wih the passage of time and when they persisted in their mission, the climate slowly changed and the people began to respond. However, the response or the co-operation that they received, came in certain order. They received the first response from the landless labourers, then the small farmers, middle farmers and then the big farmers. The money landers were the last to change. The major inhibiting factors for the big farmers were (a) renouncing their property title to the land, and (b) joining the direct democracy of the Gram Sabha. Besides these, their feudal and upper caste mentality inhibited them from reconciling to the political equality in the Gram Sabha. They were also afraid of the overwhelming majority of the poor in the Gram Sabha.

The massage of JP to the Sarvodaya workers which are equally invaluable for all social workers, was that they should work to integrate the community but not to divide it or set one group against the other. They should attempt to create community consciousness and a sense of mutual responsibility and try to bring together the different conflicting interests into mutual adjustment that would lead to a just and better social order.[16] This is a community approach. The people of the village or in the Gram Sabha should be told clearly that the village community would have to bear the responsibility towards the resolution of conflict and creation of just social order.

The firm conviction of JP was that unless village communities are built as self-governing, mutually co-operative, self-reliant bodies, the imbalance of power in the community would never be corrected and land reforms would never be complete.

REFERENCES

Narayan, Jayaprakash, The Land Grabbers; Towards Total Revolution, Vol. 3, Popular Prakashan, Bombay, 1978, p. 127.

Narayan, Jayaprakash, Face to Face, Navachetna Prakashn Varanasi, 1970, p. 15.

Narayan, Jayaprakash, Op. cit., 1978, p. 127.

Narayan, Jayaprakash, Op. cit., 1978, pp. 127-128.

Narayan, Jayaprakash, The Second Revolution, Op. cit. p. 120.

Narayan, Jayaprakash, The Second Revolution, Op. cit. p. 121.

Narayan, Jayaprakash, Land Reforms, Op. cit. p. 124.

Narayan, Jayaprakash, The Land Grabbers, Op. cit. pp. 129-130.

Bhave, Vinobha and Narayan, Jayaprakash, Gramdan for Gram Swaraj, Sarva Seva Sangh, Varanasi, 1967; See also, Dasgupta, Sugata, A Great Society of Small Communities : The Study of India's Land Gift Movement, Sarva Seva Sangh, Varanasi, 1968.

Dasgupta, S. Op. cit. pp. 16-17.

Narayan, Jayaprakash, Face to Face, Navachetna Prakashan, Varanasi, 1970, p. 7.

Mandal, B.B., Impact of Gramdan on Madhopur; Journal of Social and Economic Studies, Vol. IV, No. 1, 1976.

Sarvodaya and Development : Multi-Disciplinary Perspective from Musahari. Sachchidananda & Akinchan, S., The Sociological Perspective; Jai B.P. Sinha, The Social-Psychological Perspective; Pradhan H. Prasad, The Economic Perspective; Journal of Social and Economic Studies, Vol. IV, No. 1, 1976.

Sachchidananda, 1976, Op. cit., pp. 56-57.

Narayan, Jayaprakash, Face to Face, p. 23.

Narayan, Jayaprakash, Face to Face, p. 24.

9

JP, Agrarian Issues and Contemporary Bihar

Jagdish Prasad

The agrarian issues have attracted the utmost attention due to its predominant role in social and economic development of the country. During the struggle for Independence it was the peasantry class who played the very important role. More apparently, it was the struggle of the people of which 80 percent of the total population resided in the country side and almost the same proportion were directly or indirectly engaged in agricultural activities. The Champaran movement which may be termed as giving the strongest foundation stone for speeding up the Independence movement was totally related with the agrarian issues. This was reality that Mahatma Gandhi saw the development of the country in the development of the village. This philosophy was based on the dream of Gandhi that after Independence India could show a new path of social and economic development and "every drop of tears from the eyes of people will be wiped out."

Thus, the development of the villages was basically based on the agrarian reform. There were sufficient evidences even before the Independence that a strong peasant movement had already grown up in the name of 'Telengana Movement' since 1936. Till 1950 this movement swept through eastern India. Gradually this also led to other parts of the country. Telengana Movement was so sporadic and armed upsurge that Vinoba Bhave, a true disciple of Mahatma Gandhi started a new movement in the name of Bhoodan Movement. However, this could not be able to control the intensity of the peasant movement of which Bihar also became a seat for spreading this movement in very ugly form of agrarian conflict.

JP was also greatly distressed and anguished over the ignorance of the plight of peasantry and their movement against their exploitation. All this made him to understand the agrarian issues and believing in the philosophy of people's power. He launched his own movement based on this philosophy for combating the agrarian unrest. In this perspective, he carried on the legacy of Mahatma Gandhi. While other politicians were remained at the apogee of the state power, he symbolised Lokshakti (people's power). In fact, after Gandhi, he was the only person to expand and propagate the philosophy of 'Lokshakti' with utmost firmness and sacrifice. When the Musahari block of the Muzaffarpur district became the stronghold of the naxalite movement he launched his programme on this basic philosophy and established the people's institution for combating the naxalite problems. He was to a large extent successful as could be seen in the available evidence that the peasant of Musahari block has been now working in a coordinate fashion meaning thereby the disappearance of naxalite movement in this block. However, there are many other reasons that its success is still evident in many parts of the state.

His concept of 'Total Revolution' was basically pronounced at the time when he assumed the leadership of the Bihar movement to extirpate corruption and emerged as the Loknayak in 1974. An anatomy of this concept would reveal that 'Total Revolution' is the logical culmination of Gandhi's concept of village self rule. Today if the iniquitous agrarian system is continuing that is negation of the acceptance of this philosophy.

Though people at the helm of affairs in the Government of India and as well as in the Bihar Government owe their allegiance to his philosophy, have completely forgotten his ideology-state power must be subservient to people's power. The most sorry state of affairs is that his disciples have totally forgotten his vision for the development of Bihar. The pathetic situation of the low pace of development in the state is the by-product of unsolved agrarian problems. Today Bihar has the bad distinction of 'sick' state having the lowest rank from the socio-economic development point of view. Thus, due to persistence of agrarian problems Bihar is lurching from one crisis to another. Today people are crying for the tragic face of Bihar but little importance has been shifted to his philosophy of 'Total Revolution'. In fact, Bihar needs overhaul reform process in its agrarian economy. After bifurcation, Bihar is apparently an agrarian economy which calls for acceleration in its growth process with the aim to achieve the goal of egalitarian society. This could be brought about only with the help of JP's vision who never believed in class struggle rather he did not find any difference between caste and class. The lower caste representing the poorer faming community (proletariat class) and the higher class representing the richer farming community (propertied class). The basic agrarian issues, therefore, lie in vision for strategic solution of the varied problems of proletariat class. Whether Bhoodan movement, Gramdan-Gram Swaraj, above all land reforms, all these need to be coordinated in such a fashion that may bring about the transformation in agrarian economy of the state. This is the answer to the syndrom of non-development of contemporary Bihar.

REFERENCES

Sinha, S.P. and Prasad, Jagdish, (1980), "Special Programmes for Weaker Sections: An Evaluation (A Case Study of Programmes in Musahari Block, District Muzaffarpur, Bihar), Indian Journal of Agricultural Economics, Vol. XXXV, No. 4, October-December, 1980.

Prasad, Jagdish, (1982), "Changing Agrarian Structure and Relations in North Bihar : A Case Study of Three Villages in Musahari Block, District Muzaffarpur, Bihar", Khadi Gramdyog, Bombay, December.

Prasad, Jagdish, (1992), "Land Reform and its Impact on Land Structure and Peasant Class Relations in Bihar", IASSI Quarterly, Vol. 10, Nos. 3-4, January-June.

Prasad, Jagdish, (1993), "Land Reforms : The Case of Three Villages in Bihar", in B.N. Yugandhar and K. Gopal Iyer, (eds.), Land Reforms in India-Bihar: Institutional Constraints, Sage Publications, New Delhi.

Prasad, Jagdish ,(1997), "Land Reforms : The Case Study of Bihar", The Bihar Journal of Agricultural Marketing, Vol. V. No. 1 January-March.

Prasad, Jagdish, (2001), "Rural Uprising", The Hindustan Times, 7th April. Also see, "Peasant Movement-Why Violent", The Bihar Journal of Agricultural Marketing, Vol. VII, No. 3, July-September.

Prasad Jagdish, (2002), "Dynamics of Development in Bihar: Emerging Issues and Challenges", delivered as Second Arrupe Memorial Lecture, Bihar Social Institute, Patna, 23rd March.

10

JP and Land Reforms

Sudhanshu Ranjan

Land reforms occupy an important place in the political philosophy of JP. Right from the beginning JP was of the opinion that the village is the natural habitat of man and that the development of the village was a sine qua non for the overall development of society. By 1953 he was convinced that political parties were not equipped for nation building. He felt the Socialism had to be adapted to the needs of India. Gandhi did give a formula even though he could not delve into it because of his untimely death, but the socialists did not provide any model.

JP was solicitous about the problems of land reform since his early life. He could visualise its solution in the Bhoodan* Movement of Vinoba. In 1951 Vinoba reached Hyderabad walking hundreds of miles to participate in the Sarvodaya conference. Later, in the Nalgonda district after the prayer meeting forty untouchable families implored him to make land available to them for earning their livelihood. Vinoba appealed to people to donate land for them and to everyone's amazement one Ramchandra Reddy immediately donated 100 acres of land. This incident gave an impetus to Vinoba to start a movement for Bhoodan. He called it Bhoomi-dan-Yajna, (land donation movement), meaning worship of god through Bhoodan until an ideal condition is attained in which everyone has land only according to his needs. Vinoba launched his campaign and during his march on foot while returning he entreated the affluent landlords to donate one-sixth of their land as the share of their sixth son. He gave the slogan that he had come to plunder them with love.

As mentioned earlier JP was getting gradually drawn towards Vinoba. Earlier he was sceptic about the efficacy of the Bhoodan Movement but the fact that the movement was led by Vinova kindled his hope; "In a remote village of Telengana, Bhoodan was born. My first reaction to the event was of the usual sort; it would take hundreds of year in this manner to redistribute all the land in the country, I thought. But there were two factors in the situation which arrested my attention and forced me to give it serious thought. One was the author himself of the Bhoodan Movement. I had known Vinoba for years and often when I had occasion to visit Wardha, I went specially to see him. I always found him unusually stimulating and original. When a person like Vinoba, I thought, had started something it could not be just brushed aside as a stunt or futile gesture. The other factor was the steady growth of the movement. It was found that whenever and wherever a serious band of workers took it up, it produced results. The method was not impractical. It appeared that if as much effort was put behind the usual political movements, the result would be far quicker and sounder.

"...I decided to join Vinoba's movement. But I had a three weeks' fast impending which completed, I plunged into the Bhoodan 'Ganga' in the Gaya district of Bihar. My brief experience was exhilarating beyond expectation. Within a week nearly seven thousand acres of land were obtained as gifts, most of them spontaneous and from small holders, announced at my meetings."[1]

It may be mentioned that the communists wanted to have a foothold in Telengana as it was considered ideal for guerilla operation because of its wild, rocky, undulating terrain. It was known as India's Yenan, a province in the backwaters of China where Mao established his rule before taking over the whole of country. Social inequalities were extremely glaring in Telengana and though the communist guerillas succeeded in winning over the sympathy of the landless labourers, many of them also found their method of violence too repulsive. Vinoba, with his message of non-violence, entered the area and moved from village to village on foot. The Government offered him security but he refused.

The spectacular success that JP got at Gaya and the progress of the movement from strength to strength provided him with a glimpse to change the social structure. In the meanwhile 'Gramdan** was announced in the Mangroth village of Hamirpur district in Uttar Pradesh. Before it, JP went there to have a first-hand observation of Gramdan. He found "a fascinating picture of the future" in whatever he saw there.

In 1953 at the Asian Socialist Conference, held at Rangoon, he forcefully advocated in his speech that "Bhoodan was the solution to the land problem, the biggest problem of the country; ... there is the problem of redistribution of land. The problem can be solved in three ways; by the socialist party coming to power and legislating in that behalf; by a violent action by peasantry of by the landless workers for the occupation of the land, that may or may not succeed by a peaceful mass action by the peasantry for the occupation of those lands. Where the socialists are in power, the other two questions do not arise; but where they are not in power and where they have the opportunity to function democratically, where there are civil liberties, where there is scope for organisation and propaganda, there if we are able to move hundreds and thousands of landless people and make them peacefully squat on the lands which are owned by the landlords but which are tilled by the landless labourers and which should rightly belong to them and thereby offer resistance to the powers that be, no matter whether there are arrests, baton charges and shootings, then there is reason to believe that no power would be able to overcome that force. Even violent action will not succeed unless it is a real mass action."[2]

It is clear that JP wanted transfer of lands through peaceful means. The same year in April a Sarvodaya Conference was organised at Chandil where Vinoba delivered a touching speech. It became famous as the 'Manifesto of Sarvodaya'. Vinoba spelled out his plan: "We have to build up an independent people's power. I mean to say that we have to develop an independent people's power which is opposed to power of violence and different from power of punishment (law)... Analysing from this angle one thing strikes our mind that our style of work will have two aspects-observance of conscience and decentralisation. Observance of conscience means persuasion, appreciation of ideology and not accepting anything without understanding it. It is a pity if someone accepts our proposition without appreciating the thinking behind it... The second aspect is decentralisation. It means that all work, i.e., all the power of execution should not be concentrated in one center. Rather, the power of execution and authority should be developed in every village. If we do not decentralise power, be sure that military power will take over... The ideal of village self-rule and village planning should be a living reality. It is called independent people's power a third force."[3]

JP was so overwhelmed by the new vision that in the crowded meeting he announced, "Today all my doubts have subsided. I am prepared to call myself and to be called a disciple of Vinoba." He saw the possibility of transforming society by non-violent revolution in the Bhoodan movement. He had learnt from the Russian Revolution the savagery in which the violent revolution culminates.

At the outset his approach to Bhoodan was socialistic. He thought that it would create an atmosphere for the redistribution of land. At the Panchmarhi Conference of the Socialist Party also, JP spoke eloquently in favour of Vinoba's experiment while analysing the dismal performance of the party in the elections: "We failed because we had not put in enough work. Work is not merely waging the class struggle. There is constructive work which we have sadly neglected... We must try to understand Acharya Vinoba Bhave's efforts and not ridicule them. It is another matter whether his efforts can solve the land problem or not. One thing is certain, he is focusing the attention of the people and the Government on this problem... Vinoba Bhave is a spark of the revolutionary force of Gandhism. If this spark and the Socialist Party combine, it can shake up the whole country and start a big conflagration against injustice."[4] This suggestion was adopted by the party. Charity begins at home and JP donated half of his 50 acres of land as Bhoodan. According to Sachchidanand, JP once told Basawan Singh that the Socialist Party should ride the wave generated by the Bhoodan Movement. He was of the opinion that it would prepare the ground for the socialist movement. Actually he felt that the Bhoodan Movement had created an appetite for land among the landless which would be a great catalytic agent for the revolution. This feeling inspired his active participation in Bhoodan.

Jeevandan

In April 1954, a Sarvodaya Conference was held at Bodh Gaya. On 19 April in his passionate speech JP said that his respect for the Bhoodan Movement was growing day-by-day and it was such a movement of which dedication of one year or five years would not suffice. With these words he made an announcement of dedicating his whole life to this cause (Jeevandan) and called upon other workers also to do the same. Vinoba was overwhelmed: "Now we heard a speech. In it the heart was speaking. I was reminded of Rukmini's letter. In it she wrote to God that if she was required to take hundreds of incarnations, she would do it, but would marry only Him. The heart gets solace to hear such words of pious determination. I wish that all of us should be of strong determination like Jayaprakash Babu."[5]

Prabhavati was also delighted at JP's decision. Expressing her happiness to Vinoba she said that had this transformation in JP come in Bapu's lifetime he would have got much solace. Vinoba consoled her that it was due to Bapu's inspiration and that Bapu was overseeing all this. Out of seven hundred workers participating in the Conference, 656 also made announcement of their Jeevandan. JP's announcement of Jeevandan in 1954 has a special significance as only a year before Nehru had proposed to draft him into his Cabinet and he was seen as the successor to Nehru. So this decision speaks volumes for his iron-will, determination, sacrifice and faith.

Shortly after the Bodh Gaya Conference JP explained his position in an article 'Jeevandan' published in Janata that his decision was not an impromptu one; rather he was getting drawn towards it for several months. He clarified that it did not mean bidding goodbye to the ideals which he espoused so far but that he fervently felt that "those ideals could be achieved and preserved better through the Bhoodan or the Gandhian way,"[6] So it was not only a dedication to Bhoodan, as was often said, but to all those ideals which Bhoodan supports: "It was not the ugliness of politics that repelled me but the attraction of the new politics of Sarvodaya that drew me. For, as I have tried to show above, Sarvodaya also has a politics. But it is politics of a different kind: politics of the people as I have called it, as distinct from the politics of party and power, *lokniti* as district from *rajniti*. The politics of Sarvodaya can have no party and no concern for power. Rather, its aim will be to see all centers of power are abolished."[7]

He considered it the beginning of a social and humane movement because it aimed at transforming man, though Bhoodan may appear to be movement for agricultural reforms to the superficial observers. So, he felt, it was an experiment at the common level of the process of Mahatma Gandhi's non-violent revolution.

JP clarified that this revolutionary process could have been started in any field other than agriculture also. But the reason behind selecting the agriculture sector was that it is the prime source of production from land, land problem is the most vexed one and that it affected a large chunk of the village population.

Before this momentous decision of Jeevandan Dr. Lohia wrote to JP on 30th March that "the time to shake the country and the party was approaching and nobody else could shake it as you could. Only you can be the leader of the country and further socialism". In his reply dated 2 April, JP wrote: "You should not have made such a proposal knowing the opinion that I have at the moment. Never did I have the capacity to shake the nation nor do I have it today. Nor is it very important for me to shake it like than." He expressed his desire to keep aloof from the hurly-burly of party politics ad continue his association with the party only as an ordinary member.

After Jeevandan, JP went to different districts and urged the socialist workers to join the Bhoodan Movement. He said that after Independence the Socialist Party gave the slogan to provide twenty bighas of land and one cow to all the landless people but it failed to get the land. Vinoba got the land and so he deserves support as it will help achieve socialistic pattern of society.

JP's contemporaries and enlightened socialist leaders of other states were also raring for devoting their energies to village reconstruction. In Maharashtra, Sane Guruji called upon socialists to go to the villages. S.M. Joshi asked the people to emulate and carry out Guruji's thinking, not to erect his statue. S.M. himself led this movement and stayed in the villages. He organised a big rally at Hadpasar near Pune on 1 May, 1954 in which around 14,000 people participated including important socialist leaders like JP, Acharya Narendra Deva, N.G. Goray, et. al. JP delivered a profound and passionate speech for nearly two hours.

Communal Ownership of the Village and Villagisation

JP thought that practical form of the egalitarian society would be manifested through this experiment. At the outset he talked of collective farming and laid emphasis on the Gramikaran (villagisation) of land. It simply meant that the land belonged to the village, not to any individual. Vinoba used the term Gramdan. In fact, Vinoba wanted to imbibe the feeling of egalitarianism in dan (donation). He always referred to the Shankar's definition: *danam sam vibhagah,* i.e., dan is equitable distribution. Practically speaking there is hardly any difference between Gramdan and Gramikaran. 'Dan' symbolises piousness, while 'villagisation' sociality. JP did not use the word 'dan' as there is a social concept that the donor does not use the thing donated, e.g. Godan, Kanyadan, etc. In Gramikaran the donor does have a right as a villager in the collective ownership even after donating something.

He started the work at Sokhodeora to translate his ideology into action. He worked out a comprehensive plan for the Kawakol block, which aimed both at its economic development and at transfusing such a strength into the indigent and helpless people that it might give an impetus to revolution as well as construction. JP himself clarified it:

The non-violent revolution begins with the ideological revolution. Change in thoughts brings about change in man's life, and the society changes with the change in majority of the people.

...The first target of this work will be achieved when there would be villagisation of the total land of the village... As conceived of a non-violent society every village will be self-dependent and would import only those articles, which it does not produce. Thus, every village will have its self-rule, which will be guided by the interests of the village and that of the country. These will be our ideals of village construction.

The whole exercise was aimed at the sedulous cultivation of Gandhi's conception of village self-rule. With the effort of Gram Nirman Mandal, Samanvay Ashram and Bhoodan Yajna Committee 26,000 acres of land were distributed to sixteen thousand landless families.

Gramdan took place in four to five thousand villages of the country till 1971 and village councils and village funds were constituted there. It reinforced JP's belief that the Bhoodan Movement can deliver much better results than any law.

It seems that this belief was born out of the sad experience of the zamindari abolition which failed to bring about desired results. Bihar was the first state to take the revolutionary step abolishing zamindari system but the lands could not be distributed to the landless. Under Bihar Land Reforms Act the state government acquired the interests of intermediaries (landlords) by paying them graded compensation. There was no provision of redistribution of land in the Act and so another law, Land Ceiling Act, was enacted but by that time landlords sold much land and transferred ownership to their relatives. Another problem was that there were no proper records of land in Bihar. The Survey and Settlement Operations were conducted from 1896 to 1930. Under it cadestral survey (first survey) was conducted in 1896 and revisional survey was done in some districts in 1918-19. But it remained inconclusive. The Bengal Tenancy Act, 1885, was enacted after the 1857 mutiny which was one of the measures to pacify the peasantry. It provided that the name of a settled ryot (one who lived there for a certain period) would be recorded in the survey and rent was fixed on his land. Those who did not pay cash were registered as sharecroppers who could not be evicted by landlords. For it they were required to file suit.

After the First World War, rent was hiked. During the global depression ryots were badly affected. Landlords occupied the lands of the ryots by moving the court that they (ryots) did not pay rent or crop. These lands were called bakasht. Kisan movement was started for the restortion of bakasht land under the leadership of Swami Sahajanand Saraswati. JP addressed the Swami as his Lenin. Socialist Party played an active role in the Mokama Tal Movement.

Land dispute is a major cause of social strife in Bihar. JP favoured land reforms right from the beginning. When the Constitution was being drafted he was opposed to the incorporation of the Right to Property in the Fundamental Rights. Ultimately, because of this in the Keshavananda Bharati case, the Supreme Court gave the power to the Parliament to amend the Fundamental Rights. The court held that though the fundamental rights are unalterable, Right to Property was amendable. And since it was mentioned with other Fundamental Rights Parliament could amend them.

NOTES

** Gifting or donation of land

** Communal ownership of the village.

REFERENCES

Narayan, Jayaprakash, from Socialism to Sarvodaya A Revolutionary's Quest, edited by Bimal Prasad, pp. 203-4.

Narayan, Jayaprakash, The Ideological Problems of Socialism, op. cit., pp. 169-170.

Narayan Desai, Kanti Shah (ed.), Jayaprakash Amit Kosh, 223 Deen Dayal Upadhyay Marg, New Delhi, pp. 374-5.

Bhattacharya, Ajit, Jayaprakash Narayan : A Political Biography, Vikash Publishing House Pvt. Ltd., 1975, p. 110.

Jayaprakash, op. cit., p. 376.

Narayan Jayaprakash, Socialism Sarvodaya and Democracy, "Introduction, A Revolutionary's Quest", p. 11.

Narayan Jayaprakash, From Socialism to Sarvodaya, A Revolutionary's Quest, p. 145.

SECTION - IV
JP and Panchayati Raj

11

JP's Vision of Panchayati Raj and the Contemporary Scenario in Bihar

Sachchidananda

The vision of Panchayati Raj, JP conjured in his mind grew out of his commitment to two basic social concerns power to the people at the village level and strengthening democracy. Even before his release from prison in April 1946 he conceived of Gram Raj. A Gram Raj is a self governing village, not merely a panchayat. This was to be built up by the initiative of the people of the village and not by any governmental agency. He believed that these institutions would become centers of struggle and resistance during a revolution before the attainment of independence. But before the Gram Raj could become effective he suggested to the Congress Party members to start a cultural centre and Seva Dal and take up problems of sanitation, untouchability, communal harmony, prohibition, redressal of grievances, creation of grain bank, cooperative marketing and intensive work among women and children.

He also conceived the panchayat to exercise revenue, executive and judicial authority. At that time he believed that ownership of all land should vest in the state. The state agency could then settle pieces of land to individual families according to their needs. In this distribution the panchayat would have an important say. The panchayat would also collect the revenue for the state. Through the panchayat, the state would control the production of grains and their disposal. The panchayat could also look after cooperation, credit and handicrafts. It would also probhibit the import of manufactures that compete with handicrafts and also prevent large scale industries from infringing on their sphere. For executive functions the panchayat would have police powers and would keep village records. The panchayat would also have the power to try civil and criminal cases. In certain types of disputes such as land bound arise, the decision of the panchayat would be final. This would pave the way for *adalat mukti.*

After the advent of Freedom, there was a feeling among the common people that though Swaraj has come, it had not come to them. They were not involved in anything beyond voting in the election every five years. Common people did not explain the thrill and sensation of Swaraj. Democracy in the country had a very narrow base. It is like an inverted pyramid that stands on its head. The next step beyond government by consent is people's participation in the government or participative. It should be like real pyramid, narrow at the top and broad at the bottom. This would give people a stake in democracy.

In the late 50, Balwant Rai Mehta moved the concept of democratic decentralisation. He had the support of Sri S.K. Dey and Pandit Nehru. However, it was conceived as a procedural reform of administration at the lower level and not as a political revolution which would bring power to the people. The spirit of Panchayati Raj could not be made effective by development officers or the bureaucracy. This was the responsibility of political leaders rising above party and ideology.

JP conceived of a number of pillars of participatory democracy. The most important among them is the education of the people. This would go beyond literacy and school education. It would need the spread of political consciousness. The task could be taken up by political parties, All India Panchayat Parishad, Sarva Seva Sangh and other rural development agencies particularly the NGOs.

Organised political policies should not interfere in the working of the Panchayati Raj Institutions. People should be left in the direct control of the system.

The devolution of power to Panchayati Raj Institutions should not merely be a makeshift structure without substance. It should not be a still-born child. People must be trusted and given full responsibility. The role of government officers should be reduced to the minimum. The District Magistrate would function as a representative of the government.

At each level, the Panchayati Raj Institution should be given adequate resources. Land revenue should be collected by them. Funds should also flow to them from the state government. These institutions should not be starved for resources.

Full authority of supervision and control over government servants working in various departments of the government such as land revenue, agriculture, education, health etc. should be given to them.

Gram Sabha would have an effective role. All adults in the village would be involved in decision making process regarding the development of the area. Its meetings should be well attended and should be held at frequent intervals. This would provide a stable foundation to Panchayati Raj.

Besides developing social consciousness attention must be given to capacity building of participants in the PRIs (Panchayati Raj Institution) and strengthening the moral quality of the participants in the PRIs.

JP was highly critical about holding elections of the Panchayati Raj Institutions. He believed that if the same procedure was followed at for elections as in state and parliamentary elections, it would vitiate the atmosphere.

It would not bring self government but self ruination. He laid stress on restraining disruptive forces. For this he suggested vesting ownership and management of all village lands in the hands of the Gram Sabha. Each person should become an equal shareholder in the landed wealth of the village. He will see that land is distributed equitably among the families in the village.

JP shared Gandhiji's belief that government was the best which governed the least. People should be freed from the state interventions and restraints. It is seen that in the name of people's welfare, government is extending its control over all human and social activities. This has curtailed individual freedom which was very close to JP's heart. He believed that there is more to be done from below and less from the above. This is necessary for the preservation of the identify of the individual. Taking up of more and more activities of the government has crushed the spirit of freedom and initiative among the people. The communitarian spirit generated by the oceanic community of human beings has been completely lost.

JP's concept of Panchyati Raj is a combination of the two Gandhian concepts of government and society. Panchayati Raj begins at the bottom of the primary community. Elections cut across the community and create enduring animosities among the people. Thus the Zila Parishad ceases to function as an association of Panchayat Samities and becomes a miniature assembly with political acrobats.

Panchayati Raj was an afterthought after the draft of the Constitution had already been framed. The President of the Constituent Assembly, Dr. Rajendra Prasad wrote to the Constitutional Adviser to re-examine the whole thing and to redraft the Constitution in which the role of Panchayati Raj was defined. Dr. Ambedkar, the chairman of the Drafting Committee of the Constitution was not too enthusiastic about this idea. This was, however, not done as it was too late to do so. It was believed that the state government would create the Panchayati Raj bodies. JP made a strong plea to give Panchayati Raj the rightful place in the Constitution by amending it. This could be done by giving it the same status as the central and state government. This was also one of the conditions in the 14 points mentioned in his letter to Pandit Nehru in 1953 in connection with the latter's offer to JP for joining the Union government.

Political decentralisation is not possible without economic decentralisation. If the two parts of the policy run counter to each other, Panchayati Raj cannot succeed. A decentralised economy must be a small machine and labour intensive economy. Constant effort is needed to improve this small machine in order to enhance its efficiency and productivity without adding much to its costs. The decentralised economy must aim at full utilisation of local and regional resources both human and material. It should be seen that the rural population must not be wholly dependent on agriculture. Every village or a group of villages should be developed as an agro-industrial community JP insisted that the term agro-industrial does not refer only to activities concerned with the processing of agricultural products. It means an organic blending of agriculture and industry by including cottage industries such as marufacturing of radio and cycle part, small machine and electrical goods. The organisational pattern of decentralised industry and trade must also be different from that in the centralised sector whether private or public. It should largely be of the owner worker of cooperative type. The essential thing is that it should not be bureaucracy ridden or exploitative. It is in this background that Panchayati Raj Institutions will have to play an important role in economic development. Decentralised economy is desirable not only because it would be more democratic but also would bring immediate benefits to the masses through employment and making available wage goods to ordinary consumers.

Disruptive forces in society have to be kept in check. Caste, land, money lending and trade generate injustice and exploitation. They do not permit a community of interest to develop.

There should be clear distribution of powers at all the three levels. Each should also be given equal importance. The Gram Panchayat should have all the powers it is competent to administer. The Panchayat Samities and the Zila Parishad should not be merely coordinating and advisory bodies. It should not be only an executive arm of the Zila Parishad.

Top political leadership in the country should be interested in building up and strengthening the edifice of Panchayati Raj. Greater attention should be given to the Gram Sabha and the Gram Panchyat as they are the foundation of the entire super structure.

JP was highly apprehensive of vesting powers in the state government to supervise and control and take disciplinary action against PRI functionaries. While he conceded the need for exercise of such powers by someone, he thought that it would be dangerous to vest them in the state government. Such a measure would seriously detract from the autonomy of these bodies and tend to reduce them to mere agencies of the state government. It would also throw open Panchayati Raj Institutions to the incursion of party politics, groupism and the struggle for power. Such an apprehension is very human. Sometime party interests may not be identical with people's interests. There would be constant effort by political party leaders to capture these institutions. It will be necessary to keep them away from becoming pawns in the power game. Past experience also supports the contention that local self government institutions have sometimes been superseded entirely for partisan reasons.

In view of all these considerations JP recommended that the work of assisting, guiding and supervising the functionaries of PRIs should be given to a non-political autonomous body headed by a person of great integrity, who is outside the administrative set up. The Pachnayati Raj Commission should not function merely as a negative body. It will have full powers of taking disciplinary action, including supervision and control of Panchayat elections. It would also be the task of the Commission to make Panchayati Raj strong, self reliant and competent.

Current Panchayati Raj Scenario in Bihar

It will be useful to review the experience of Panchayati Raj in Bihar with a view to find out the extent of the fruition of JP's vision. JP's plea for giving Panchayati Raj a Constitutional status was accepted by the government through the 73rd Constitutional Amendment in 1992. Bihar was one of the first states to pass the Panchayati Raj Act in August 1993. However, on account of reservations for Scheduled castes Scheduled tribes, Backward Classes and Women, there were many legal hurdles before holding of the elections. It was only in the year 2000 that the legal hurdles were cleared and a decision was taken by the state government to hold elections for different functionaries in the Panchayati Raj Institutions. Elections to the Panchayats were conducted in six phases over a period of about three months starting from 7th February 2001. The first polling was held on the 11th April 2001. It was apprehended that there would be large scale violence during the elections. In 1978 elections the casualty figure was 700. However, at the end of the 2001 elections the casually figure was not more than 200. Of these, more than half emanated from group clashes occurring far away the polling stations. In spite of the call for boycott given by the Naxalites, polling figures were quite high in areas under their influence. More than 40,000 women candidates have been elected and much larger number of women contested. Going by the large turn out and high voting percentage and the response of the voters belonging to the weaker sections the elections were by and large free and fair. It is true that as in the elections of state legislatures and Parliament, muscle and money power did have an important role. However, since the bulk of the functionaries represented small constituencies the amount of money spent per candidate was not very large. Ordinary voters could not be lured by money. In many cases muscle and money could not win votes and some real grass-root workers who had a record of social service in the area were elected. As regard the entry of criminal elements in the system, this could not be entirely eliminated. Newspapers report the killing or arrest of Mukhiyas every now and then. However, till 15th November, 2002, 45 elected members of PRIs have been declared disqualified. Out of these 36 are Mukhiyas, 4 are Panchyat Samiti members, 3 are Gram Panchayat members and 2 are Zila Parishad members.

In the elections for most of the posts people in the age group of 31-40 have been elected. It is clear that the younger generation have taken leadership roles. The Mukhiya is the Kingpin in the Panchayati Raj set up. Among the elected Mukhiyas, 93 percent are matriculates and above. Although there was no reservation for women for the post of Mukhiya, 78 women including those belonging to Scheduled Castes and Scheduled Tribes have been elected as Mukhiyas. Persons belonging to the backward class have got the lion's share in Mukhiya's election. They have cornered 56 percent of the total elected posts. Among the Pramukhs, 37 percent are in the age group of 31-40. They are highly educated and 47 percent are graduate and post graduate degree holders.

The stakes were very high in the post of Adhyaksha of the Zila Parishad. Nineteen percent of the Adhyakshas is above 50 and about 43 percent of the Adhyakshas are degree holders.

Although the elections were not held on partly lines, political parties did influence the election of Adhyakshas. Thus JP's dream of electing PRI functionaries by consensus has not been translated into action.

The co-option of MLAs, MPs and MLCs in Block and Zila Panchayats as member with voting rights may have a demoralising impact on the elected functionaries. They would tend to control the activities of the Panchayati Raj Institutions and party interest might supersede people's interest.

The Bihar Act seems much more oriented to Zila Parishad than to Gram Panchayats so far as the division of functions among the three tiers is concerned. There may be a tendency to centralise the regulatory and controlling role of the state government. The purpose of the new Panchayats is not to ensure people's participation in development activities and achieving special justice. They must function as vibrant units of participating democracy. They must articulate people's will and people's power at the grass-root level.

JP's idea about the creation of the Panchayati Raj Commission has been given a burial. The state government has a stranglehold over the Panchayati Raj system. The colonical hangover is still there. It is reflected in various sections of the Act, such as relating to the removal of the Mukhiyas and the Pramukhs on grounds of corrupt practices or inefficiency. In these cases the concerned functionary is required to tender his resignation to the Panchayat Officer in case of the Mukhiya or to the B.D.O. in case of the Pramukh. Another section of the Act provides for the dissolution of Panchayats, Panchayat samities and Zila Parishad son the grounds of inefficency and misuse of power. It is also provided that the Zila Parishad has similar power as the State to dissolve Panchayats. This makes Panchayats subordinate to Parishads.

In the Panchayati Raj set up the role of Gram Sabhas has been sidelined. This is the only non-elected body and reflect people's will and articulates their real needs and urge for development. The Mukhiyas seem to have arrogated all powers for themselves. The role of Ward members should also be clearly understood. They could bend their efforts to make the Gram Sabhas in their area real and vibrant institutions. At present they function as silent functionaries.

State government departments like education, health etc. are still dragging their feet in the transfer of control of their staff to the Gram Panchayat. The employees themselves are also resisting this as they feel insecure in the new set up. Efforts must be made to hasten this process and to disabuse the minds of the employees of their misgivings.

Capacity building of the newly elected members of the PRIs is essential so that they have a clear idea of their responsibilities and the limits of their power. This has to be done through training. At present training is being provided only for account keeping. In the training programme NGOs should be involved in a large measure as the task is vast.

The attitude of political leaders towards Panchayati Raj ranges from apathy to animosity. There are two reasons for this. Party politicians have a strong disbelief in the Panchayati Raj system itself. They doubt the capacity of Panchayat functionaries in delivering the goods. The success of Panchayati Raj would detract from their influence and clout in the political affairs. They do not like to share the political space with Panchayat leaders. Such lack of support from the political parties and their leaders in contrary to the expectations of JP, who hoped that national and state leaders would lend their support in strengthening the exercise of people's will and people's power for the well being of the masses. No effort for economic decentralisation is visible. In JP's view this is a pre-requisite for the success of Panchayati Raj.

Thus the functioning of Pachayati Raj in Bihar does not reflect JP's vision. In the present set up one cannot expect results which JP had envisaged. Both in letter and spirit, there is much that the wanting. However, this is the first step in this direction and even in this murky atmosphere some good work is being done in certain pockets. In course of time, the spread effect of success will build up some pressure and momentum. The shortcomings in the legislation may be removed after some experience has been gained. With the rise in political consciousness, this process will be accelerated and people will be able to manage the development process according to their own will.

12
Musahari and the Gramdan Panchayat Model

K.K. Sinha

The most dangerous development on account of the failure of Panchayati Raj in Bihar has been the growth of crime and corruption in villages along with poverty. JP had started feeling that the Bhoodan Movement was losing its fire and the Sarvodayists were becoming stab and flabby in spirit. The need therefore was a more rigorous panchayat movement to fight poverty as well as growing naxalism and violence. The idea of Gramdan tagged with gram sabhas was thus to institutionalise a process of change in villages. JP took up the Musahari block in 1970 for this experiment. This was a traditionally poor block with big landholders and Mahajans controlling the rural life. There were some killings and notices were served, to loot sweet potatoes of some rich land holders and also to some Sarvodaya Mandals.

There were already statutory panchayats working in this area as agents of districts for some functions (land revenue collection, settling petty cases, receiving grants etc.) under the Balwant Rai Mehta scheme of 3-tiered panchayat system and community development. This system was officialised, and that added strength to it, to compete with any other system of reform or change by voluntary organisations on mere ethical grounds. But the Sarvodayists thought they could do it.[1]

The underlying message of the Musahari Experiment was the reconstruction of a Panchayat society where freedom is not compromised for "the glory of the state or for anything else' and the realisation that 'the socio-economic reality in the village is, on a close examination, ugly and distressing in the extreme'.[2] The Musahari Experiment was thus a parallel experiment with the statutory panchayats already existing.

Concept of Gramdan Panchayats

The above two tenets – freedom from government and freedom from poverty gave rise to the Musahari Experiment which was for exploring the Bihar Gramdan Act, 1966, creating gramdan villages, and carrying the Bhoodan Movement through a new set of panchayats. This was a village to village movement with no infra-structure except a few voluntary organisations and a selective gram sabha which was not a general body of villagers,[3] and which depended on its president, secretary and treasurer.[4] Though the short term problem of containing naxalism was thrown on the law and order function of the state, the basic ailment was taken deeper than that. JP undertook the reforms within the limits of the Gramdan Act.

The difference now from the simple Bhoodan approach was that Bhoodan was converted into Gramdan in the sense that 51% of village land was owned jointly with the gram sabha. It was not denial of individual possession but only a formal change of legal ownership by Agreement. Villages thus become catalysts of change, and ownership of land becomes a limited right to possess and transfer. If you made an agreement with the gram sabha to this effect, you do not lose the land but only a small part of it and the right of absolute consumption by family. Thus you have to agree to spare one kattha in every bigha (i.e. 1-20th) for redistribution to the landless and 1-14th of the produce for the village fund. You could also transfer your land subject to the permission of the gram sabha.

Here a panchayat unit would grow up enforcing land sharing without the confiscation of land by State, what the Russian communes enjoyed. The gramdan panchayats were opposed to strong power-wielding state and tried to achieve a communitarian order as people's choice. Communitarianism was thus opposed to communism and made the panchayats of neighbours, and not the State, the carrier of change.

The terms of ownership were much softer than even cooperative farming. Here the family farms were retained and managed personally but ownership was conditioned to some social or neighbourhood sharing, which anybody with a little larger land than others, could easily like to accept. This was more true to those landholders who did not till themselves or were absentees. Thus gram sabhas and not cooperative farms were to be the new centers of communitarian sharing and community development.

The second merit of the Bihar Gramdan Act, 1966 was that a single village gram sabha could amalgamate with two or more gram sabhas, (sec. 11). Thus a gramdan village could extend to the statutory panchayat size, which covered 5-6 villages on the average. It is true that the Musahari Experiment did not explore that part of the Act, nor the possibilities of making gram sabhas a general body with agreed functionaries. The gram sabhas remained membered and too small. Under the Act, the gram sabhas could be registered as cooperative societies (Sec. 27) or could be empowered by Government through Gazette, as a panchayat, (under the Bihar Panchayati Raj Act, 1947) when the statutory panchayat would cease of function in the said area (sec. 28/2/I). Thus, gramdan villages could be convertible into gramdan panchayats through a given process.

Yet another merit of the Gramdan Act was that the functions of gramdan villages in the Act were more concrete and transparent than the long list of formal and shared functions of the panchayats in the Bihar Panchayati Raj Act, 1947. It is mainly land management and agriculture and village crafts and poverty issues which belonged to the gramdan panchayat and which were specific and most suited to them. Similarly on the financial side, gramdan panchayats had to create a Gram Nidhi or Village Fund with 1-14th share in agricultural produce from the landholders and one day wage per month from the workers. This was a more pragmatic and participatory form of rural finance than the house taxes and profession taxes and fees given to panchayats in the Panchayat Act, which were urban in nature and British in origin.[5]

An Assessment of the Musahari Experiment

All this shows the potential merits of the Musahari Experiment, though there are reasons for a mixed experience, mainly on account of the parallel functioning of a panchayat system sponsored and run by the state government and aided by ad hoc grants under the Plans. Unfortunately the character of the Gramdan Act was not compulsive but optional and this was bound to put the gramdan panchayats in a statutory disadvantage. Had this Act been conceived along with the Panchayat Act, a much better world could have been created.

In fact the Musahari Experiment faded out with JP leaving it after one year of his stay there. Though some positive signals of reconstruction were appearing, the over all picture was one of 'gentle persuasion' without a bite. If there was Agreement why could it not have the force of Law? JP was disillusioned and actually took up in 1974, a new fight straight against the law makers, the government itself, which had become power-corrupt and was playing with a 20-point programme for the rural poor. The strategy of Bhoodan or Gramdan thus took a new turn towards people's struggle by 1974. What was added to the theory of gramdan village now was organising pressure groups against the state to bow down to more decentralised governance at the grassroot and more egalitarian norms for rural reconstruction. Thus, whereas building gramdan villages was reconstructional, resisting the centralised and oppressive state was a struggle.

The failures of the Musahari Experiment as surveyed in a 1976 Report[6] should be evaluated against this background now. The Gramdan Movement by JP, termed 'Sarvodaya Movement by Sarvodaya workers' in the above report, had to face a hasty comment that "it has its impact on strengthening rather than weakening of semi-feudal bondage."[7] This remark is not fully corroborated by some other positive features in the Report, but the writers feel that the gram sabhas of gramdan panchayats 'belonged to the higher castes' and 'intended to maintain the status quo by tinkering here and there in the system.'[8] The failure is thus more a comment on the poor provisions of the Gramdan Act regarding the constitution of the gram sabhas than the ideology of 'gentle persuasion'. It is a comment when gramdan was facing its teething trouble and was facing the challenges of a parallel system of panchayats, which was statutory and status quoists. If gram sabhas of needed orientation were not coming up, the generosity of landed people in giving some gifts in a personal way, no doubt, reflected only a Raja-praja relation. The institution of gram sabha has to be a general body and if it is not, where is the Agreement and between whom? Gramdan is based on such Agreement with a gentle bite of Law. If you write an Agreement, you are bound by it. If there is no such thing, the process of change stopped at the initial step, and there is neither Gramdan not its ideology. So the experiment could make no march ahead of the Bhoodan strategy. This however, in no way, rejects the ideological base of the Gramdan Movement nor could suggest an alternative in Naxalism as posed in the Report.[9]

Sarvodaya was already reoriented to Antyodaya-development of the poorest and if the effort did not click, it was not any ideological failure but the existence of strong pro-rich lobbies in the law-making power centers of state and central governments. This was reflected locally in the dual system of panchayats, which was working in the area, one under voluntary organisations and the other, under the State. The two could not go together. The statutory panchayats were swallowing Musahari groups as they were running parallel in villages and Blocks with their state patronized order and privileges. The feudal bondage surveyed by the Report was, thus, not the result of the experiment but a symptom. The statutory panchayats ruled over such small gramdan organisations which were all the time looking for state grants which statutory panchayats used to get. The JP effect was too short-lived to give any result. Further, Sarvodaya was oriented to Antyodaya, and the Sarvodaya Movement generally lacked the rigour implicit in such orientation. It could not be just an ethical persuasion without a struggle.

The internal conflict between the two forms of panchayats still continues. This is confirmed by a recent study.[10] The study by the author indicates that by 1992, 4256 villages in 147 Blocks had applied for grant of gramdan status. Out of this 3344 cases confirmed to the required specifications. But only 1776 villages got the approval while only 1568 villages were notified in the Gazette. Of this only 32 gram sabhas were empowered with the panchayat status while 182 did not get it even after complying with all the formalities. Thus, there was a rush for getting the status of a panchayat though the gramdan spirit was almost dead and on paper only. The inherent weakness of such development was attraction to get the privileges of he government-run panchayats, which, in 1993, obtained Constitutional status.

Unfortunately the new Bihar Panchayati Raj Act, 1993 after the 73rd Constitutional Amendment does not make any provision for the gramdan villages so that there was no case for erecting the Musahari super structure any more. The new elected panchayats seem to have completely swallowed the gramdan element of panchayats, and unless they are themselves restructured on the gramdan lines, they cannot any more assume the nature of social changers in favour of the rural poor. Fortunately they still leave fuller scope of empowering the gram sabhas for such reforms.

Case for a Struggle

JP's Bihar Movement during 1974-77, to which he switched over, was actually a new step taken to face this state of affairs and the growing despotic and feudal character of the higher governments in states and in Centre. For changing a social order, it is the State, which must be tackled first. The movement termed as Total Revolution, took this orientation for a class and mass struggle. This movement succeeded just as Gandhain freedom movement or Lenin's class movement, but the reconstructional part of all these movement could not be worked out well, the former due to state control of local panchayats and the latter due to state regimentation of the local communes. State power thus ruins the whole process of reconstruction and change, whether it is democratic or socialist.

The success of JP in turning the Bihar Movement against the central rule was achieved by 1978 when the authoritarian governments cracked down in a nation-wide election. It was said to be a second movement of freedom after Gandhi. But after a new party and government came in power, the panchayat issues were left behind. JP lived to see that within the next two years the movement-born governments at the centre and states started growing strong and dictatorial again with little regard to a communitarian order at the bottom, to which they were committed.

Of course the movement-borne governments also took up several anti-poverty schemes for the village poor, but they were nothing but 'bribes' to the poor for facing poverty and the status quo. The newly elected panchayats by 2001 remained defunct and toothless as no basic reform of the gramdan type was conceived. Panchayat election, made mandatory under the 73rd Constitutional Amendment, was not a sufficient condition for effective Panchayat Raj. The new relation between the state and panchayats remained as before, that is, as one of giver and taker, so that there was no bargain except passive acceptance. Panchayats had to function with whatever is given to them.

This has suppressed the urge for land reforms and communitarian sharing of the village resources among themselves. A Musahari situation is thus recreated and the norms of a panchayat reconstruction still seek desperately a Gramdan orientation in the new Acts.

Prospects of Revival

JP's idea behind the Total Revolution after the 1977 elections was more reconstructional once a government was dismantled, because only then could people keep the centralised governance under control. This was what the Leninists thought by way of local communes. But they allowed an intermittent state power as a pad to feudal resistance to change. Gramdan panchayats were not to have the same metal as the communists had. JP here conceived of a resistant class struggle joined by the poor and doubly by another pressure group of youth and intellectuals. This could create a change of the rural order and the ownership structure of land in villages and an urge for helping the poor for rural upliftment. Empowerment of the gram sabhas against its inbuilt feudal content, and suppression by the higher governments in their own political interests remains still the crux of reconstruction.

Thus JP's Total Revolution can be treated as total if there was a combination of struggle with reconstruction.[11] Reconstruction meant a communitarian sharing for equality. "Danam samvibhagah" (Land donations for equality) was what departed from the simple norm of Bhoodan. Added to it now was a continuing struggle for people's power against the rising power of the State. The experiences of Musahari would still make a case for 'gentle persuasion' but with a bite of law for giving statutory powers to the gram sabhas and of the pressure groups of the common man. Not only that the religious tenets were for it and against stocking and self-consumption, the poorer class was religiously devoted to fighting this struggle without violence and civil war.

People have started feeling more than before, the need for organising themselves in neighbourhoods for a better life. In communist countries the idea of living in self-governed small communes flopped in spite of disappearance of land rights. Communes became a part of the state, which and collectivised land and were only tuning people to live in communes under the dictates of the state. The naxal movement took some hints from this method, which was only half-baked and alien in Indian villages.

Rising Expectations

Gramdan villages could be much less reactionary device for a basic egalitarian change in social relations against growing urbanisation, centralism and violence. There is a clear evidence of rising expectations in the village people in various forms. The village situation could develop as a struggle, if a movement of rising expectations could take place in villages with the creation of egalitarian and cooperative panchayats. There are some positive signals towards this.[12]

Firstly, pressure from grassroots is increasing to supplant governance from the top with governance at the bottom.

Secondly, local communities and voluntary organisation are coming up to shake off their dependence on governments.

Thirdly, financial devolution is becoming pressing on the state itself, which would give local bodies more authority to levy taxes and control their resources.

Fourthly, direct democracy through gram sabhas, as opposed to representative democracy in legislatures or parliament, is getting more acceptable and more prevalent, and finally, a better educated and better informed electorate is increasingly demanding its rights and is increasingly critical of non-performing governments and the representatives above.

Further, as the State never withers away, whether it is democratic or socialist, it will always move to rebuild itself once it is dismantled, and so JP thought that communitarian panchayats could keep a permanent check on State getting powerful. The need was for a continuous struggle for change and for decentralised governance at the grassroot. JP had the gramdan norm for reconstructing society right from the panchayats. It was actually institutionalising a process of change through people's empowerment at the village levels.

One could see now the inbuilt quality of a gramdan movement to promote an egalitarian system so that it could be tried again and again. In villages, 10 percent land holding families are holding about 40 percent of land, so that the remaining small holders have 60 percent of it in uneconomic sizes. A panchayat could easily be sponsored by 75% of village people because, with 40 percent of village population as landholders, the next 40 percent are landless and 20 percent are artisans and traders. This gives a broad picture of easy sponsorship of such a panchayat. The bigger landlords (10% of land holders, though in minority) could agree to spare small portions of their land and of its produce to the gram sabha pool. Even the poorer sections would be sparing one-day wage in the common pool. This would give a mutually supported social group where each group benefits the other. There will still be sharecroppers because redistribution is never a foolproof solution of a system where land is the main occupation. But the panchayats can plan poverty eradication in a much better way with structural changes and self-help and mutual-aid cooperatives in non-farm occupations, which are already showing results.

The basic flaw in recent panchayat reforms seems to lie in marginalisation of the small villages, the Tolas and the poor people living in it. The violent organisation have only roped this situation, going deep in villages where nothing reaches except poverty. Such violent organisations surprisingly have failed in creating any organisation of the local poor. They have created a situation of terror and mass killings instead. Murders by one group are retaliated by mass killing by the other. This is in no way a struggle for power for the poor people. The Panchayat Act could give a statutory power to Tolas and the gram sabha constituting them, so that the districts could not rope the situation with force of the State.

Towards Amalgmation of the Panchayat Acts

JP's experiment of Bhoodan panchayats in Musahari block was a trial and error effort and no model building. A Bhoodan Yagya Samiti had already been created under the spell of Bhoodan Movement of Vinoba Bhave in 1954, when Bihar had taken a lead. A Gramdan Act was passed under it in 1966 to institutionalise Bhoodan under the gram sabhas. Under the Gramdan Act, gram sabhas and Agreement of land holders and others shoul have a force of Law instead of being persuasive and dependent. This could be possible only if the gram sabhas were made statutory and open. The rest of the provisions were too accommodative to be unacceptable to any sections. Small land holders could not be land donors by very nature, while the landless could be donating a little of their wages while big land holders could easily rcconcile with their donations for more peace in return.

Land reforms do find a place in the newly created Panchayat Act, but the issue is blurred with too many functions enumerated in the list of all the tiers of panchayats and districts seem to dominate over the lower tiers. The village tiers are thus preventive from playing the role expected from them in matters of rural change.

The attack on sharecropping was made by the Bengal panchayats under the Barga Operation and land was given to the tillers. But a smoother process was devised in the Bihar Gramdan Act when land reforms could be pursued by agreement and choice of rural people. The feed back of Musahari Experiment explains both success and failure. Most of the village heads of Musahari were proud to tell that they were not subordinate to the official Hakims and could run their village on their own. This was a symptom of increasing distance for a state-run system in villages. But a gramdan panchayat was a one-village unit of 200-500 families. This was only a revenue unit, too small as an administrative or planning unit and lacked the needed statutory powers. Of course this could extend to 5-6 villages constituting the gram panchayat and a simple provision in the new Act to recognise such units as full-fledged panchayats does not disturb the Act. There is nothing to restrict the present panchayats to reintroduce the gramdan commitments under the Gramdan Act, under its own Rules of Conduct. It this is realised, a vibrant panchayat system of the communitarian variety could still be resurrected at par with the rest.

Unfortunately the Bhoodan Yagya Committee, which is expected to promote and pilot such gramdan movement of panchayats, is only looking to the State for its existence. It should, instead, be part of a state Panchayat Development Body as a policy making and promoting institution. The feeling that the Gramdan Act of 1966 is still valid, does not give some villages the status of a panchayat unless such provisions are incorporated in the new Panchayat Act of 1993. To give a new life to the Gramdan Act, it is rather expedient to draw the attention of the government to amalgamate this with the general Panchayat Act. This will make all the panchayats sponsored locally and running locally for a cause, and would give sufficient power to gram sabhas for land reforms. Fortunately there are no partisan elements in Bihar panchayats to distort the system for their own power game. This should be strengthened further through pressure groups and voluntary organisations.

REFERENCES

For the two systems, see Sachchidanand et al, Sarvodaya and Development, ANS Instt, 1976, p. 32.

Jayaprakash Narayan, Face to Face, 1970.

Sachchidanand, op. cit. pp. 16, 64-68.

Ibid, p. 71.

K.K. Sinha, Uma Sinha, Panchayat Strategy, Vora, Bombay, 1979.

Sachchidanand, op. cit.

Ibid. p. 96.

Ibid. p. 109.

Ibid. pp. 49, 51.

K.K. Sinha, Panchayat Dilemma, A Senior Fellowship Report sponsored by ICSSR, Delhi, 2003.

K.K. Sinha, JP Centenary Lecture on Foundations of Total Revolution, Econ. Assoc. of Bihar, 2002.

For a ref. See India Vision 2020, Planning Commission of India, Report of the Committee on India Vision, Economica India, 2003.

13

JP's Approach to Panchayati Raj : Towards Participatory Democracy

Vijay Ranjan Dutta

Introduction

JP pointed out the contradiction between representation and participation for a meaningful discourse on democracy. With the increasing role of the state for performing a number of activities parliamentary democracy with its representative principle tends to become centralised with a powerful bureaucracy. As a result, people are losing their liberty and initiative and they do not appear to be the masters of their destiny. To put it precisely, the representative principle of parliamentary democratic state overshadows the participatory element of democracy. People are mainly voters during periodic elections in parliamentary democracy. This shows that the principle of electoral participation is confined merely to the consent of the people and it does not look beyond. The scenario today shows that the frequency of elections either for state assemblies or Lok Sabha has put democracy in a limited framework of legitimacy but it does not inspire the common people to take initiative for enriching the parameters of democracy and development which are required for a country like India with its agricultural base: It seems that in the Westminster model of parliamentary democracy as manifested in the people, has lost its operational significance. In this context, Bryce has rightly laid emphasis on people's sovereignty for nurturing genuine democracy: "The sovereignty of the people is the basis and watchword of democracy. It is a faith and dogma to which in our time every frame of government has to conform and conformity to which every institution is tested."[1] Today, the centralised structure of parliamentary democracy shows that people's sovereignty has diminished.

Further, the Westminster model of parliamentary democracy is restricted to political domain. And, the economic aspect, i.e. industrialisation with economism and large scale technology flourishes in parliamentary democracy. It seems that parliamentary democracy permits such industrial civilisation which disintegrates the village community and thereby man becomes an alien among his fellowmen. Parliamentary democracy does not take the problem of social disintegration into serious consideration which is really the by-product of industrial civilisation. Besides this pitfall, social democracy is not widely discussed and little attention is paid to people who are living in unequal conditions. Thus, people are unable to participate in politics of parliamentary democracy on the basis of equality and freedom.[2]

Significantly, it was within the value-concept of truth and non-violence that Gandhiji viewed democracy in a holistic manner. He laid emphasis on village panchayat with *self-reliance* (Gram Swalamban) and *people's participation* which would lead the villages of India towards *Gram Swaraj.* Gandhiji made a distinction between 'Political Swaraj' and 'Village Swaraj' (Gram Swaraj). To him, freedom from the British rule was merely 'political swaraj' and once he termed it as 'parliamentary swaraj'. Gandhiji was of the opinion that 'Gram Swaraj' was the foundation of democracy and it had to be achieved. He stated: "True democracy can not be worked by twenty men sitting at the centre. It has to be worked from below by the people of every village."[3] For true democracy, parliamentary democracy symbolising 'political swaraj' has to be transformed into 'village swaraj'. Gandhiji envisioned *panchayat* as *village republic* for all-round development of village life and thereby it epitomises 'village swaraj'.

JP, one-time Marxist and later, turned a Gandhian thinker, derived major ideas from Gandhiji's speeches and writings and developed further his approach to Panchayati Raj with the ultimate goal of participatory democracy. It may be mentioned that the ideas of JP about village reconstruction or Gram raj may be traced even during his socialist phase, particularly to his letter addressed to the freedom fighters just after his release from imprisonment of the British rulers in April, 1946 and again to the ideas on panchayats stated briefly in the election manifesto of the Socialist Party. He was concerned with the centralising tendencies of the state power in the Westminster model of parliamentary democracy which adversely affected the creative potentiality and participation of the people for the reconstruction of society. But, it was during late fifties and sixties that JP put forth the ideas of Panchayati Raj and participatory democracy in the conceptual framework of the ideas of Gandhiji. He was also influenced by the ideas of 'radical humanism' enunciated by M.N. Roy, particularly to Roy's critique of the party system and the importance of political education and consciousness of the people. JP admitted it in the Introduction of his small book *Swaraj For the People*: "I am indebted not only to Roy, but to many others–most of all to Gandhiji."[4]

I

Conceptual Framework

JP presented a critique of parliamentary democracy and delineated his ideas of Panchayati Raj which he considered as a step towards attaining, the goal of 'participatory democracy'. He welcomed the three-tier Panchayati Raj Scheme of Balvantrai Mehta Committee introduced in 1959. The aim of this experiment was restricted to obtain public cooperation in the execution of development programmes but its implications were deep. Therefore, JP put emphasis on driving this movement of Panchayati Raj further in the following words: "There is still need of arousing popular enthusiasm about this measure, and of making people realise that what was intended was not a procedural reform of the administration at the lower levels, but a political revolution of the greatest significance for the people; that, in effect, the intention and the attempts were to bring swaraj to the people".[5] For transforming Panchayati Raj into a 'participatory democracy', JP was of the opinion that "Panchayati Raj" must not be terminated at the district level but extended forward upto New Delhi. Although this cannot be done immediately, it should be set clearly as the goal."[6]

JP was critical of the centralised trend of parliamentary system and stated that democracy today is just like an 'inverted pyramid' which stands on its head and the base of the structure becomes very narrow. If the foundation of democracy is weak and top layers are strong, the edifice may topple down. And, the voters are like heap of particles of sand thus, the disorganised voters are not capable to build up 'participatory democracy'. Therefore, the base of the pyramid of democracy should be made strong. JP suggested: "The broad upper levels of present-day democracy must be drastically sawed off and large portions of the vast upper floors brought down to earth, so that the pyramid of democracy could become a real pyramid 'narrow at the top and broad at the bottom. Such a system of democracy could give people a stake in democracy as well as the sensation of swaraj".[7]

Apart from political pyramid, the 'economic pyramid' of society also shows the same fantastic picture. For setting the inverted political pyramid on its right place, fair attention has been paid to political decentralisation. But the economic aspect, i.e., economic decentralisation has been neglected to correct the inverted 'economic pyramid'. And, political decentralisation cannot be effective without economic decentralisation. It is by ways of decentralising the economic institutions and processes of society that the pitfalls of inverted 'economic pyramid' can be corrected. In this context, JP suggested five major ways for economic decentralisation:[8] (i) The process of production should primarily be based on small-machine and labour-intensive economy; (ii) Decentralised economy must aim at full utilisation of local and regional resources human and material; (iii) Villages should be developed as 'agro-industrial' communities. It means an organic blending of agriculture and industry; (iv) The decentralised pattern would overwhelmingly be of owner-worker or cooperative type; and (v) Panchayati Raj institutions will have to pay an important role in the area of economic decentralisation.

II

Dimensions of Panchayati Raj

There are five major dimensions for understanding, JP's approach to Panchayati Raj. These dimensions discussed by JP in his writings pave the way o reach the goal of 'participatory democracy'.

Mass Society and Communitarian Society

It was with a distinction between mass society and communitarian society that JP unfolded his basic presumptions of participatory democracy. It is in the process of industrialisation and economic order that the Western society along with parliamentary politics has become an atomised mass society. It was in the context of parliamentary politic, that JP analysed it further by stating that in a mass society the political system falsely proclaimed the sovereignty of the individual. The reality appears to be different. It may be observed that the individual is alienated and becomes a nameless digit who is being manipulated by the political and economic masters for power, profit and glory. The state of affairs reflects that political democracy has been reduced to counting of heads. In such circumstances, political parties built around power-groups establish government by party and not government by people. As a result, participatory principle of democracy is endangered and even the representative principle is confined only to small competing power groups. Daya Krishna rightly states the phenomenon : "Except for direct democracy, there can be no such rule of the people or by the people. If the propositions 'of' and 'by' the people are taken seriously, all the mass societies of today are condemned to be undermocratic."[9] Contrary to alienated individual in mass society, the communitarian society treats the individual as a distinct personality living with other personalities. In a communitarian society, man does not live like a particle of sand in an inorganic heap, but as a living cell in organic community. JP derived some ideas from Gandhiji to substantiate his viewpoint. First, it is by living in community with others, his rights flow from his responsibilities. Second, the relationship between individual and community is strengthened by the readiness of the individual to die for community and the community for the individual. By implication, the point may be deduced that it is the sense of community which inspires people to participate in the affairs of the community in a meaningful way. This promotes participatory democracy or communitarian politics.

Primary Community and Participation

It is only in the primary and face-to-face community at the panchayat level that the individual feels one with the community. When the individual lives in community with others, he learns ethical values like adjustment, conciliation, harmony and co-operation. Primary or small organic group promotes co-operation or what Karl Manheim calls as self-regulating power or shared control. Manheim states that the alternative of co-operation represents a creative principle. This method of social control is one of the most significant inventions in the field of social techniques.[10] The self-regulating power and shared control, as manifested in the principle of co-operation infusing creativity, ultimately turns individuals as community-minded. The community spirit motivates individual for participation in the affairs of the community.

The question arises: What would be the size of primary community? There cannot a cut-and-dried answer. It is in the context of India that JP considered that *revenue village* would be appropriate unit which is commonly known with understood definition. It usually consists of a number of hamlets and all the inhabitants feel a sense of belonging to one another. Therefore, the revenue village may be taken as the primary community in India. For participation, *Gram Sabha* would be the assembly of the village and all adult males and females will be its members. For its working, JP devised three basic principles:[11] (a) The executive or panchayat will be formed by the Gram Sabha by general consensus; (b) No individual should hold the same post for more than a definite period of time; and (c) The Panchayat will function through sub-committees. It is to be noted that there is a scope of creating primary community even in large towns and cities also. To JP, *Gram* denotes simply a primary community urban or rural. The large towns or cities are made up of smaller areas which correspond to primary communities. The *Mohalla* is usually known like such area in North India.[12]

JP viewed that people's participation at the village level symbolised direct democracy. He stated: "*If there is any level of self-government at which the fullest participation of the people is practicable, it is at the village level. It is only there that direct democracy can adequately function.*"[13]

Concentric Circle of Communities

JP's emphasis on village as primary community does not mean that his approach to participatory democracy is limited to the primary unit. He visualises a circle of communities, beginning from the primary community at the village level to the world community to ensure the participation of the people in decision-making at different levels. All the communities are interrelated and thereby an integrated community may be established in human society. JP derived the idea of concentric circle from Gandhiji's view on this concept which the latter termed as *'oceanic circle'*. It would be relevant to cite the statement of Gandhiji which forms the basic premise of JP's proposition.

> "In this structure composed of innumerable villages there will be everwidening, never-ascending circles. Life will not be a pyramid with the apex sustained by the bottom. But it will be an oceanic circle whose centre will be individual always ready to perish for the village, the later ready to perish for the circle of villages, till at last, the whole becomes one life composed of individuals, never aggressive in their arrogance but ever-humble sharing the majesty of the oceanic circle of which they are integral units. Therefore, the outermost circumference will be wield power to crush the inner circle but give strength to all within and derive its own from the centre."[14]

It was on the basis of the concept of *oceanic circle* that JP worked out the details of concentric circle.[15] Each circle of community will do what may be possible with its competence and internal resources. Each primary community (Village Panchayat) will provide primary school, primary health services, small irrigation works like wells and tanks and village industries. A regional community (regional panchayat) will be formed out of a number of primary communities which will look after a high school, an indoor hospital, a power station and servicing centre, larger industries, larger irrigation works, etc. But, again, there are many things which are beyond the competence of regional community like techno-agriculture college, a major irrigation project, production of electricity, manufacturing of machine, etc. In order to undertake these tasks a number of regional communities will form a district community. Likewise, provincial community and national community will be formed. The national communities may also federate to form the World Community.

JP's communitarian polity based on concentric circles provides utmost scope for the people to participate in the decision-making at different levels. From the point of participatory democracy, there are certain principles which will guide the polity. First, each community in its sphere of activities is equally significant. Second, as one proceeds from inner to outer circles, there is less and less to do for the outer communities. Third, the level of outermost circumference does not suffer from a sense of superiority to crush the inner levels of the circle. Fourth, there will be co-operation and mutuality among the different concentric circles.

Agro-Industrial Community

For inculcating participatory culture among the people village community and other communities at different levels are considered as economic units. JP presents a picture of decentralised economy, with different levels of the polity serving as economic units in which village industries, block industries, district industries, state industries and union industries would exist. Of course, some of the State and all the Union industries will be of large scale nature.[16] In view of the man-land ratio and rate of population growth, the rural population cannot depend solely upon the land. Therefore, JP was of the opinion that some industries should be integrated with agriculture so that every village or every small group of villages is developed as an agro-industrial community which means a blending of agriculture and industry. Such agro-industrial community would not only process wheat and paddy, fruit and vegetables, sugarcane and cotton but it would also manufacture radios, cycle parts, small machines, electrical goods, etc. The decentralised pattern of agro-industrial community would be of the owner-worker or co-operative type. Thus, there is a wide scope of participation of the people in such agro-industrial communities which will be more egalitarian than the centralised sector.

JP's idea of panchayat bodies at different levels are agro-industrial communities which will be nourished by the fundamental principle of Gandhi's aphorism- 'production for the masses, not mass production'. This requires a vision for adopting appropriate technology. To Gandhiji, *"machinery has its place...But it must not be allowed to displace necessary human labour."*[17]

Tradition of Self-government an Need for Social Engineering

For justifying the case of direct democracy at the Panchayat level or what is called participatory democracy, JP made attempt to take cue from the strong traditions of self-government and self-help as manifested in the village republics of India in ancient and medieval periods. Community in ancient India had two forms–territorial community of the village or town and functional or occupational community. The two forms were integrated together which used to strengthen self-determining pattern of village republic. Although JP referred to the glory of the ancient village republics, he never advocated to copy it in toto in the modern time. He was of the opinion that panchayat as units of self-government and participatory democracy would not work unless the disruptive factors of the village community were not removed. Therefore, he laid stress on the need for 'social engineering' in order to introduce radical changes in the life of village community. In this context, JP expressed his views. "The experience of recent social engineering may and should be drawn upon, but the main mould of life must be indigenous and consistent with the genius of Indian social organisation".[18] Today, social and economic factors require necessary alteration. And, the glaring defects of caste system based on social hierarchy are required to be changed. Economic factors like money lending and land reform measures remain on paper in most of the states and they should be implemented to remove inequality and exploitation. From the point of view of social engineering, the statement of JP may further be cited:

> "A social hierarchy represented by the caste system marked differences in land holding, the great division between the landed and landless elements, these circumstances are bound seriously to defeat the objectives of democratic decentralisation. Mitigation of caste system is not so much a matter for state action as of internal reform of Hindu society, but it is a pity that land ceiling legislation has been so tardy and so halting and rural industrialisation so badly neglected."[19]

It is thus obvious that the success of Panchayati Raj as participatory democracy with the objective of communitarian society - the main mould of life in the Indian social organisation–depends on social engineering. This requires a psychological revolution also among the people so that they may be prepared psychologically to subordinate their narrow interests (individual, family, caste, class, etc.) to the good of the community. Legislations alone are not sufficient for mass awakening. Political and social workers have to come forward to undertake this task.

III

Autonomy, Participation and Performance

As a pragmatic leaders, JP made attempts to put up some practical measures for improving the three-tier Panchayati Raj system introduced in 1959 on the pattern of Balwant Rai Mehta Scheme. Those measures are applicable also to the present phase of Panchayati Raj (PR) which has taken shape on the basis of 73rd Constitutional Amendment Act, 1992. As suggested by JP, the following measures are important which need immediate attention today for due autonomy, participation and performance of Panchayati Raj System—

(i) In the power-structure of the state level, there are two partners–the ministers and the higher bureaucracy. It is a common observation as well as general complaint of elected officer-bearers of panchayat bodies that ministers and bureaucrats surrender power in words but they withhold it in deeds. Therefore, it would be desirable to set up a non-political autonomous body or commission headed by a person who does not belong to the civil service. The Panchayati Raj Commission will look after the performance of PR bodies as per provisions of panchayat legislation : (a) Allotment of funds from the state and Centre are properly paid out and utilised; (b) The higher tiers do not unduly interfere with the lower; (c) The administrative staff should function under the democratic control as per law but at the same time the interests of officials are protected; and (d) Proper corrective or disciplinary action is taken against any offending office-holder or institution of the PR bodies. It is to be noted that the functions of the commission should be positive and it is the duty of the commission to help the PR institutions and individuals for better performance.[20]

(ii) The state government has the right to frame the necessary Rules under the State Panchayat Act. It has been noticed that sometimes some provisions of the State Act are too vague and thereby the Rules framed by the Executive of the State acquire more importance than the Act itself. Therefore, the State Legislature has to take care of this problem.[21]

(iii) It has been observed that the village is a disharmonious community on the basis of caste, class, family and other types of factions. But, 'community spirit' is required for proper development. JP cogently remarked. "Self-government through faction-fighting will not be self-government, but self-ruination. Let it be remembered that the village is a primary, face-to-face community where the people are physically thrown together to share their joys and sorrows."[22] For maintaining the harmony of face-to-face community, contests at elections to panchayats must be avoided and thereby the entire village community may be mobilised for the task of reconstruction and development.

(iv) For the sake of vitality and participation of the people, organised political parties should refrain from either setting up party candidates or putting pressure on elected members of PR bodies to become party members. No doubt, as consciousness grows at the ground level, elected panchayat members will be less and less liable to be moved as pawns by political parties and their leaders.[23]

(v) For participation and development through PR bodies, people should be imparted education by non-partisan agencies. Even political parties can undertake this task of education in a non-partisan spirit. Schools, libraries, co-operative societies and all-India non-governmental agencies can do the work of educating the people for participation and development by producing literature, conducting surveys, studying problems, etc.[24]

IV

Conclusion and Observation

JP's emphasis on the role of panchayat bodies at different levels as 'agro-industrial' communities is significant from the point of view of participatory democracy and development. It gives a new meaning to 'self-government' for panchayats which has now been made mandatory by the 73rd Constitutional Amendment Act, 1992. The deep implication of 'self-government' denotes 'gram swaraj' which, in turn, promotes people's participation as well as self-reliance (gram swalamban) of villages in *basic needs* of life. It was in 2003 that the Central Government has announced to draft a new Constitutional Amendment Bill to improve the Panchayati Raj system in terms of due autonomy, financial resources and performance. It would be a progressive step if the new constitutional amendment makes attempt to spell out the meaning of 'self-government' in the conceptual framework of 'gram swaraj'. And, the core of 'gram swaraj' is vibrant 'agro-industrial' communities at different levels of Panchayati Raj. Further, the new Amendment may also include the provision of an autonomous Panchayati Raj Commission in every state to look after the work of panchayat bodies as suggested by JP for due autonomy and better performance of panchayat bodies.

JP was of the opinion that panchayats as units of self-government and participatory democracy would not work unless disruptive factors of village life were not removed. For this, JP suggested a scheme of *'social engineering'* in order. to introduce radical changes in social and economic life of the village community. He assigned the responsibility of mitigating the caste system and its hierarchy to Hindu society itself. And, for implementation of land-ceiling legislation and the programmes of rural industrialisation, JP considered state action as a necessary step. Despite pronouncement, states like Bihar has to do a lot in the area of land-ceiling law and the distribution of surplus land to landless people. Of course, caste hierarchy is breaking fast but the category of caste itself is still a disruptive factor. It may be mentioned that Bihar has a record of doing exemplary work by holding conferences for eradication of caste system, particularly by the Samyukta Socialist Party in 1967 under the leadership of Dr. Ram Manohar Lohia and again by raising the issue of untouchability and graded caste system during the Bihar Movement in 1974-75 under the leadership of JP. A social movement is still needed to move further for a new resurgence.

For gradual transformation of Panchayati Raj into 'participatory democracy', *Gram Sabha* at the panchayat level should be made active. This ensures *transparency* in the development work and it also prevents misuse of power by elected office-bearers and members. JP laid stress on *Gram sabha* as the bottom tier of Panchayati Raj. It has been observed that gram sabha is not active and people are not conscious enough to attend its meetings. In this context, the role of NGOs are important for launching awareness development programmes. It maybe recalled that it was during sixties that JP tried to build a bridge between voluntary organisations and Panchayati Raj Institutions. In his presidential address of a seminar on the *Role of Voluntary Agencies in Democratic Decentralisation* held in April, 1960 at Bihar Vidyapith, Sadaqat Ashram, Patna, he pleaded for a significant role of voluntary organisations in activating the people for their participation in the Panchayati Raj system. It is noteworthy that eminent Gandhian thinker and social activist Acharya Rammurti is doing exemplary work for awareness development programmes among the elected members of Panchayati Raj bodies in Bihar. Apart from the role of eminent social activists and NGOs, teachers of schools, colleges and universities can high-light the basic ideas of Panchayati Raj for participatory democracy and development. International organisations like UNICEF can also play a major role in awareness development programmes among the elected members of PR bodies. It may be mentioned that the Bihar branch of the UNICEF organised a two-day workshop on Panchayati Raj at Patna on 22-23 June, 2002 and the discussion of the workshop laid stress on some crucial issues in relation to Bihar as well as on some broad features of PR bodies of Madhya Pradesh and Kerala. This was a good attempt to draw some meaningful conclusions in a comparative perspective for future guidelines.

Today, the delay in transferring due powers as per 29 subjects listed in 11th Schedule to panchayat bodies is a matter of concern. Cases under PIL in some High Courts in this regard indicate that the process of decentralisation is not an easy task. Strangely enough, in Bihar, District Planning Committees in 36 districts have been constituted after two years and the matter was taken up by the concerned department of the state government after intervention of the Patna High Court under a petition of PIL. How can development plan for a district be drafted without duly constituted District Planning Committee? Apart from this problem, we cannot overlook the ground realities of the rural scenario which are not satisfactory. Zila parishads in some districts are not functioning well due to factionalism among elected members and there is always a threat of no-confidence motion by a faction against the chairman of a particular zila parishad. Is it possible to check all these problems with the formation of an autonomous Panchayati Raj Commission as suggested by JP. The pros and cons of this proposed body may be examined.

Today, panchyats as 'agro-industrial' units cannot work in isolation and they have to take notice of the macro-level economic institutions and the changing world scenario. The recent trend of market economy under globalisation may shatter the vision of the participatory 'agro-industrial' panchayat bodies. It is a dangerous phenomenon that the *modus operandi* of production and marketing processes even in the sphere of agriculture will lie somewhere else and people on the forum of panchayat will in due course become dumb spectators. Thus, from the perspective of people's participation, the market economy under globalisation may damage the roots and parameters of democracy. Is it not a sort of 'neo-colonialism' of a few developed and highly industrialised nations entering as big brothers into developing and poor countries having agriculture as the backbone of their economy? It is worth mentioning that JP briefly noted with concern about the dangers of 'neo-colonialism' in *Prison Diary* during his imprisonment in Emergency in 1975. He also suggested for a deep study of 'neo-colonialism' in the context of India.

It appears to be a dangerous trend that the common people will remain far away from the decion-making process relating to the basic issues of human life which are now decided by a super body like WTO in the name of globalisation and economic reforms. Significantly, farmers and representatives of NGOs of developing countries led a protest march against the supremacy o some developed and highly industralised countries regarding the policy in the sphere of agriculture at the WTO meet held recently at Cancun, Argentina. In the context of India, it is a redeeming feature in our political development that there are now 32 lakh elected representatives including ten lakh elected women members in the rural area at the third stratum of the Indian polity, i.e., Panchayati Raj Institutions and they are the saviours of 'participatory democracy' and 'agro-industrial' panchayat bodies. In future, panchayats of

India as 'village republics' or 'little democracies' will counter-balance the saddening impact of 'neo-colonialism' under the garb of globalisation.

REFERENCES

James Bryce, Modern Democracies, Vol. I, The World Press, Calcutta, 1962, p. 161.

Neera Chandhoke, State and Civil Society, Sage, New Delhi, 1995, pp. 163-64.

M.K. Gandhi, Panchayati Raj (Compiled by R.K. Prabhu). Navajivan, Ahmedabad, 1959, p. 16.

Jayaprakash Narayan, Swaraj For the People, Sarva Seva Sangh, Varanasi, Fourth Printing, 1968, p. VII.

Ibid, p. 11.

Ibid, p. 39.

Ibid, p. 6.

Ibid, pp. 31-33.

Daya Krishna, "What is Democracy", Democracy in the New States (Rhodes Seminar Papers), India Printing Works, Bombay, 1959, p. 57.

Karl Manheim, Freedom, Power and Democratic Planning, Routledge & Kegan Paul, London, 1959, p. 16.

Jayaprakash Narayan, Socialism, Sarvodaya and Democracy (Ed. Bimal Prasad), Asia Publishing House, Bombay, 1964, p. 229.

Jayaprakash Narayan, Swaraj For the People, op. cit., pp. 23-24.

Ibid. p. 15.

M.K. Gandhi, Village Swaraj, (Complied by R.K. Prabhu), Navajivan, Ahmedabad, 1963, p. 70.

Jayaprakash Narayan, Socialism, Sarvodaya and Democracy, op. cit., pp. 212-214.

Jayaprakash Narayan, Swarj for the People, op. cit., p. 31.

M.K. Gandhi, India of My Dreams (Compiled by R.K. Prabhu), Navajivan, Ahmedabad, 1995, Fifth Reprint, p. 30.

Jayaprakash Narayan, Socialism, Sarvodaya and Democracy, op. cit., p. 207.

Jayaprakash Narayan, Communitarian Society and Panchayati Raj (Ed. Brahmanand), Navachetna, Varanasi, 1970, p. 61.

Jayaprakash Narayan, Swaraj for the People, op. cit., pp. 25-26.

Ibid, p. 24.

Ibid, pp. 18-19.

Ibid, pp. 12-13.

Ibid, pp. 11-12.

SECTION - V

JP as a Hero of Past and Hope for Future

14

The Ideological Legacy of JP and the Future of Democracy in India

Bimal Prasad

I

Jayaprakash Narayan popularly known as JP, occupies a unique position among the galaxy of political leaders produced by India in modern times. He played a major role not merely in the struggle for freedom from foreign rule, but also in shaping the minds of people as well as events after the achievement of Freedom, attaining a stature next only to that of Jawaharlal Nehru. Yet he never aspired to hold any office or position of power and was content to serve society as an ordinary citizen. Among the causes he cherished, some belonged to the lost category and had no chance of success. Sometimes his stand on certain issues, like, for instance, Kashmir, made him extremely unpopular among large sections of the Indian people. He, however, did not care and stuck to his path so long as he was convinced that path was the right one. Towards the fag end of his life his exertions for the restoration of democracy in India did attain success, but he was aware, more than anyone else, of the limitations of that success. For his exertions had been directed towards a much higher goal-Total Revolution- and he knew only too well how far away India was from it. What made things worse for him was that most of the people who had come to power with his blessings and support soon forgot all his ideas and plunged into a naked pursuit of power and wealth as per the pattern set during the past few years.

Confined to bed by a serious kidney ailment which afflicted him during the last years of his life JP had no option, but to watch this situations helplessly. The one thing which mitigated his misery during those days was the hope that the ideas propounded by him from time to time might inspire some people in future to strive for a better life for all. For he remained convinced till the last breath of his life that it was not the destiny of his fellow men and women to always live amidst poverty, squalor, exploitation and degradation and that it lay within their power to secure a better deal for themselves if only they strived seriously for it and followed the right path. He, of course, did not claim that he had said the final word on what that path would be like. He indeed believed that no one could do so. He did, however, hope that his ideas in this regard would be of some use to those who might be interested in bringing about a radical transformation of society. In the opinion of the present author, there is no doubt that JP's ideas constitute a most valuable legacy left by him. They are particularly capable of illumining the path of all those who may be interested in safeguarding democracy and rebuilding our social order on the basis of the ideals of freedom, equality and peace.

The quintessence of JP's ideological legacy is contained in his vision of Total Revolution. Almost all those who either eulogised or attacked that vision immdediately after JP had mentioned it at a public meeting at Patna on June 5, 1974 thought that JP had for the first time used the term Total Revolution. Many still continue to think and write in the same vein. Actually it was Karl Marx who had first used this term more than a century and a quarter before JP popularised it in India in 1974-75. Writing in *The Poverty of Philosophy* (1847), Marx remarks: 'Meanwhile the antagonism between the proletariat and the bourgeoisie is a struggle of class against class, a struggle which carried to its highest expression is a Total Revolution.'[1] In a different sense, i.e., signifying a radical transformation not merely of our material conditions but also of the moral character of the individuals the idea of Total Revolution was implicit in many of Gandhi's writings and speeches.[2] Vinoba carried the idea further. As early as 1951 he declared: 'My aim is to bring about a three-fold revolution. First, I want a change in people's hearts; secondly, I want to create change in their lives; and thirdly, I want to change the social structure.'[3] In the sixties he spoke in this vein frequently enough to warrant the use of *Towards Total Revolution* as the title of a book containing his speeches, edited by Suresh Ram and published in 1968.[4] At least once Vinoba had also used the term 'Total Revolution'.[5] It has been aptly observed in a recent study that JP's movemnt of Total Revolution was a 'continuation of the preceding movement for non-violent revolution through Bhoodan and Gramdan'.[6] JP was fully justified in remarking on one occasion: "There is hardly any difference between Sarvodaya and Total Revolution. If there is any, then Sarvodaya is the goal and Total Revolution the means. Total Revolution is basic change in all aspects of life. There cannot be Sarvodaya without this".[7]

Without using the term 'Total Revolution' JP himself had been emphasising since the mid-forties, if not earlier, the need for a social revolution which would not merely bring about a change in the structure of society, but also an improvement in the character of the individuals comprising it.[8] After he joined the *Bhoodan* Movement in the fifties he laid particular stress on it. In course of an article published in 1969 he also used the term 'Total Revolution' to describe the objective of the Sarvodaya movement in India. Referring to the *Bhoodan* and *Gramdan* programmes he observed: "Gandhi's non-violence was not just a plea for law and order, or a cover for the *status quo,* but a revolutionary philosophy. It is indeed a philosophy of a total revolution, because it embraces personal and social ethics and values of life as much as economic, political and social institutions and processes".[9] It is, however, a fact that the term 'Total Revolution' became a recurrent theme of JP's speeches and writings only since 1974 and it is only since then that it has taken its place in Indian political discourse.

II

What led JP to give a call for Total Revolution in 1974? More than a quarter of century of experience of public life in independent India, first as a socialist and later as a Sarvodaya leader, had convinced him that piecemeal reforms of the socio-economic and political system operating in India since the achievement of Independece would not be able to bring about any significant change in the lives of mass of the people and that what was required was a radical transformation of the entire social system. That system, according to him, had hardly undergone any change since Independence. He, of course, recognised that zamindari had been ended, certain land reform measures had been adopted by the various legislatures and untouchability had been abolished by law. But most of the Indian villages still continued under the grip of the bigger and medium landowners, generally belonging to the upper castes. The majority of villages in almost all parts of India consist of small and marginal farmers and landless labourers, comprising Harijans and other miserable. Harijans were still burnt alive. The condition of Adivasis was similar and they continued to be mercilessly cheated and exploited by the money-lenders.

The condition of the urban poor was hardly better. True, a number of industries, banks and life insurance organisations had been nationalised. Railways had been nationalised long ago, during the period of British rule. A number of large industries had been set up in the public sector, free from the control of capitalists and fully owned and controlled by the state. But all this had only added up to state capitalism, marked inefficiency, waste and corruption. The general people had no role in the public enterprises except as workers and consumers. This was not socialism. Nor could socialism be equated with nationalisation.

Turning to the educational system JP found that in spite of several committees and commissions it had remained basically what it was under British rule: 'class education designed as an escalator to reach the top.' 'There was no change also in the customs, manners, beliefs and superstitions of the mass of the people. Some change in these field was noticeable among the elite, but that was largely superficial'.

From the point of view of social and economic development the picture was frightful. Population had gone on rising, so had poverty. More than forty percent of our people were below the poverty line and denied some of the barest necessities of life such as drinking water, food and clothing, housing, education and medical care.

The question was: could a radical change in this gloomy picture be brought about by merely a change of government or the enactment of some laws by the legislatures concerned? JP's emphatic answer was 'No'. This answer was based on his understanding of India's economic and social development since the achievement of Independence. Several progressive measures had been enacted by the legislatures in the socio-economic field, but they had remained largely on paper. Among the examples of such measures mention might be made of laws providing for the imposition of ceiling on land-holding and for the protection of the homestead land of the landless labourers. The same applied to measures against dowry in marriage and corruption in administration which had gone on increasing in spite of the enactment of several measures to curb them. A radical change in the situation, therefore, could come only through 'a systemic change in society' as a 'revolution in every sphere and aspect of society'. In other words, a Total Revolution.[10]

III

This systemic change is to be brought about neither by legislation nor by force from above, but through public-education and non-violent struggle by the people from below. In those countries where revolutions had been attempted through violence or force, power had passed into the hands of a coterie and people at large had failed to secure control over government. JP repeatedly warned the Indian people against being tempted by the example of such revolutions. 'My conclusion after a study of violent revolutions', he observed in 1969, 'is that violent revolution does bring about a revolution in the sense that it uproots the old social order and destroys it from its foundation. But it fails in achieving the objectives for which the revolution is made'.[11] During the same year he again stressed in course of an article dealing with the theme of revolution that 'once the revolutionaries of the day seize power, the people are inescapably subjugated to the juggernaut of the party and the state'.[12] Explaining why this happens, he further added: 'it is not that the violent revolutionaries deceive and betray; it is just the logic of violence working itself out. It cannot be otherwise.'[13] In a successful violent revolution, there is a widespread unorganised revolu-tionary violence which succeeds in accomplishing the destruction and uprooting of the old order. After this accomplishment, however, it becomes necessary to organise a force to stop further violence and to protect and consolidate the gains of revolution. Whoever controls that force wields supreme power. It is thus that power passes from the hands of the people to a small coterie, sometimes even to one individual, who rules in the name of revolution and keeps the people out of power.[14] Such an outcome can be avoided if a revolution is brought about through non-violent methods. Describing the characteristics of this method JP observes:

"The most important characteristic of this method is that its means must be in harmony with its ends. If the end is a non-violent society, the means also must be non-violent; if human freedom is the end, coercive means (except moral coercion) are ruled out; if man is end himself he cannot be used as a means; if truth is to be the basis of the new life, untruthful means are inadmissible; if the end is dispersal of power the means cannot be...centralised power".[15]

While referring to Total Revolution in course of his speeches and writings in 1974-75, JP continued to lay stress on the fact that such a revolution had to be brought about through non-violent methods and care had to be taken to see that the democratic structure of the state was maintained intact. Indeed, one of the objectives of Total Revolution was to strengthen democracy by ensuring direct participation by the people in the work of government as far as possible. As JP put it in his notes on 23 August 1975 while in prison: "Total revolution has to be peacefully brought about without impairing the democratic structure of society and affecting the democratic way of life of the people".[16] He, of course, realises that this would prevent radical changes from being introduced at one go, as may be possible through a violent revolution and would delay the process of social change. He, however, prefers this slower process in order to avoid violence and ensure more permanent results. He also feels that in revolutionary times the period of transition can be shortened, though not to the same extent as in a violent revolution. As he puts it in his prison-notes in 1975: "The revolution being peaceful, it was not to happen suddenly and swiftly. It would take time, but the times being revolutionary, not too much time–perhaps a space of a decade or two".[17] This is, on the whole, not very different from the thinking of Gandhi and Vinoba, who also looked forward to a social revolution through non-violent means.[18]

IV

JP's thinking is, however, not wholly identical with Vinoba's. He, for instance, differs from the latter in assigning priority to systemic change over change in the thinking and behaviour-pattern of the individual. JP had, of course, been consistently emphasising the importance of the latter since the mid-forties and this had, indeed, been partly responsible for his shift from Socialism to Sarvodaya. Some Marxist strain in his thinking, however, always remained and he realised that although efforts must continue to change the individual along with society, systemic changes in society must be accorded priority. Thus even while accepting that a non-violent social revolution is likely to require a longer span of time than a violent revolution in order to accomplish its objectives, he observes: "The basic systematic changes would happen first and the individual and group adaptations, mostly psychological, later".[19] Vinoba has a different approach to revolution. "Merely a big change", he observes, "does not make for a revolution. As long as there is no revolution inside, there can be no revolution outside. Change in mental attitude is termed as revolution."[20] According to him: "changes in individuals come first and then these lead to systemic change. Social revolution is secondary to individual revolution and is the sum total of individual revolutions."[21]

Behind this difference between JP and Vinoba there lies a divergence in their respective approaches to the role of state power in society. Because of the continuing Marxist strain in his thought JP, while always emphasising the importance of people's power as against state power from 1954 onwards, has a more realistic conception of the latter.[22] It is this realistic conception which on the one hand led him to devote so much time and energy to the fight against the growing threat of authoritarianism in India between 1973 and 1977 and on the other made him visualise, under certain circumstances, a positive role by the State in the movement for Total Revolution.

JP too, however, constantly emphasises that the future of such a movement primarily depends not so much on what is done or not done by the State, but what is done by the people at large. The votaries of Total Revolution, according to him, would have to pay their major attention to working among the people. This would involve not merely the spread of the gospel of revolution and constructive work, but also struggle may not always be necessary. In his speeches in 1974, JP remarked more than once that the movement of Total Revolution need not necessarily lead to a fight against the government of the day. For there might also be a government sympathetic to the cause of such a revolution. However, he realises on further reflection that though not impossible such a development is highly unlikely. He, of course, welcomes a struggle for he thinks that during a period of struggle the message of revolution would be widely scattered among the people and this would contribute significantly to their awakening.

A struggle, JP takes care to warn, cannot be conjured up at will. It can be started only when the people are in a state of disaffection. Leadership and organisation will also have to play a vital role in 'bringing out of the revolutionary situation a revolutionary movement'. In the absence of proper leadership and organisation such a situation may end in chaos or the imposition of dictatorship. While under certain conditions help on such occasions may be taken from such political parties as may come forward in support of a struggle for Total Revolution, efforts must be made to build up a cadre of workers fully wedded to the cause of such a revolution and trained in its dynamics. JP particularly put his faith in the youth. During the Bihar movement (1974-75), he founded the *Chhatra-Yuva Sangharsha Vahini* (Student-Youth Struggle Brigade) with a view to building up a trained cadre of young workers for the cause of Total Revolution. He also sought to promote the formation of *Jan Sangharsha Samitis* (people's Struggle Committees) at various levels and *Janata Sarkars* (People's Governments) in villages with a view to spreading the gospel of revolution among the people. The work of organising these bodies was, of course, rudely interrupted by the imposition of emergency in June 1975. By the time the emergency ended (1977), JP was too crippled by ill health to do anything effective to revive them. He did, however, renew his call for the formation of people's committees in all parts of the country and did whatever he could to put fresh life into the *Chhatra-Yuva Sangharsha Vahini*.

This acceptance of the need of struggle in certain situations on JP's part further distinguishes his concept of a non-violent revolution from that of Vinoba. For the latter never appreciated the need for struggle against the government and thought that in the conditions obtaining in India after the achievement of Independence a social revolution could be brought about by changing the consciousness of the people through the power of thought.[23] Thus addressing a meeting of the Sarva Seva Sangh in December 1973, he observed: "In Gandhi's days, there was no freedom of thought and expression... But in India today we enjoy the highest measure of freedom in the world...Everyday the newspaper brings to us the highest indictment of the government...Satyagraha as practised by Gandhi has, therefore, become quite irrelevant in India'.[24]

JP not merely realised that the road to Total Revolution may, in certain conditions, lie through a non-violent struggle against the government of the day, but also, towards the end of his life, advocated what amounts to a non-violent class struggle. Elaborating the programme of work which he had in mind for the *Chhatra-Yuva Sangharsha Vahini* as the vanguard of the forces working for Total Revolution, he told the present author in course of an interview in 1977:

"I expect them of work in close cooperation with the villages and ward sabhas or people's committees, consisting of all citizens of the area, and to function as their vanguard in fighting against all types of injustice and oppression. In particular, they have to engage themselves in organising the Harijans and other weaker sections of society. Apart from this they are expected to work for the acceleration of social change and the introduction of necessary structural reforms in the economic life of the people of the area. If and when a situation develops calling for a local regional or national struggle either by way of protest against injustice and oppression or for ushering in a new social order, they are expected to playa leading role in it. I must make it clear that I do not see any prospect for total revolution without a long-drawn-out struggle and without the masses participating in such a struggle."[25]

In 1978, JP went even further and openly expressed himself in favour of supporting the consolidation of the suppressed and backward sections of society in their struggle against the exploiting classes. He further remarked : "People have asked me whether this would not lead to class struggle; I say that class struggle is inevitable...A struggle is implicit in change... We would only ensure that, in this struggle, those who are suppressed triumph, those who are backward advance in society."[26] Such views further widen the gulf separating JP from Vinoba. For the latter had absolutely no use for the concept of class conflict and indeed regarded it as alien to India and quite destructive.[27]

Needless to add, while JP thus differs from Vinoba on the methods to be adopted for ushering in Total Revolution and adopts a position which shows the continuing presence of a Marxist strain in his thinking that position cannot be characterised as un-Gandhian. It was certainly not Gandhi's position that after the achievement of independence there could be no situation calling for a struggle against government. Thus he observed in 1930: "May non-violence would (not) prevent me from fighting my countrymen on the many questions which must arise when India has become free". He further added: "I know that if I survive the struggle for freedom, I might have to give non-violent battle to my own countrymen which may be as stubborn as that in which I am now engaged."[28] It is, of course, a fact that during 1946-47, Gandhi warned on several occasions against resort to civil disobedience on a national scale against the Government of free India, based on democracy. However, it has been rightly pointed out by competent authority that "it would be wrong to interpret Gandhi's position solely on the side of caution and to rule out Satyagraha in a democracy, for all practical purposes".[29] JP's position on the legitimacy of a general mass struggle on non-violent lines even in a democracy might not have been fully anticipated by Gandhi, but it certainly represents a natural extension and development of Gandhi's ideas on Satyagraha. This can be substantiated by referring to some of Gandhi's observations about the time of the achievement of independence. Thus he affirmed in July 1947:

> It is not...claimed that all the laws of Satyagraha have already been formulated. I cannot say either that I myself know all the laws. This I do assert that every worthy object can be achieved through Satyagraha. It is the highest and the most potent means, the most effective weapon. I am convinced that socialism will not be reached by any other means.
>
> Satyagraha can rid society of all evils political, economic and moral."[30]

The same applies to JP's views on the need to support the suppressed and backward classes in our society in their struggle against the exploiting classes. Gandhi, or course, would have been happy if the exploitation of the poor by the rich was ended without any conflict between them. But if ever a clash arose, and he was intelligent enough to realise that it would, he left no one in doubt as to where his won sympathies lay. Thus in his speech at the Round Table Conference in London in 1931, he observed that every interest in India which was worthy of protection must subserve the interests of the 'dumb millions' whom the Congress was pledged to serve. Further, if there was any real clash between the latter and any other interest he had no doubt that the Congress would 'sacrifice every interests for the sake of the interests of these dumb millions'.[31] Much has been made of Gandhi's opposition to class war and of his theory of Trusteeship, If his writings on these themes are carefully studied, however, the conclusion will be inescapable that he was opposed to class war because in his mind it was associated with violence, not because he was not interested in organising the poor or helping them to secure justice in their struggle against the rich. Indeed, he himself advocated what can legitimately,be described as non-violent class struggle. For he again and again emphasised that if all efforts to persuade the rich to live as trustees failed, the only way open to the poor was to organise themselves and resort to non-cooperation and civil disobedience in order to secure their just rights. Thus he wrote in the *Harijan* of August 25, 1940:

> "If... in spite of the utmost effort, the rich do not become guardians of the poor in the true sense of the term and the latter are more and more crushed and die of hunger, what is to be done? In trying to find out the solution to this riddle I have lighted on non-violent non-cooperation and civil disobedience as the right and infallible means."[32]

V

What about the content of Total Revolution? In other words, what is the nature of change which Total Revolution is expected to bring about? As noticed earlier, such a revolution will be all-inclusive and touch all aspects of life. According to JP, it will be a combination of seven revolutions-"social, economic, political, cultural, ideological or intellectual, educational and spiritual."[33] There is nothing sacrosanct about this number and it can be reduced or increased through regrouping or change of words. What is important is the emphasis on a thorough-going change in all aspects of life. JP could not spell out these changes in detail, except to point out again and again that the problem facing India could not be solved nor a new society created merely through a change of rulers or even of a system of government, but only through a radical transformation touching all aspects of life. However a picture of the social order he was aiming at is available in some of the tracts he wrote in the late fifties and early sixties, particularly: *A Plea for Reconstruction of Indian Polity* (1959) and *Swaraj for the People* (1961).[34] That he stuck to the picture drawn there even while talking about Total Revolution is confirmed by the fact that while containing a few points not touched upon earlier, the outline of his ideas on the nature of the new social order, which he jotted down in his notes in prison in 1975, conforms to that picture in all its essentials.[35] He also told the present writer in course of an interview in 1977 that his picture of the new social order remained broadly the same as depicted in the two tracts mentioned above.[36] The latter, therefore, constitute the best guide to the content of Total Revolution.

In *A Plea for Reconstruction of Indian Polity,* JP rejects the Western model of democracy on the ground that it does not give full scope to the people to participate in the management of their affairs and is based on an atomised view of society, the State being an inorganic sum of individuals. In its place he pleads for a model of democracy, based on an integrated concept of society and providing the fullest possible scope to the individual to participate in the management of his affairs, without the intermediation of political parties. The latter, according to JP, function without any control over them by the people or even by their own members and are the source of many evils. It is not, however, the party system that is the main culprit, but parliamentary democracy, which lies at its back and which cannot work without it. In JP's ideal society, therefore, parliamentary democracy will be replaced by a new kind of polity which he describes as a communitarian or partyless democracy.

The problem of devising a new polity is, however, part of the larger problem of social reconstruction. Modern industrialism has resulted in the disintegration of human society and made man an alien among his fellowmen. The problem is how to remedy this situation and "put man in touch with man, so that they may live together in meaningful, understandable, controllable relationships. In short, the problem is to recreate the human community". The essential attributes of a true community are sharing, participation and fellowship. The new socio-political system must be so devised as to provide a congenial, environment for the fostering of these qualities.

The base of the new social organisation will be the local or primary communities, neither so small that a balanced development of communal life and culture become difficult, nor so large that life in them becomes impersonalised. They will be neither rural nor urban, but agro-industrial, based on a balance between agriculture and industry. The existing big cities will have to be reorganised and made federations of smaller-sized communities. Where this is not possible, they will have to be endured, care being taken to see that they do not become bigger and no new big cities come up. Just as a number of families come together and cooperate among themselves to tackle common problems and build the regional community. A number of regional communities will in their turn join together to form the district community. The district communities will federate to form the provincial communities, and the latter will join hands to form the national community. As we proceed from the base upwards, there will be less and less to do for the bigger communities, so that, when we reach the level of the national community, it will deal only with such matters as defence, foreign relations, currency and inter-state coordination.

The political structure of the community must correspond to its social structure and rise storey by storey from the foundation, which will consist of 'self-governing, self-sufficient, agro-industrial, urbo-rural local communities'. The existing villages and townships can be converted into such communities if sincere efforts are made in this direction. The development of the rest of the political structure, however, need not wait till this task is completed. The work must begin at all levels simultaneously; otherwise it will not succeed at any level. The most important political institution of the local community should be the village assembly – *Gram Sabha* – with all the adults of the community as its members. The executive – *Panchayat* – should be selected by general consensus of opinion in the *sabha,* without anybody standing for election for any office. The *sabha* and the *Panchayat* should be given responsibility to manage things that really matter. For instance, it should be their duty to ensure that no one in the village goes without food, clothing and shelter, every child receives primary education and everyone receives primary medical care. The next level of the political structure will be that of the regional community, with the *Gram Panchayats* integrated into the *Panchayat Samiti*. Similarly, the *Pancyayat Samities* of a district will be integrated into the District Council, the District Councils into the State Assembly, and the State Assemblies into the National Parliament. Thus, the political institutions at each level will be an integration of the institutions at the lower level. There will be indirect instead of direct election.

The issue, however, is not merely one of strengthening local self-government or of introducing indirect elections. 'It would be wrong to suppose', warns JP, 'that if local bodies were given more powers and the direct system of election were replaced with an indirect one, and the rest of the social organisation were left as it is, the resultant would be the kind of polity that is being advocated here. The polity herein suggested is not a graft on the existing body of society, but an organic part of a radically transformed social order'. Such a polity cannot be built in a day and there will have to be a period of transition. To begin with, elections should be so conducted that political parties do not play any role in them up to the district level. Even at the state and national levels the candidates must be selected by the people themselves and not by the parties which, during the period of transition, may be allowed to support particular candidates after their selection by the people. Thus will the role of the parties in our political process be gradually reduced and that of the people increase, leading eventually to the establishment of a communitarian or partyless democracy.

The problems of the transition from the old polity to the new are dealt with more fully in *Swaraj for the People.*

In what manner should Panchayat Raj be extended to higher levels? Here JP suggests a procedure slightly different from that suggested by him in *A plea for Reconstruction of Indian Polity,* two years earlier. In the latter he had suggested that each lower level should elect the immediately higher through a system of indirect election. But after further thinking he changed this view, as indirect elections might encourage parochialism and retard the growth of a national outlook among all the citizens. Besides, such a system might be more liable to be corrupted by moneyed interests, as the number of electors would be small, except at the lowest level. He, therefore, formulated a method of election which would be direct, yet so organised as to give the institutions of Panchayati Raj at every level a definite role in it. Thus it will be possible to have the advantages of direct election without affecting the organic nature of the new polity.

The role of the political parties should be restricted as far as possible and the people enabled to select their own candidates for election through popularly constituted Electoral Councils. Every constitutional and educational device should be adopted to encourage these councils to set up not more than one candidate for every seat, thus avoiding contest. For it is necessary for the fulfillment of democracy – no matter what its kind – that its process is 'as little divisive as possible, or, to put it positively, as cohesive and unitive as possible.'

VI

The political structure sketched above will require for its base a new kind of economic structure. While the satisfaction of the material needs of man will be its objective, it will not endeavour to satisfy the insatiable hunger for more and yet more which modern industrialism – capitalist, Socialist and communist – has created. JP strongly argues in favour of this view in *A Plea for Reconstruction of Indian Polity.* "I believe", he observes, "that for man really to enjoy liberty and freedom and to practice self-government, it is necessary voluntarily to limit his wants. Otherwise, the greed for more and yet more will lead to mutual conflict, coercion, spoliation, war and also to a system of production that will be so complex as to bind democracy hand and foot and deliver it to a bureaucratic oligarchy". If the present science of economics comes in the way of the development of an economy based on a voluntary limitation of wants, a new science of economics may have to be created, together with new methods of planning and new techniques of industrial organisation.

These new methods and techniques come in for more detailed discussion in *Swaraj for the People.* Here JP reiterates his view that the old belief of socialists that nationalisation of the means of production, distribution and exchange would automatically usher in economic democracy is no longer valid. In fact, the experience of communist countries has shown that even the complete nationalisation of all these means results not in economic democracy, but in the most rigorous economic dictatorship, giving rise to new forms of economic exploitation and inequality. The only way out is economic decentralisation. What would be the essential features of a decentralised economy in India? According to JP, such an economy must be a small-machine and labor-intensive economy, care being taken to constantly improve the efficiency and productivity of the small machine without adding much to its cost. Secondly, there must be regional surveying and planning so that the resources of a particular region might be utilised to the full to satisfy the needs of that region, though, of course, surpluses of one region should continue to be exchanged for those of others. Thirdly, there must be launched a programme of rural industrialisation so that every village, or at least every small group of village, is developed as an agro-industrial community, based on an organic blending of agriculture and industry. Fourthly, the organisational pattern of decentralised industry should be such as to keep it free from both bureaucratisation and exploitation. Fifthly, the institution of *Panchayati Raj* should play an important part in the development of such an economy.

JP makes it clear that his objective here is not to preserve the traditional methods of production. On the contrary, what he is suggesting is, in fact, a most modern type of economy, the like of which does not exist and has not existed anywhere and the creation of which would require a new machine technology as well as a new socio-economic technology. He also emphasises that he has been pleading for a decentralised economy not only because it would be democratic, but also because it would bring immediate benefit to the masses by offering employment on a mass scale and producing wealth in a manner that would ensure its wide distribution and make 'wage goods' immediately available to ordinary consumers.

During 1974-79, when JP constantly used the term 'Total Revolution', he made only two or three important additions to the picture drawn above. In the first place he again and again stressed that along with a change in the political and economic systems, there was need also for a radical transformation of the social customs and institutions. In particular, he pleaded for the abolition of the caste system and the practice of dowry at the time of marriage. The other important point stressed by him was the need for a radical transformation of the educational system by including the mass of the people within its scope and relating it to the real needs of the people, particularly those living in the rural areas. He also stressed the need for a cultural revolution to bring about a change in the lifestyle of the people.

JP also made an important clarification during these years. When he had pleaded in 1959 for the abolition of the party system and the replacement of parliamentary democracy by partyless democracy, many thought that he wanted the immediate end of the former. When he began to lead the students' movement in Bihar and to talk of Total Revolution in 1974 many again thought that his immediate objective was the establishment of a partyless democracy. It is against this background hat he clarified that when he talked of Total Revolution he realised that all the ingredients of its programme could not be implemented immediately. The establishment of a partyless democracy was far away in the future and the Bihar Movement had nothing to do with it.[37] Actually JP went even further and in order to meet the situation created by the emergency himself inspired the formation of a political party – the Janata Party – and actively canvassed for it in the general elections of 1977, without actually joining it.

Finally, JP took pains to stress that the goals of Total Revolution, as also its form and programme, would go on changing with the change of times. Certain tasks may appear urgent at a given time. But after they are accomplished new tasks are likely to emerge and the votaries of Total Revolution will have to attend to them. As he put it in 1976: "Total Revolution is permanent revolution. It will always go on and keep on changing both our personal and social lives. This revolution knows no respite, no halt, certainly not a complete halt".[38]

VII

To sum up, the concept of Total Revolution has had both Marxist and Gandhian origins and is indeed as old as the concept of a social revolution. For the latter is always expected to be total, touching all aspect of life. However, it is a fact that it is JP's use of this term which has made it a part of the Indian political terminology. Besides, he had his own distinct concept of Total Revolution, including both its methodology and content, the basic elements of which have been noted earlier. JP developed his concept of Total Revolution on the basis of a synthesis not merely of the Marxist and Gandhian concepts of social revolution but also of the principles of Western Democracy. For he was very keen to see that the struggle for Total Revolution should not in any way impair the working of the democratic institutions in the country. He had, of course, his own concept of democracy and preferred what he termed as communitarian or partyless democracy. But he realised that was only a distant goal and an abrupt transition to it was neither feasible nor desirable. As with partyless democracy so with several other goals of Total Revolution, like the abolition of the caste system or the end of all exploitation of the weaker sections by the stronger sections of society, the struggle for Total Revolution is bound to be a very long one. The final end may never be achieved. Indeed, there is nothing like a final end. For Total Revolution of JP's conception is a permanent revolution and is expected to move on towards higher and higher goals.

It may be freely admitted that there is a good deal of the element of utopia in these goals. But that is true of the ideals placed before humanity by all great revolutionaries and path finders. If partyless democracy seems utopian, can anything different be said about the Stateless society which was the ideal of both Marx and Gandhi? As the latter used to say there is no harm, but every good in an ideal being idealistic. For in trying to reach that ideal humanity is likely to come nearer and nearer to it without ever completing the journey. The same may be said about JP's concept of Total Revolution. In spite of being partly utopian it is full of constructive and practical guidelines for making our society much more democratic and just than it is at present. Thus, for instance, although political parties cannot be wished away in a democracy, it will be all to the good if they are not influenced by partisan considerations all the time and show their willingness to work together in dealing with some of the urgent problems facing the country. Moreover, if democracy is to be really valued by the people, it is necessary for them to have a hand in selecting the candidates for elections and not merely in voting for them. The present situation in our country in which the candidates even for state legislatures are selected by the central leaderships of the various parties is quite unsatisfactory and cannot be called democratic. If the people have some day to be given a hand in selecting the candidates for election, the method suggested for this purpose by JP in *Swaraj for the People* will be found extremely useful. Besides, the foundations of democracy will become much stronger that at present if, through political and economic decentralisation, on the lines suggested by JP, the masses are given an opportunity to manage their affairs themselves through the *Panchayati Raj* institutions and thus help transform our present representative democracy into a participatory one. It will also help if the political parties keep themselves away from the *Panchayati Raj* institutions and allow the people to hold sway in them. Again, while our economic system must continue to nurture a sufficiently strong base of heavy industries – an essential requirement of modern times – there is an undoubted need to lay much greater emphasis than heretofore on the small machines and the programme of rural industrialisation, both for removing unemployment and for fostering balanced development. The same may be said about JP's emphasis on ending some of our outdated and ruinous social customs and overhauling our educational system, with a view to founding a new social order based on freedom, equality and human fellowship.

NOTES

1. K. Marx, F. Engels and V. Lenin, *On Historical Materialism* (Moscow, 1972), p. 83.
2. For a synoptic view see B.N. Ganguli. *Gandhi's Social Philosophy* (Delhi, 1973), pp. 145-261.
3. Vishwanath Tandon, ed., *Selection from Vinoba* (Varanasi, 1981), p. 91.
4. Suresh Ram, ed., *Towards Total Revolution* (Thanjavur, 1968).
5. Jayaprakash Narayan, *Towards Total Revolution,* Brahmanand, ed., IV (Bombay, 1978), p. 115.
6. Geoffrey Ostergaard, *Non-Violent Revolution in India* (New Delhi, 1985), p. 207.
7. Ibid., p. 404.
8. Bimal Prasad, ed., *A Revolutionary's Quest; Selected Writings of Jayaprakash Narayan* (New Delhi, 1980), pp. 115-18.
9. *The Times* (London), October 13, 1969.
10. Jayaprakash Narayan, *Prison Diary* (Bombay, 1977), pp. 31-34.
11. Prasad, No. 8, pp. 285-86.
12. Ibid., p. 290.
13. Ibid., p. 294.
14. Ibid.
15. Ibid., p. 295.
16. Narayan, No. 10, p. 33.

17. Ibid., p. 21.
18. Failure to notice this has led a sympathetic critic to stress that JP' concept of Total Revolution, unlike Gandhi's vision of gradual social change, runs counter to the principle and practices of democracy. See Amritananda Das, "Democracy and Revolution: JP's Synthesis" in S. Das Gupta, ed., *Total Revolution: A Symposium* (Calcutta, 1978), pp. 68-84.
19. Narayan, No. 10, p. 21.
20. Tandon, No. 3, p. 91.
21. Ostergaard, No. 6, p. 389. See also *People's Action,* June 1973.
22. See Geoffrey Ostergaard, "Vinoba's 'Gradualist' Versus Western 'Immediatist' Anarchism" in R.R. Divakar and Mahendra Agrawal, eds., *Vinoba. The Spiritual Revolutionary* (New Delhi, 1984), pp. 94-95.
23. See Tandon, No. 3, p. 95.
24. Cited in Ostergaard, No. 6, p. 63.
25. Prasad, No. 8, p. 388.
26. *Gandhi Marg* (Hindi), April 1978, translation by S.R. Gupta.
27. See Tandon, No. 3, p. 101.
28. *Young India,* 30 January 1930. The word 'not' is missing in the first sentence cited above both here and in *The Collected Works of Mahatma Gandhi,* XLII (New Delhi, 1972), p. 436. However if seen in conjunction with the second sentence cited above, which follows the first in the same para, it should be clear that it is a printing error.
29. Raghavan N. Aiyar, *The Moral and Political Thought of Mahatma Gandhi* (Oxford, 1973), p. 321. See also Buddhadeva Bhattacharya, *Evolution of the Political Philosophy of Gandhi* (Calcutta, 1969), pp. 340-41.
30. *The Collected Works of Mahatma Gandhi,* LXXXVIII (New Delhi, 1971), p. 16.
31. Ibid., XLV (New Delhi, 1971), p. 16.
32. See Nirmal Kumar Bose, *Studies in Gandhism* (Culcutta, 1962), p. 50-51.

33. Narayan, No. 10, p. 87.
34. For texts see Prasad, No. 8, pp. 209-71.
35. See Narayan, No. 10, pp. 61-64; 88; 95-96.
36. See Prasad, No. 8, p. 396.
37. Ibid., p. 338.
38. Ibid., p. 369.

15

JP—A Practical Idealist

Ramjee Singh

JP has been widely respected but often misunderstood. Some of us feel that he was simply a dreamer of dreams, while to the less sympathetic, his is a career of "Missed Opportunities" and his Gandhian–Bhoodan Mission is mostly an escape from active politics. These are also those critics who do not hesitate to brand him as political opportunist and too much vacillating in his ideological framework and action-strategy. He is said to have change his horses too often in a most unpredictable manner.

Taking his whole life into consideration, he can be at least called a visionary or idealist but not an utopian. He was, no doubt a saint among politicians scrupulously following the path of "Goodness Politics" akin to the Gandhian concept of "Spiritualisation of Politics". For JP politics has never been an untouchable thing as it was also not to Gandhi, because "Politics is the coil of a snake which he cannot escape therefore he must wrestle with it." JP like Gandhi, Vinoba and M.N. Roy did believe in partyless democracy but he did not overlook the transitional steps in strengthening the parliamentary democracy including "Opposition Unity" or openly, fighting emergency and personal dictatorship. Hence he was both a saint and a warrior, a Moralist as well as a Realist. Like wordsworth's skylark. JP was true to the kindred points of heaven and home. He was, a master of ideas as well as a man of mission. Apart from his refreshing ideas and action, he had introduced a third dimension-motivation and inspiration into his strategy of social action which made him a hero for all times. He never lived in the past but in the present as well as in the future through his prospectival vision and world-view. Hence we find him a romantic Robinhood during the Freedom Struggle as well a charismatic hero at his advance age of 74 years during Bihar Movement in 1974-75. Even during Bhoodan Movement under Acharya Vinoba Bhave, JP struggled like a legendary Abhimanyu taking all his political ambitions by offering the supreme gift of his whole life of dedication called Jeevandan. This was heroism par excellence. Thus he galvanised very dimension of this social and political enterprises, whether it was his Kisan struggle or his All India Labour Movements, Grass root Panchayat Democracy, or interlocking voluntary organisations (AVARD), his peace missions in Nagaland, Kashmir and elsewhere. He worked like angel during communal carnages in Jamshedpur, Rourkela, Ranchi, Ahmedabad etc. He could not remain a silent spectator during liberation movement of Goa or Bangladesh. Tibet, Czechoslovakia or Hungary. He was versatile and a social scientist genius and a sophisticated intellectual but he was not an arm-chair drawing-room-politician. His nature was such that he never shirked to take risks or accept challenges with the greater humility and sincerity of which he was capable of whether it was during chivalrous escape from prisons from Nepal and Hazaribagh during Freedom Struggle, Naxal threat to the lives of his humble Sarvodaya workers in Muzaffurpur. Infact he was more an inspirer like Sardar Bhagat Singh, Netaji Subhas Chandra Bose rather than a professional politician or stateman. Hence we recognise JP not only as a hero of the past but a *hero-eternal.* JP and heroism sound like identical terms. This was indeed his Gandhian cum revolutionary legacy. His was a life of long and continuous fight against injustices. Had he been alive today, JP would not have remained an onlooker to the engulfing corruption, collapse of civil society and worst criminalisation of politics. These revolutionary adventures were not a gift given to JP by anyone, it was in-built in his being. Hence his contribution is not only intellectual and actional but also emotional.

For the constraint of time and space, I wish to analyse the niche of his instrument of social change through youth-power about which he has written in his Prison Diary known as his *last testament*. JP was a great inspirer of youth and he was convinced that for a total revolution, it is the power of youth which can bring tangible results. He visualised a prophetic vital urgency in youth power without which we cannot achieve revolutionary change bereft of vested interest. Revolution needs asceticism and no vested interests. JP had tried and tested all agencies for social change. He had launched a new political forum and latter a new political party called Socialist Party to achieve social and economic justice and take the place of the Congress Party, which had almost completed its historical role of providing a common platform for freedom movement. Even Gandhi is his last testament had asked the Indian National Congress to wind it up so that when India gets Freedom, people should choose its own political framework for the reconstruction of the nation. During 1952 general election, JP's Socialist Party appeared like the most viable alternative to the Congress. But after the great debacle in the election, JP had a taste of the same moral degeneration, unhealthy cut throat competition and lack of missionary zeal in politics. All these are cross materialism which can offer no incentive to goodness. To him politics without morality was a death trap and it cannot yield any real revolution. Besides, the parliamentary politics is rooted in a structure, which has its own limitations. A party looks to a part of society only hence it cannot do justice to the whole society. The western democracy based on the Westminster model is only so called. It is diluted Fascism and Nazism. Party bosses and caucuses usurp the power of the ordinary party members and rule through forming cliques and groups.

All decision making jobs are in the hands of only a small party oligarchy who select candidates for election, provide funds, create groups, distribute rewards and spoil. Hence the representative democracy of today is neither representative in character or in functioning. There is no participatory and no grass-root democracy. Hence parliamentary democracy ceases to be "of the people" or "by the people" and hence it can never work "for the people". It is not "People's democracy" which JP had in mind. It falls short of its Jeffersonian-Linconian ideal but as an instrument of making a people's republic and degenerate into a craftsmanship of power politics based on materialistic consideration of self interest, Hence, this is most deficient in its structure.

Party system tends to turn the whole political system as anti-people as well as anti-democratic. Hence, JP left traditional politics of power and party and instead tried to develop people's politics through grass-root work. He tried his best to set up a communitarian non-party village government in Musahari block in Muzaffarpur. Like a true social scientist, JP had his mind open about the Gramdan republics and he tried his best to find out its potentiality for a new dispensation. But he could not find adequate response and dynamism in Gramdan experiment too. The Bhoodan-Gramdan movement also suffered from some organisational and structural defects. There was an ugly pressure to complete the target of gramdan villages resulting in a mega hoax of Bihardan. This was anti climax. Had Gramdan experiment been executed in a scientific, systematic and dynamic manner, perhaps it would have yielded some tangible results. But Vinobaji being the Field-Marshall of Bhoodan-Gramdan movement, JP could neither openly disassociate with it nor conceal his disillusionment and reservations in pathway of real social revolution. He was always in search of a tool or agent which could further this cause. Earlier he had tried Kisan Movements and fought with feudal and conservative power. But it was not enough for an upheaval in whole society. Similarly, he tried to organise the labour-force and was president of such powerful associations like the Railway Men's Federation. All India Post and Telegraph Employees Union, All India Dock Workers Union, but JP discovered a serious moral flaw in these organisations. They had, no doubt the zeal for struggle against their employers and a militant fighting spirit but they became more interested in their pay, pension, promotions and perks rather than ushering the total revolution. They themselves are in the habit of developing their vested interests. For example, the three-day total bundh call given by JP during crucial struggle of Bihar Movement, he was disillusioned to find that the industrial workers in Bihar could not try to go for even a one day sympathetic bundh at their own place, where as youth in Bihar gave up their studies, examinations, carreer-courses etc to make the call a complete success.

All these evidences led JP to think that the youth force is the most appropriate and effective revolutionary instrument of change. There are both psychological and sociological reasons for this inherent revolutionary urge in the youth power for ushering total revolution. The reasons are as follows :—

Firstly, the youth power has the least vested interest both structurally as well as emotionally. They do not have any pay, promotion or pension interests. Then the youth power has an additional advantage of having the surplus energy also. They have both desire and energy to work day and night for any social-political upheaval. A grown up or an elderly man with settled life needs comforts leisure and rest but the youth because of their inherent surplus energy can work with greater gusto and strength. A revolutionary situation does need greater time, energy and speed of action. Revolutionary work demands a madness, an untiring effort, for which the youth-power is greatly inclined. A youth is generally a dynamo of energy.

They are more free agents of social changes. A Government employee or factory servant, an officer or a teacher, a doctor or a businessman has liabilities enough which find them to their vested interests but students and youth have no specific responsibility to take care of except their studies and future career about which only an uncertainty looms large.

So, the youth power can shoulder more risks. Any person with a job or business will think thrice in order to plunge into the vertex of revolutionary movement because he has to loose them but the youth has no such mental constraints except a distant one. So he can take greater risks and adventure. By nature youth-power is sensitive and also romantic. Revolution demands sensitivity to the suffering of the people. Those who do not posses a kind and sensitive heart cannot be a sincers partner in the people of social revolution.

The suitability of youth power for being a favourable agent of a major social change is also due to the fact that even numerically they form a big chunk of society. If any problem catches their attention, they can mobilise a greater number of their friends and comrades. From the age group of 12 to 40 years, the youth force form the most formidable wand wagon of social change. Besides they can mobilise the other sections of society, with the result that they have the capacity to shake up the entire social fabric.

History also provides the evidences that the youth power when arises and awakes, humbles the mightiest politicians and power brokers on the earth. Greatest rulers of our time like General De Gaulle, Ayub Khan, Sukarno and Indira Gandhi were humbled when the students and youth power became the vanguard of the revolutionary change. Even in India during 1942, it was the youth force which kept the flame of Quit India Movement burning when all the elderly leaders were put behind the prison bars. Even during the Bihar Movement of 1974-75, it was the youth power which worked predominantly as its vanguard.

Besides we can attribute a spiritual factor also for the greater suitability of youth force for being the true agent of revolution. It is generally believed that the young mind is generally free from all prejudices and evil thoughts. Child is supposed to be nearer to God so youth power is likely to have more purity, and stronger moral fibre than the grown up people who develop many complexes and vested interests.

Considering the above socio-psychological and spiritual factors in favour of the youth power, JP in his quest of real revolutionary agent, started his programme of "Youth against Democracy" much before the Bihar Movement. Perhaps he was visualising the perils on Indian democracy due to the growing authoritarian tendencies in the ruling party under the Titan–Indira Gandhi. There was no intra party democracy left and there was no scope for dissent. On the other hand, the opposition parties were not also divided and discredited. The people in general had become almost disinterested and inactive. Such a situation was dangerous for the functioning of a democratic system. So JP thought to go to the students and youth around the country to guard against the erosion of democracy. JP could not compromise with individual freedom for anything else. Individual was the supreme consideration. JP wanted to usher a revolution of man. For this, he chose the power of youth, which was the appropriate instrument of change. So in his last testment, JP expresses his last wish that if the manifold obstacles in the path of the progress of youth are somewhat removed, he will be quite satisfied in his mission of life.

16

Marx, Gandhi and JP

K.K. Sinha

Taking that JP Movement or the Bihar Andolan of 1974 (named Total Revolution-a Gandhian variant) was for recall of the rulers in government and dissolution of the legislature, the struggle aimed at reasserting people's power against the increasing coercive power of the Indian state only after 25 years of freedom. State power should have given way to people's power, so that the state withered away and social changes took a leap in society of common people. This was what Marx and Gandhi too visualised. In this sense, the element of struggle of Gandhi and Marx or JP had a close semblance. What unites Gandhian System with the Marxian is, more than anything else, the eventual 'withering away of the state' in the so called, synthesis phase.

But in Russia this never happened though the class struggle under Lenin seized power in favour of the worker's party, the Bolshevics. The principle of recall was laid down by the Bolshevics themselves to assure leader's agreement to his subordination to people. Actually what happened in Russia after the 1917 revolt was a re-establishment of a still ruthless government and a dictatorship of the proletariat. Gandhi was very critical of almost similar political changes in India, which changed the spirit of the Freedom Struggle to centralised power with the new rulers. The European anarchists who stood close to Marx always forewarned that a struggle for change must lead to "all power to the communes or the local soviets". Power with the state tends to grow and get corrupt, making the rulers a class in themselves. JP's Total Revolution was an effort to overthrow an oppressive rule in the same sense.

The Common Elements of the Class Struggle

To say that changing an oppressive government was not the basic purpose of Total Revolution is to deny the essence of social change implicit in it. Both, Marx and Gandhi alike, had an aversion to an all-powerful state, democratic or oligarchic. To both, a multiparty parliament looked like "a sterile woman and a prostitute" as it was always under outside pressure and changing loyalties with powerful parties. The individual members have "neither real honesty nor a living conscience"[1] Gandhi found that it was a seat of self-interest in which the wealthy and powerful enjoyed all the privileges and supported status quo in the name of justice and neutrality. But Gandhi was not in favour of a single party rule of the proletariat either. His choice in the so-called synthesis phase of Marx was a Ram Rajya where a moral quality and habitual adherence of Truth always expressed the collective will.[2] This is not any one-man or one-party rule but a state of enlightened anarchy in which each person will become his own ruler, without hampering the well-being of his neighbours. This is actually the withering away of the state with no political institutions and no political power.[3] JP also felt that if state grows and strengthens itself, people lose, and so a constant struggle is needed to keep the powers of the state in check.

Marx thought of a commune pattern (later developing as Paris Commune, 1871) of local self-government after the capitalist state machinery was smashed. But the Marxists missed the point that setting an interim dictatorship of the proletarian state with a vanguard Party and armed workers would not promote the communes but swallow them. They misconceived that in the early phase of change, the birth pangs of a bourgeois society required some rules of law to enforce a change. It is true that by scrapping private rights of property a socialist equality of wealth was assured and could help the growth of a decentralised society. But for a communist equality, Marx felt that everybody must get according to his need and everybody must work according to ability. So it was thought that such system would come only through gradual reforms so that the government of persons would be replaced by administration of things at the local levels. The Marxists felt that this required an interim dictatorship of the proletariat to make public use of the capital so appropriated and to intervene ordinary market payments and earnings for the ultimate goal. The class view of factory owner versus workers would disappear under a proletarian state so that the communes would run and administer freely in due course with no class remaining to oppress. The disappearance of the state was thus notional rather than actual, dying out a natural death when time was ripe.

But here the dictatorship of the proletariat set up after a violent struggle created inbuilt seats of power which was strengthened by state planning. The insistence on large scale investment of the vast amount of capital seized overnight would only make state enter the shoes of the private capitalists. It was almost a reversion back to the Adam Smith's economics, of course with the additional advantage of controlled market, administered prices and restricted consumption. This was sure to lead to an empire building, like capitalism, but in a state garb. It became a prerogative of the state to nationalise and use the resources for rapid industrialisation. This entailed strict restrictions on consumption. To some, it was this Stalinist state in Russia following Lenin that caused the eventual failure of Russian communism. And the dictating state could have never wither away in favour of administration by the local communes or soviets.[4]

There was a big debate among the Marxists on this part of Marxian theory during the 1870s, just as was the Cultural Revolution debate in China during the 1970s. Lenin felt that withering away of the state had to be gradual, but the Anarchists (viz. Bukanin) felt that creation of worker's communes meant instant abolition of the state. Lenin differed from this because it repudiated politics of the central power and arming of the communes to pursue the central policies. The anarchists wanted autonomy to the communes, and no authority as the Marxists felt. It was this difference which made local councils quite easy and natural in the anarchist system but impossible in the Marxist.

Lenin refuted the social democrats (viz. Bernstein) too; who developed the idea of a federal parliament and adult franchise with a network of communes as participatory democracy. Lenin found these authors as renegades and opportunists, who were undermining Marx's concept of revolution. To him the concept of a democratic state was unscientific, which would be a tool of subjugation of the minority over the majority. Further, democracy as a right of self-determination was impossible under capitalism and superfluous under socialism.[5] Democracy was a superstitious reverence for the state and its lucratively positioned officials[6] which rids the people from monarchy. Lenin was thus making a case for a wider, free and more open form of the class struggle to continue till the communes settled into administrative units. The state and democracy both withered away in the eventual era of peace or what is known as communism.

The fragile part of this concept of democracy was that it was treated redundant in socialism and oppressive in capitalism, i.e. instrument of oppression of one class on the other.[7] The concept implied that the early communes would be only what capitalism gave birth and would mature into complete democracy only after a longer period. "The more complete it is, the sooner state will become unnecessary and wither away of its own accord."[8]

In the Gandhian system, what withers away is the state, but not democracy, which exists with least governance and as democracy of the people. Marx also meant the same. In The Economic and Philosophical Manuscripts, which Marx wrote in 1844, though published late, he had pronounced aversion to anything which impaired man's liberty and this spirit was represented better by the humanist Shekharov, who had to leave Russia for his political opinion, than Andropov who occupied the seat of power in Russia.[9] Marx was a Hegelian in his book Grundrisse or Outline of National Economy as translated in English in 1930s. Alienation and not exploitation was the central theme here, and alienation talked of many classes, each alienating the other. What was now missing in later Marx and Engels was a theory of Mediation to show how to move from an abstract to the concrete lives of individuals.

But in the later Marxian system democracy remained only as a natural history of development of a proletarian society and not a maturing of a capitalist society. Gandhian people's democracy had to accept a capitalist and feudal base as remnants of the past and improve on it with rigour. It has its strict resemblance with the anarchist order of cooperatives and communes. When panchayats take control of administration, the higher circles, risen out of the panchayat wave or circle would represent the poor and not the rich. And such panchayats cannot be anything but proletarian with land and small industries as their communitarian base.

The skepticism of Gandhi about a parliamentary socialist democracy was almost Marxian. The popularity of the political groups involved in the Freedom Struggle in India made them powerful vote-catchers entering into the shoes of the former despotic rulers. Gandhi had visualised this when he said that there could be English rule without the English man and state capitalism, without the capitalists, Gandhi's choice for village republic was therefore against a capitalist democracy.

But what made Gandhi differ from Marx was that he was not in favour of a proletarian dictatorship either.

The State Never Withers Away!

What makes the state not committed to its own destruction is the easy and natural greed for power. Even if private property is appropriated by revolution, the political instruments of the revolution establish their own authority to property and a faith system blindly tied to the new set up. Thus property and religious faith reappear in a state garb. The issues of social equality as conceived by Marx also tended to retain the state, since, if left on natural order and market, it would become impossible and with a statist order, it necessitated an all-powerful state to enforce it.

The problems in non-communist states, where private property is allowed, remain almost similar. Any struggle for change, changes only the government and not the vested interest of property which captures the state. Naturally the state reappears to counter the change and maintain a status quo. The rigour for bringing about even basic equality between unequal people loses its tooth. Gandhi and JP therefore looked for a state which was least governed and which devolved its powers to people organised in small neighbourhoods and derived its powers from those organisations themselves. It is not that there was no state in this system but surely the state had no special privileges apart from what people wanted them to have. This in a sense meant a withering away of state and its commitment to sacrifice its powers to the local organisation of people.

It may be noted here that both, Russian and Indian revolutions for change in the system for an egalitarian goal, succeeded in changing governments but there were no signs of withering away of the state. In Russia there was continuance of a "barrack socialism" (Kautsky) and barbaric and "an atavism belonging to lower culture and civilisation" (Bernstein)[10] The soft state in India also gained strength after the Freedom through state corruption and state crimes.

In sum, the two systems, Gandhian and Marxian, rejected the role of state in their preference to local councils but were not rid of it. Gandhi wanted that democracy could evolve itself out of the local republics as an inverted pyramid or power at the bottom. Marx thought of an intermittent state committed to its destruction in due course. But both these concepts did not materials and have failed in their ultimate aim of raising a local people's base against a nation-state. They failed not in their struggle phase but in the phase of synthesis or reconstruction. It is being lately realised that the cause for failure in both cases has been the over-stress on power politics and under-stress on decentralised development of the society.

Reconstruction Aspect of JP Movement

For establishing a people's socialism at the grassroots, JP had taken the thread of a communitarian system from Gandhi for the constructional phase of Total Revolution. Marxian dictatorship was too strong and the Gandhian choice for building up from below was too feeble a concept for the eventual withering away of the state. It was this situation which prompted JP to a movement for systemic change in society, which naturally included change of government as well as a rebuilding of people's power at the grassroots.

This naturally meant an overall change of social relations and systems. JP thought a double pronged attack on the system, one on the state and the other on the iniquitous social relations. It became a movement with struggle and peaceful change or reconstruction. Gandhi's satyagarh was nothing less than a struggle but it had become blunted by the later Gandhians. JP sharpened it, accepting class struggle between the weak and strong, which can be said to be a Marxian effect on him. The ultimate aim here also was the building from below, again as Gandhian or Marxian as it could be. Unfortunately both had failed in achieving it, former due to ignoring class struggle and the latter, due to its statist stance.

In fact Gandhi did want a movement to continue for detracting people from private ownership of property specially in matter of land relations. A land socialism could build up local societies into homogeneous group at decentralised neighbourhoods. This was more strategic than the violent struggle and nationalisation of land by the decree of the state. Unfortunately the Gandhian land socialism could not come forth, as land ownership had become sticky. Vinoba's Bhoodan lost its teeth soon on that account. Gandhi had such apprehensions. He once remarked that :—

"If I thought class conflict inevitable, I should not hesitate to preach and teach Marxism".[11]

This only signifies that Gandhi did not like the process of change to be slow and statist. Similarly, Marx also felt that class violence could not be protracted indefinitely. Both seem to believe, however, that the growth of consciousness or change of heart alone could decide the speed of change. To quote Lenin,

"We set ourselves the ultimate aim of abolishing the state, i.e. all organised and systematic violence against people in general... In striving for socialism, however, we are convinced that it would develop into communism... since people will become accustomed to observing the elementary conditions of social life without violence and without subordination". (Lenin, op cit., p. 79).

But there remained in Marxism a vagueness in dating such process," as there is no material for answering these questions".[12] We do not, and cannot know when the higher phase of communist society could be attained, since basic equality (from each according to his ability and to each according to his needs) is utopian. Lenin finds that this depended on the "level of technique" and development of productive forces of human society[13] Gandhi felt that it depended on empowerment of villages themselves, since the village units were more likely to have a proletarian culture. It appears here that Lenin was denying the non-violent Gandhian situation to usher in just after empowerment, and Gandhi denied the need of force after such empowerment. In Hegelian terms Gandhian dialectics was idealist, Lenin's materialist. But the challenge to both remained oriented to a changed society free of violence. Not ignoring the Gandhian maxim of non-violence and the Marxian radical elements of struggle as a class issue, JP's Total Revolution brought the two systems closer, what in spirit was actually a pacifist Anarchism.

Now, when the communist countries had reverted back to the market mechanism with sufficient element of private capital in their productive system, the need based equality of communism loses ground. In a market system the emerging problem to both of the systems, socialist and capitalist, would be the emergence of sub-national identities in many countries due to the growth of multi-national companies. It would transcend the boundaries of nation-states and keep the interest of the shareholders above every thing, giving a challenge to both the systems alike.

The futility of centralisation of power in a nation, which consists of a number of sub-nationalities, has to be directed to minimum power at the centre and maximum at the decentralised units of small people. Thus there is a unity of purpose in the systems, Gandhian and Marxian, i.e. the reconstruction of society at the bottom as self-reliant and classless units of administration. This alone can be a necessary safeguard for people from the onslaught of growing imperialism and state power. The alternative would be wars as Lenin theorised in terms of the decaying phase of monopoly capitalism. But it was true to state monopolies too, what made Mao Tse Tung hostile to Russian imperialism.

What is needed now was a democratic state and a socialist society as a synthesis of Gandhi and Marx. (Rammurti). This will be a guarantee against political power becoming oppressive and against inequality of status and capabilities in society growing wild. What would prevent such reconstruction seems to be the possible growth of state power on the one hand and the rise of multinational companies on the other. Both are inimical to the growth of peripheries and small societies. A lot of experiments is needed now in place of dogmas and faith attached to Gandhi and Marx. Some authors feels that fixed notions tended to grow due to the charisma attached to these great thinkers and people liked to depend upon a frontline leadership opposed to each other (P.H. Prasad). Now, with new quest for suitable paradigms for development, a lot of information and feed backs may be available in light of new spread of information technology (Siddharthan). This may be a safeguard against the mere faith systems and dogmatism implicit in both the systems in small and poor societies.[14]

The restoration of people's power would depend on the empowerment of small village units in Gandhian system and the devolution of state power to the local councils or communes in the Marxian system. It is therefore contended that the two systems could converge to give out a system where poverty could be taken as a systemic feature of development, and villages as the new organisations of systemic change. This may allow a democratic state with minimal functions. This would be a land socialism and a dualistic development, not as a trickle down but as a trickle up from the bottom.[15]

The question of Gandhian notion of Trusteeship was superfluously taken up by those who thought of development of capital sectors.[16] It was a milder equalitarian norm and Gandhi himself felt that it has yet to prove its worth.[17] But for village economy this concept grew strong in the face of the Bhoodan Movement. It is where the total revolution of JP gained ground and momentum.

What is doubted is the Marxian stress on arming the local units in the intermittent period,[18] just on the ground that, without it, the local units will not attain the authority to administer due to the feudal or bourgeois forces lurking around even after being vanquished. But the Freedom Struggle in India was overall a non-violent process and took a long period of 100 years to change the alien rulers. Some extra time could be worth allowing to avoid violence. But the delay in changing over to local councils after changing the government was due to power-seeking politicians. Even those in struggle seek a reward in power after the struggle was over. JP therefore schemed the Total Revolution as a second struggle of freedom after Gandhi's, and wanted it as a permanent feature of struggle, since whenever the state rebuilds itself, it has to be resisted again and again. Thus this experiment hits at a chronic feature of state power.

The British oppression was more overt and hence the resistance to it gathered strength, but democratic governments after freedom, based as they were on elections, got so cunning and strong that people become defunct and least organised to win the battle against their own governments. The village society soon became accustomed to a status quo and were completely shattered and broken. This further weakened a people's movement. Even the Maoist strategy of change through arms failed in Indian villages as the hardened leaders would not get the needed support of the poor, generally a peaceful and mute rural folk. Now conceiving a process of violent struggle could only be sporadic as the Naxal violence is. It seems alien in origin with borrowed slogans of alien situations.

The Total Revolution of the JP variety could still hope to sustain itself as a "positive anarchism", which should continue and would never die out. But the base of it had to shift to villages where the pangs of poverty would keep the fire of revolt burning. There will always be a proletarian work culture. This was to be bought in action by a double pronged pressure, one by the suffering masses and the other by youth and intelligentsia. This resembled the mixing up of different classes into one in the Marxian system, as JP visualised it.

Lenin felt that religion would mar the spirit of forcing a change, while non-partisan politics in small communities will become toothless to effect autonomy.[19] Here Gandhian norms seems to have been refuted only for the fear that they would renounce the spirit of struggle and stupefy the people.[20] But after a long period of suppression of the village folk in India the rising expectations of the village people seems to be high, as indicated by coming up of the village elite in many villages. Further, religion in the Gandhian sense means service to people and not any superstition of the primitive society. Thus the two systems can now easily reconcile on the issue of devolution of the state power to local bodies, what Total Revolution carries as a cultural revolution or an education to transform religion into spiritual strength.

Villages as the Vanguard of Systemic Change

The question is-will people's movement sustain itself? In the context of new situation of the colonial group of countries, a peaceful class struggle makes out a case for a rural mobilisation under a panchayati system of neighbours. This is plausible because poverty is a rural syndrome and urban poverty is only a reflex of rural poverty due to rural spillover and evacuation. Even those settled in towns and its slums or dirty surroundings are actually village dwellers with nothing in towns except beggary, illegal activities or very low paid jobs like hawking and rickshaw pulling. Villages are characterised by their remoteness from the urban nodal points of growth. Such growth has an in-built quality of impoverishing the villages by over-concentration in cities due to various spread factors including infrastructure and social amenities like education and health. The trickle down theory of economics recently floated seems to be falsified, as nothing trickles out the rich centers of growth except some doles or low paid jobs in towns. Even the political set up shifts to the towns with no social workers left in villages. This caused the migration to, and slum dwelling in, towns and a backwash in villages.

In fact this happened even in Europe by 1850, which witnessed growing mass poverty and extreme uneven distribution of wealth causing a drift from villages to cities with uncertain business, though production rose with cities. This was due to the profit culture of these countries and it is why the classical logistics explained production assuming away any mal-distribution and exploitation of workers. In fact what explained wealth was not sufficient to explain poverty and this led to the emergence of Marx. In a more developed stage of capitalism after the World War, the issue of wider poverty at mass scale in the colonies went beyond the classical and even the Marxian range and this led to the emergence of Gandhi.

Thus, poverty issue has to be taken as a micro problem of colonial states with little semblance with the industrial west. This had remained a case of neglect under a bourgeois democracy with no proletarian local councils (in the Marxian sense) but only subordination of a political minority over the majority. It is worth pondering whether reconstruction of panchayats will need the Marxist-Leninist route of vanguard party and violence or the intensive Gandhian resistance (Satyagrah and civil disobedience) by people at large.

Total Revolution of JP stressed at radicalising the Gandhian concept of villages and the poorest of the poor. The long struggle for freedom under Gandhi left out the issue of class relations of Indian rural economy. But after freedom this was to be main problem to solve. Of course, by organising the poor in villages, class-consciousness for the poor could create Satyagrahis for a cause. But the option for arming the village bodies would either be roped by the naxalites or lumpen elements. If panchayats and their gram sabhas are fully empowered to take up the work of reconstruction, it will make a real change at the bottom.

What is needed as an extension or second generation of Total Revolution is therefore a *panchayat movement*. The fight is again to be targeted against a power-corrupt state represented now by the landed middle class and the politically dominant caste groups, who will naturally be against the empowering of panchayats.

Chinese Cultural Revolution: Some Lessons

Chinese communism takes its birth in 1949, embarks upon the commune model with all round collectivisation by 1957 and fearing the bourgeois restoration (as the leadership end) declares a civil war in 1967, known as the Cultural Revolution. Thus it is thought that class struggle, as a part of communism has to continue indefinitely in a guerilla spirit, externally against imperialism and internally against the non-changers. The fear of opportunism and revisionism thus becomes an accepted part of the theory of dialectical materialism, which Lenin also conceded. Mao declared a civil war to check the going back from the path of struggle and make compromises. In China even those belonging to the anti-feudal liberation army seemed to detract. The first such class was the new managerial and administrative elite in large state farms who had elevated their cooperatives to a large-scale whole sale business. The second class was the petty bourgeois revolutionaries who "loved dragons but when a live dragon came down the road they ran away as fast as they could".[21] They went against feudal power but were engaged in capitalism. The third were the conscious revisionists and believers in Khrus-chev's theory of peaceful coexistence, peaceful competi-tion and peaceful transition, (i.e. the Shao Chi group). More rebellious were the vanquished landlords and the expropriated compradors and the underworld gangs and lumpen elements under them, who were supported from abroad, the imperial powers.

This development created a cultural crisis between experts versus revolutionaries. Thus "technique in command" challenged "politics in command", that is, a fight between those who preferred production and those who wanted self-reliance and driving the imperialists. This was the same Leninist apprehension, which had to be crushed ruthlessly. The Shao Chi group argued that "whether the cat is white or black makes no difference so long as it can catch mice." And the tree would prefer calm, but the wind refuses to subside-was what Mao preached to help the upsurge in the Third World and also within China against the Russian and American imperialists. The Chinese Cultural Revolution thus went to mobilise the left, win the middle and isolate the diehard, which meant uniting almost 95 percent of the masses. This was the theory behind the movement—"from the masses to the masses".

The way it was carried-may have some lessons for Indian politics but the political changeover in China later on gave a blow to the whole process of cultural revolution and to the effort of dictatorial leadership of brain washing through education and hero worship of the leader, when the successor of Mao snatched the mantle of leadership through a coup, and initiated liberalisation in 1979. (The pro-market new dawn was quite a different event from what the Naxalites dreamed about in their grim struggle in India.) Nevertheless, but for denial of democratic openness and freedom and excesses of Cultural Revolution in terms of human rights and one-child rule, the Chinese dialectics had prepared a redistributive ground work which gave great strength to the market system which followed.[22] Further, the stress of the revolution on village communes and "building on the worst" brought in the masses in the decision-making, and industries and education in rural areas became oriented to the disadvantaged. To quote —

"In many ways, Maoist ideology rejects the capitalist principle of building on the best...While capitalism strives one-sidedly for efficiency in producing good; Maoism in numerous ways builds on the worst. Experts are pushed aside in favour of decision-making by the masses; new industries are established in rural areas; expertise or work proficiency, in the narrow sense, is discouraged, new products are domestically produced rather than imported "more efficiently"; the growth of cities as centers of industrial and cultural life is discouraged; steel, for a time, is made by every one instead of by only the much more efficient steel industry". (John G. Gurley, 1971, Capitalist and Maoist Economic Development, Monthly Review, Feb. pp. 23-24).

This was a village fetish which is very much Gandhian. The rural education was made basic to the needs of rural production what the "Buniadi Talim" of Gandhi signified. The natural distaste for such education was however checked in China by promoting a cadre of workers with socialist consciousness and culture. Students were selected from among workers and peasants and should return to production after a few years of study. This was a way of Chinese resistance to imperialism and looks very much like the Swadeshi (use of home goods) movement of Gandhi and Chhatra Sangharsha Vahini of JP. But in absence of a revolution spirit in India after the JP Movement (1974-78) and little structural and proletarian changes in villages, the building from below could not become the engine of growth by its own.

Total Revolution: Some Lessons

It may however be interesting to treat Total Revolution as a similar Cultural Revolution in India under JP in 1974, almost coinciding with the Chinese Cultural Revolution. The purpose here also was to check the culture of political and social corruption, which was countering the immediate need for a pro-people change in the system. In China the movement was state sponsored and had the force of state resources, where as, in India, it was an anti-Congress (ruling party) upsurge at a mass scale. It was again 'from the masses to the masses' type of movement for egalitarian changes in the system with the Gandhian jolt.

The movement was able to pull down the government in power through a democratic voting method. The success of the movement was the polarisation of all political parties against the ruling party dictatorship. The 'total' in its connotation did mean the change in the cultural and political and socio-economic base but the strategy was first to change the government, (and not to maintain the government as in China). This made the difference between the two. In democracies the state must be prevented from being oppressive with a ruling party without a truly democratic intent. This became a protest of neutral (non-partisan) forces under JP who was a Bhoodan leader, and an outsider to state politics. The Chinese revolution was pro-poor but not pro-democracy. The JP revolution resulted in restoration of panchayats, a real participatory democracy with a vanguard party (Janata Party) "pledged" to the people, and in growth of numerous voluntary social organisations to take up the muddles of mis-education, corrupt elections an redistribution of land. The real question was-could changing a government bring about a systemic change? JP felt that "once the revolution of the day seize power, the people are inescapably subjugated to the juggernaut of the party and the state." JP was very skeptic about political parties, which must degenerate with power, and hence he wanted to create cadres of student workers to carry the struggle for change, as Gandhi wanted Sewa Dal in place of party workers.

This distinguished JP's revolution with Vinoba Bhave's Bhoodan Movement. Both were Gandhian variants, but JP wanted systemic changes first while Vinoba was for individuals to change first. JP therefore wanted a class struggle, of course, through Gandhian tools.[23] What worried JP was the slowness implicit in Bhoodan, and it was due to the lack of will at the state end and corruption all round. The only way was for the poor to organise themselves and protest through non-cooperation and civil disobedience, the Gandhian tools.

The movement gave a jolt to an unchanging system but it was only like "climbing a mountain" as JP said. In fact the spirit fizzled out in 5-6 years and a status quo was restored with little devolution of state power to the people. The utopia of a "total change" persisted but its burden went back to a power centred state. Of course there were now one lakh and odd voluntary organisations along with a few older Gandhian and religious organisations. They can be said to be the remnants of the Total Revolution. Many of them were funded from outside and some others grew non-functional over time. There were some constitutional enactments for reviving the village panchayats but it lacked the movement spirit.

JP however, had given some blue prints for a reconstruction of the polity long back. It was neither dictatorship of the proletariat nor the western parliaments with supremacy of party leaders. It was a decentralised polity what he called a communitarian democracy, not any commune models as strong party bases, but partyless local models with communitarian ownership of land and cultivation rights to the *kisans,* the tillers. The government at the centre, if created by the partyless local units would only be a partyless democracy, with parties remaining just as educative institutions and not centers of power.[24] But these thoughts were not the product of the revolution but its forerunner. The new government, which was the product of the movement, lost the spirit of change sooner than expected.

Thought the task of the revolution remains incomplete, this revolution for communitarian panchayats, as an alternative to the reappeared state power the ongoing Naxal movement got a firm base. But the dilemma of organising the poor still remains unresolved.[25] The social changes through Bhoodan seemed to usher in land socialism but the failure of Total Revolution could not push up the already slow going movement in land relations and rural organisations. The rural poverty has been increasing while there is an outflow of resources to the urban centers. This has been the main cause of the simmering discontent in villages and of urban-rural frictions with the seeming eclipse of Total Revolution.

The friction further increased after the spate of economic and market reforms of liberalisation and globalisation in the 1990s with its statist stance. This brings us to the crux of the problem of continuing poverty in villages and lack of proper organisation for the poor. Myrdal under similar situations talks about the movement of rising expectation as a non-Marxist strategy. This is very akin to Gandhian Satyagrah or a Total Revolution. Myrdal quotes Jan Tinbergen who recommended the Gandhian line of development based on simplicity and austerity.[26] This amounts to some village growth models with austerity of the rich class. This meant a social revolution in the weaker section (Antyodaya) and a psychological revolution in the elite. JP talks of a communitarian reconstruction in villages which would create a system of in-built growth among the self-governing society of neighbours and a changeover from private ownership to communitarian ownership, i.e. land to the village. Gandhi had talked about Trusteeship where the property owners treated themselves not as owners of the social surplus but as just its social trustees. This could still be the new rule for a land socialism allowing individuals the using rights on land but no ownership. All this requires a serious rethinking when poverty is taken as a Marxo-Gandhian debate, and local councils (panchayats), as the last hope.

Need for a Continuing Struggle Against State Power: Enlightened Anarchism

JP's object in converting Sarvodaya or the Bhoodan Movement into Total Revolution was actually prompted by slowness of the Gandhian changes, over-growth of state power and the rise of naxalism in villages with growing poverty and worsening class relations. In his "Face to Face", published in London in 1970, he seems to react against growing officialisation of panchayats and even of the Bhoodan Movement itself under a power-corrupt over-centralised state. It was during his stay in a village block Musahari that Total Revolution as a 'positive anarchism' was conceived. Though pacifist in content, it brought in class struggle of the weak against the powerful as a new Gandhian variant. JP had also conceived failure of all revolutions unless their post-struggle phase took up social reconstruction outside the corridors of state power. But for that it required a band of workers and pressure groups at local levels. The commitment to a communitarian order has however to be made the immediate concern, media and information groups in form of the vast voluntary organisations which have grown under the impact of Total Revolution. European anarchists could create the Paris Commune but succumbed to the rising systems of nation-states in Europe. The pressure of voluntarism in Indian situation however reassures the possibilities of gaining grounds for local institutions.

REFERENCES

Gandhi, Hind Swaraj, in Collected Works Vol. 10, Pub. Div., Govt. of India, pp. 17-8.

Collected Works, Vol. 35, pp. 489-90.

Gandhi, CW, Vol. 68, p. 265.

V.M. Tarkunde, 1992, Why Communism Failed in the Soviet Union, M.N. Roy Memorial Lecture, Indian Renaissance Instt., New Delhi.

Lenin, 1985, State and Revolution, Progress Pub. p. 75.

Ibid. p. 77.

Ibid. pp. 77-9.

Ibid. p. 85.

V.M. Tarkunde, op. cit.

Quoted, Sushila Ramaswamy, 1993, Theory of State-the Blind Spot in Marxism. Statesman, Delhi, 17 June.

V.B. Kher, ed. 1957, M.K. Gandhi, Economic & Industrial Life & Relations, Navjiwan, p. 74.

Lenin, op. cit. p. 92.

Ibid, p. 93.

For references, see, Rammurti, 1991, Marx & Gandhi; also P.H. Prasad, 1999, Marx and Gandhi; also K.K. Sinha, 1983, Marx and Social Change; a Crtique of Methodology, IEJ conf.; also P.C. Joshi, 1985, Gandhian economics today, IEJ, Dec. also N.S. Siddharthan, The Gandhian Thought and Information (Fourth Industrial) Revolution, Ibid. Also, K.K. Sinha, Nature and Significance of Gandhian Economics, Key Note, Bihar Economic Assoc., 1999, Conf., to be printed.

K.K. Sinha & Uma Sinha, 1985, Had Gandhi a Theory of Planning, IEJ, Dec.

Pradhan, op. cit. No. 18, p. 98.

Gandhi, Harijan, quoted V.B. Kher, ed. 1957, Economic and Industrial Life and Relations, p. 71.

Engels, quoted Lenin, State and Revolution, op. cit. p. 72.

Lenin, op. cit. p. 73.

Ibid.

Mao Tse Tung, quoted, Hinton, op. cit. p. 15.

Sen A., Econ. Dev. & Soc. Opportunity, op. cit. pp. 58, 65.

Bimal Prasad, ed. A Revolutionary's Quest. 1980, pp. 285-86, 339; also Bimal Prasad, 1991, JP Memorial Lecture, Mahila Charkha Samiti, Patna.

JP, 1959, A Plea for Reconstruction of Indian Polity; also JP, 1961, Swaraj for the People.

J.D. Sethi, a Gandhian suggested five ways for organising the poor, (in Population, Poverty and Hope, 1983) (a) Rural unionism, (b) Social mobilisation by political parties and by education; (c) Highly decentralised system of power with tempered bureaucracy; (d) Cooperativisation and (e) Voluntary grassroute organisations).

Quoted, Myrdal, op. cit. p. 765.

17

Jayaprakash Narayan as Hero of Past and Hope for Future

Nil Ratan

I

On the front door of JP's room in Kadamkuan, Patna, there is a touching Urdu couplet written in Hindi:

"Malik Teri Raja Rahe Aur Tu-Hi-Tu Rahe,

Baki Na Main Rahu Na Meri Araju Rahe".

II

As the world celebrates Jayaprakash Narayan's Birth Centenary we Indians salute him as one of the tallest leaders in India. He occupies a unique position in the galaxy of Indian leaders like Gandhi, Nehru, Subash Chandra Bose etc. Like Gandhi, he was a moral force. JP was the true heir of Gandhi. JP was in many ways a mirror of his times. His teachings and thoughts stand as a beacon for generations of Indians. JP is an icon, a living legend and an evergreen hero. He symbolises a person of creativity, intellectuality and great wisdom. He never aspired for any post or position in his entire span of public life. He lived for the masses and died for them. He worked for empowerment of youth, women, and weaker sections and less privileged. He was dynamic in his words and deeds. He struggled hard with the might of a titan against the dark forces of power politics, massive corruption, demon of communalism, bureaucratic dominance and moral bankruptcy. He lived the life of a hero.

An action man, who faced the brunt of lathi to pursue cherished path of truth, democracy and freedom. If Mahatma Gandhi gave this country freedom from colonial masters, then Loknayak Jayaprakash Narayan gave us our Second Freedom. He renewed the legacy of freedom, civil liberties, pluralism and mass social & political movement. He was a true selfless server of people and a remarkable nation builder. He is role model for Indians. His values and thoughts can be emulated in the reconstruction of caste and communal ridden society.

JP's contribution to philosophy, thought and world of ideas are landmarks in evolution of a thought and practice process in modern Indian political thought. JP was an early bird to picking up the sensitivities of social and political dynamics of the society. He was a true student of great Indian tradition of observing the societies, their contradictions and antagonistic social realities. It was his involved anxiety for the common man that earned him the public prefix "Lok Nayak", which led him through Marxism and Socialism to Gandhian path. JP was a born revolutionary, a socialist thinker, freedom fighter, institution builder and hero of past and today's hope for future. Loknayak Jayaprakash Narayan's contribution to the social and political growth, to Freedom Movement, his solution to socio-political problems, his approach towards Total Revolution and his suggestion for radical reforms are footprints in sands of history.

Ajit Bhattacharya writes that the change from his own early Marxist phase is reflected in the contrast between his praise for State power in 'Why Socialism', written in 1935 and his censure of it in 'From Socialism to Sarvodaya', more than 20 years later. But, he later went further to find Sarvodaya inadequate in remedying deep-rooted social ills and stressed the need to mobilise mass struggle. He grew increasingly impatient and justified violence if the Government failed to perform, as he announced in New Delhi in 1969.

III

Phases of JP's Life

Early Life (1902-1930)

Jayaprakash Narayan was born on October 11, 1902, in Sitabdiara, a village on the border of Uttar Pradesh and Bihar. His father Harsudayal was junior official in the Canal Department of the State Government and was often touring the region. JP, called Baul affectionately, was left with his grandmother to study in Sitabdiara.

Ajit Bhattacharya writes that JP was still in school in his early teens when a companion, Chotan Singh, introduced him to a youthful revolutionary from Bengal. They met in secret in a deserted stretch beside the Ganges River. The revolutionary told him about the terrorist exploits in Bengal and gave him some pamphlets as well as a book (Desh ki baat) that described how the British were exploiting India. He told him what dangerous lives they led and the tests initiated to prove their loyalty. JP was impressed by initiation rite-holding a finger in a candle flame without flinching and found himself attracted by dreams of reviving the country's historic glory. They met several times, but one day the revolutionary disappeared. And soon the police arrested Chotan Singh. Many years later, he could recall how they tied his hands with rope, inspite of his being a youth, they marched him to the Police station.[1] This episode left a deep impression on his youthful mind.

While in school, JP read magazines like Saraswati, Prabha and Pratap, book like Bharat-Bharati, and poems by Maithilsharan Gupta and Bharatendu Harishchandra which described the courage and valour of the Rajput kings. JP also read the Bhagwad Gita. He excelled in school. His essay, "The present state of Hindi in Bihar" won the best essay award. He joined the Patna College on a government scholarship.

JP was married to Prabhavati, daughter of lawyer and nationalist Brij Kishore Prasad in October 1920. Prabhavati was very autonomous and on Gandhiji's invitation, went to stay at his ashram while Jayaprakash continued his studies.

JP, along with some friends, went to listen to Maulana Abul Kalam Azad speak about the Non-cooperation movement launched by Gandhi against the passing of the Rowlatt Act of 1919. The Maulana was a bright orator and his call to give up English education was like leaves before a storm. JP was swept away and momentarily lifted up to the skies. That brief experience of soaring up with the winds of a great idea left imprints on his inner being. JP took the Maulana's words to heart and left Patna College with just 20 days remaining for his examinations. He joined the Bihar Vidyapeeth, a college run by the Congress.

JP studied in the U.S., where he came in contact with radical socialist ideas. At age 20, JP sailed aboard the cargo ship Janus while Prabhavati remained at Sabarmati. JP reached California on October 8, 1922 and gained admission to Berkeley in January 1923. To pay for his education, JP picked grapes, set them out to dry, packed fruits at a canning factory, washed dishes, worked as a machanic at a garage and at a slaughter house, sold lotions and accepted teaching jobs. All these jobs gave JP an insight regarding the difficulty the working class faced.

JP was forced to transfer to Iowa State when fees at Berkeley were doubled. He was forced to transfer to many universities thereafter. He pursued his favorite subject, Sociology and received much help from Professor Edward Ross, the father of Sociology.

In Wisconsin, JP was introduced to Karl Marx's "Das Capital". The accomplishment of Russian Revolution of 1917 made JP determine that Marxism was the way to mitigate the suffering masses. He explored into books by Indian intellectual and Communist theoretician M.N. Roy. His paper on Sociology, "Social Variation", was declared as the best of the year.

During Freedom Struggle (1930-1947)

JP had to cut his doctorate short when news came that his mother was seriously ill. JP returned to India in November 1929. For JP, it was not enough that the nation attain political freedom. To him, the definition of freedom was freedom from social and economic malaise.

While JP became a believer of the Communist school of thought, Prabhavati became an ardent Gandhian. He respected Prabhavati's choice and did not force her to change her views. In 1929, both JP and Prabhavati left for the Congress session at Lahore under Jawaharlal Nehru's presidentship. There Nehru invited JP to join the Congress, an offer that JP gladly accepted. He began to work in the Labour Research Cell of the Congress at Allahabad.

Following the 1930 'Dandi March', most of the top Congress leaders were arrested. JP immediately set up an underground office at Bombay to continue Congress work. He travelled all over the nation, printing, distributing and organising secret meetings. After an underground meeting of the Congress Working Committee in Banaras, JP went to Madras where he was arrested. The next day the newspaper headlines screamed, "Congress Brain Arrested!"

In the Nasik jail, JP had the opportunity to meet thinkers like Ram Manohar Lohia, Asoka Mehta, Minoo Masani, P. Dantwala and Achyut Patwardhan. All of them were impatient for freedom and agreed to steer the

Congress towards the goal of Socialism. Jayaprakash was released from jail in 1933.

In 1934, JP and his friends formed the Congress Socialist Party under the Presidentship of Acharya Narendra Deva and Secretaryship of JP himself. The group intended to function as the Socialist wing within the Congress Party and aimed to make socialism the goal of the Congress. In a book "Why socialism?" (1932), JP explained why socialism would be right for India. He was adored by the youth for his idealism.

JP was arrested for speaking against Indian participation in the Second World War in February 1940 and sent to Deoli detention camp in Rajasthan. JP was appalled at the conditions in Deoli. He organised a hunger strike to protest the conditions in 1941. The Government immediately released him. He was again arrested in 1942 for participating in the Quit India Movement. In November 1942, Diwali night, JP along with five others escaped the prison by scaling a 17 feet high wall while the guards remained distracted by the festivities. A Rs. 10,000 reward was offered for JP's capture, dead or alive. JP escaped to Nepal and organised a guerilla army called the "Azad Dasta". JP and Ram Manohar Lohia were captured briefly but were rescued by the Azad Dasta members, who set fire to a hut to distract the guards. Both freedom fighters escaped to Bihar. Finally the British closed in on JP in Amritsar when he was on his way to Rawalpindi to meet Khan Abdul Gaffar Khan. Jayaprakash was taken to Lahore Fort, notorious as a "Torture Chamber" on September 18, 1943. 16 months of mental and physical torture followed. JP was put in solitary confinement for the first month. Then came interrogations, physical torture and humiliation. JP was released from jail on April 12, 1946.

JP returned to a nation he could barely recognise. Talk of partition and riots between Hindus and Muslims dominated the atmosphere. JP rushed to Bihar to assist in curbing the riots. He pleaded with the Congress Working Committee not to accept the partition plan.

Independence finally came on August 15, 1947. Within a year Gandhi was assassinated. Prabhavati hid her sorrow behind the spinning wheel, but JP's mind churned (with) grief and horror. He began to see the wisdom in Gandhi's insistence on truth and non-violence.

As Political and Social Reformer (1948-1973)

The Socialists led by JP lost to the Congress in the 1952 elections. Nehru invited JP to join the Cabinet. When Nehru could give no assurances on the implementation of JP's 14 point plan to reform the Constitution, the Administration and Judicial system, nationalise the banks, redistribute land to the landless, revive Swadeshi, and setup cooperatives, JP refused the offer.

JP turned his attention to the trade unions he was President of. He, along with the unions was able to get a minimum wage, pension, and medical relief and housing subsidy introduced. At the same time, JP was keenly watching events in Russia. The bloody purges and imprisonment convinced JP that Communism was not for India. He realised that Gandhi's success in the Freedom Struggle had showed that it was possible to bring about change without sacrificing one's values.

On April 19, 1954, at a meeting in Gaya, JP made the dramatic announcement of dedicating his life (jeewan daan) to Vinoba Bhave's Sarvodaya movement. He renounced all self-interest, gave up his land in Sitabdiara, and withdrew from all personal activities to devote the rest of his life to the movement. Prabhavati was delighted at this declaration. JP set up an ashram a poor and backward village in Nawada district. He gave Gandhian concepts a new dimension by using modern technology to uplift the village.

JP believed that every village should be like a small republic-politically independent and capable of taking its own decisions. It was a marriage of Gandhian-Indian concepts and modern Western democracy. His thoughtful, well-researched and brilliant book, "The Reconstruction of Indian Polity," won him the Raman Magsaysay Award.

The Social Responsibilities of Business

In 1968, JP asked his old comrade and friend, Minoo Masani, to organise a seminar under the auspices of the Leslie Sawhny Programme (LSP) to work out a Declaration on the Social Responsibilities of Business. He had an eye for all issues.

JP's Free Kitchen Movement

JP as the Chairman of the Bihar Relief Committee, was the lone voice to suggest an in-depth study of the 'Palamau Experiment'. He said, "Any aid delay would amount to aid denied".

In 1966, JP was the only name on the lips of government officials and the drought-stricken people all over Bihar and UP.

According to JP, 35 million people were starving in Bihar during that famine in December, 1966. He feared that the number of hunger-stricken people would swell by another ten million in the coming months. Drought had turned into scarcity and scarcity into famine.

JP's 'Free-Kitchen Movement' in this area saved hundreds from dying of hunger. At the 'Free Kitchens', there were many in the crowds with bowls in their hands. Probably this was the first time in their life, that they had been forced to stand in a food line.

JP appealed to the nation:

"I regret very much to say that although the need of the drought-stricken people of Bihar is enormous, the response from the country has not been encouraging. This may be due to lack of adequate information about the severity of the situation. Please remember that this is not an ordinary drought. This is an unprecedented drought, the like of which this part of the country has not seen in the past centuries. At present, the most pressing need is for clothing and blankets. I appeal to all of you to spare from your ration whatever you can, as some people are already doing. There is need for cash contributions, small and large, with which we can buy whatever is needed".

Among the political leaders in India, JP was the only one who was alive to the grimness of the situation. Under his direct supervision, the 'Free Kitchen' service was now increased from 1,000 to 1,400 and on an average, about 700 people were fed daily from each kitchen. As the situation worsened, he increased the facilities within his available resources. It was a great human effort and yet another of JP's great feat to serve humanity.

Musahari Experiment

In June 1971, Sarvodaya workers in Muzaffarpur, Bihar, received a letter threatening to kill them. The area was continuously threatened by Naxalites, which was made up of young men. JP walked into the heart of Naxal territory armed only with love and sympathy. He knew that the cause of the violence was that the youth were frustrated because of poverty and unemployment. He lived in Musahari block for many months and experimented to alleviate the problems of the Naxals.

JP was also a key person in the surrender of dacoits in the Chambal Valley.

On April 15, 1973, Prabhavati died of cancer, leaving JP alone.

Towards Total Revolution (1974-1979)

The main quest, however, remained where and what it was, namely a relentless confrontation against corruption, money power and misuse of political authority which seemed to dominate the national scene even after years of parliamentary democracy.

1974 ushered in a year of high inflation, unemployment and lack of supplies of essential commodities. JP was asked to lead a peaceful agitation by the Nava Nirman Andolan of Gujarat. On April 8, 1974, at the age of 72, he led a silent procession at Patna. The procession was lathi charged. On June 5, 1974, JP addressed a mammoth crowd at Gandhi Maidan in Patna. He declared, "This is a revolution, friends! We are not here merely to see the Vidhan Sabha dissolved. That is only one milestone on our journey. But we have a long way to go... After 27 years of freedom, people of this country are wracked by hunger, rising prices, corruption...oppressed by every kind of injustice...it is a Total Revolution we want, nothing less!"

On June 12, 1975, the Allahabad High Court held the Prime Minister, Mrs. Indira Gandhi, guilty on charges of corrupt practice in her election. JP advised her to resign until the Supreme Court cleared her name. Instead, she clamped Emergency on June 26. JP was arrested and sent to Chandigarh where he was kept as prisoner in a hospital. "My world lies in shambles around me", he cried. As his health worsened, he was moved to a hospital in Bombay.

Finally, in January 1977, the Emergency was lifted. Fresh elections were declared. Under JP's guidance several parties united to form the Janata Party. The party incorporated all of JP's goals in its manifesto.

JP was weak and helpless by that time. He felt his work was done, but he had to sorrowfully witness the collapse of the Janata Party government. JP died on

October 8, 1979. People hailed him as "Loknayak" or leader of the people.

IV

JP's contribution can be illustrated by understanding his concept of Total revolution. Following Gandhi, JP recognised the prime necessity of change in the individual who takes upon himself/herself the task of changing the society. In this lies the whole philosophy of JP's Total Revolution. The gist of this concept is presented in his letter to people of Bihar and an extract from the *Notes on Bihar Movement,* both written in 1975. Earlier, he had also pleaded for reviving the ancient concept of dharma to suit democracy so as to ensure that the main mould of life remained indigenous. His basic objective is succinctly told in the text reproduced from JP's weekly, *Everyman's.*

JP has himself thrown light on the subject. He says that "I have used the word "Total" in the sense of a comprehensive revolution affecting all aspects of social life including individual life. If there were a Total Revolution of my concept, the individual man would also undergo a revolutionary change. So it is the Totality that undergoes the change including the individual. I think the specific nature of a Total Revolution at any particular time would be governed or determined by the needs of the time, the situation that obtained in the country and the forces that were contending for power. So at different times, a total revolution might take different forms, even different meanings in the sense that its contents might also be different. In the present context, a total revolution in India should mean a revolution from the village upward to the largest urban concentration. There must be a total change in civic life. Civic relationships, civic institutions, civic relations and as we go beyond the sphere of civic life, we enter larger spheres of the state of the national life; we have innumerable spheres in which the changes will have to be brought.[2]

JP expounded a new paradigm of political thought, which was revolutionary and evolutionary in ideas and contents. He spelled a new meaning to social order and social change. As he wrote, "I have been saying that a Total Revolution is combination of seven revolutions-social, economic, political, cultural, ideological or intellectual, educational and spiritual.[3]

JP had a vision of change and betterment of the society, which would encompass all segments and give social justice to all. He was true champion of down-trodden and underprivileged, because he writes "I visualise the movement as Total Revolution that will bring about fundamental changes in the social, economic, political, cultural, educational and moral spheres...the changes in the economic sphere will have to be such that the uplift of the Harijans, Adivasis, Muslims, agricultural labourers, landless farmers and such others will come first..."[4]

JP wanted a change in totality, which would metamorphise the society into an egalitarian order where there would be no place to inequity and deprivation or discrimination. He in his genius of Total Revolution concept feels the pulse of Indian society and its undercurrents, which needed change.

V

JP was a great innovator and was always in process of giving alternative to an institution of a political, social and economic process for providing a better society and social equitable environment. Thus, in giving a huge direction to the debate on political sustenance of existing political system and process, JP pleads that we must seriously set about to find a better type of democracy".[5] JP made a great incisive and penetrating observation on parliamentary democracy and its processes. JP writes, for power, political parties have to indulge in corruption and malpractice. They, indeed, try to exercise the passions of the voters. They make dishonest but pleasant promises before the voters. As a result of all these the voters become unable to cast their vote dispassionately. Moreover it is well known that many political parties terrorise the voters to capture the polling booths. Consequently, the voters are deprived of their franchise."[6] He expressed his view about corruption in political process when he said that huge amount is spent on the elections which affected system adversely. It brought corruption and paved way for malpractice.[7]

JP did not rest at the issue of political institution and process in India by drawing the demerits and fallacies of parliamentary democracy but took great pains to spell the political paradigm which he thought deemed fit for Indian context. He expounded the necessity of introducing participatory democracy, as a political model. The cornerstone of his ideal was Panchayati Raj model, which would be a three-tier structure. The primary community of the rural area would be village panchayat as the lowest body of administration. The villagers would directly participate in its activities. JP says, "I have been emphasising here the element of people's participation, a true measure of democracy. Now if there is any level of self-government at which fullest participation of people is practicable, it is at the village level. It is only there that direct democracy can adequately function. He further expressed that "if they accepted the idea that it was in the best interest of the village to choose uncontested panchayats, that should become a challenge to them, and they should all join together to educate and persuade the villagers to do a challenging and creative task.[8]

VI

In every sphere of society, JP's contribution can be recalled. A chronology can be drawn of this hero like JP and Marx, JP and Gandhi, JP and Sarvodaya, JP and Freedom Struggle, JP and economic philosophy, JP and socialism, JP and people's movement, JP and Bodh Gaya Math struggle, JP and Musahari Experiment, JP and rural development, JP and Panchayati Raj, JP and land reforms, JP and civil society movement (PUCL/PUDR), JP and the events of 1974 and after, till his death.

The list is long and exhaustive. JP is one of the greatest heroes of our times, and his contributions are of great relevance in contemporary time as in the past.

REFERENCES

Bhattacharya, Ajit, Jayaprakash Narayan: A Political Biography, Vikash Publishing House, and New Delhi, p. 34, 1975.

Narayan, JP, and Total Revolution: Some clarification in Brahmanand (ed.) Towards Total Revolution, Popular Prakashan, Bombay, and pp. 107-198, 1978.

Narayan, Jayaprakash, Towards Total Revolution, Volume One, (ed.) Brahmanand, popular Prakashan, Bombay, p. 192, 1978.

Narayan, Jayaprakash, Towards Total Revolution, (ed.) Brahmanand, p. 68, 1978.

Narayan, Jayaprakash, Youth and Democracy, Everyman's, New Delhi, Vol. 1, and No. 25, 22 Dec. 1973.

Narayan, Jayaprakash, Communitarian Society and Panchayati Raj, Varanasi, 1970, pp. 71-90.

Narayan, Jayaprakash, A Plea for the Reconstruction of the Indian Polity, Varanasi, 1969, pp. 85-107.

ACKNOWLEDGEMENT

1. Transforming the Polity —Centenary Readings from Jayaprakash Narayan: Selected and introduced by Ajit Bhattacharya; Rupa and Co., 7/16, Ansari Road, Daryaganj, New Delhi-110002.
2. Jayaprakash Narayan: Selected Works: Vol. I (1929-1935)/edited by Bimal Prasad. Delhi, Manohar, 2000, 300 p., ISBN 81-7304-354-X.